Economic Reforms in India and China

Economic Reforms in India and China

R.K. Mishra
Zhou Shaopeng

ALLIED PUBLISHERS PVT LTD.

New Delhi • Mumbai • Kolkata • Lucknow • Chennai
Nagpur • Bangalore • Hyderabad • Ahmedabad

ALLIED PUBLISHERS PRIVATE LIMITED

1/13-14 Asaf Ali Road, **New Delhi**–110002
Ph.: 011-23239001 • E-mail: delhi.books@alliedpublishers.com

47/9 Prag Narain Road, Near Kalyan Bhawan, **Lucknow**–226001
Ph.: 0522-2209942 • E-mail: lko.books@alliedpublishers.com

17 Chittaranjan Avenue, **Kolkata**–700072
Ph.: 033-22129618 • E-mail: cal.books@alliedpublishers.com

15 J.N. Heredia Marg, Ballard Estate, **Mumbai**–400001
Ph.: 022-42126969 • E-mail: mumbai.books@alliedpublishers.com

60 Shiv Sunder Apartments (Ground Floor), Central Bazar Road,
Bajaj Nagar, **Nagpur**–440010
Ph.: 0712-2234210 • E-mail: ngp.books@alliedpublishers.com

F-1 Sun House (First Floor), C.G. Road, Navrangpura,
Ellisbridge P.O., **Ahmedabad**–380006
Ph.: 079-26465916 • E-mail: ahmbd.books@alliedpublishers.com

751 Anna Salai, **Chennai**–600002
Ph.: 044-28523938 • E-mail: chennai.books@alliedpublishers.com

5th Main Road, Gandhinagar, **Bangalore**–560009
Ph.: 080-22262081 • E-mail: bngl.books@alliedpublishers.com

3-2-844/6 & 7 Kachiguda Station Road, **Hyderabad**–500027
Ph.: 040-24619079 • E-mail: hyd.books@alliedpublishers.com

Website: www.alliedpublishers.com

© 2011, Conference Convener

ISBN: 978-81-8424-683-4

Published by Sunil Sachdev and printed by Ravi Sachdev
at Allied Publishers Pvt. Ltd. (Printing Division),
A-104 Mayapuri Phase II, New Delhi-110064

Preface

China and India are two largest countries of the world in terms of population. The two countries are considered as two powerful engines that will lead the world to the Asian century. The two countries could further add to their socio-economic and political mite by understanding the dynamics of economic reforms through exchange of experiences and confabulations on the future strategies to lift the rate of growth and at the same time remove social dissentions. China and India are the two largest countries of the world in terms of population. The two countries are considered as powerful engines that will lead the world to the Asian Century. Both the countries are booming with high rate of economic growth and face the social and political challenges of consolidation. China and India are engaged in re-writing their economic history and creating a great economic history and creating a great economic future by transforming their respective economies and societies. In this backdrop, the Institute initiative of a dialogue with the China National School of Administration, Beijing during the period 2004-07 translated itself into an agreement of organizing a two way seminar on 'Economics Reforms in India and China'. The first part of the seminar was conducted from 2-4 June, 2008 at the CNSA which also organized. The seminar was attended by 30 participants from India and China.

In this context, this edited volume contains select papers presented at the seminar. The seminar was coordinated by Prof RK Mishra, Director, Institute of Public Enterprise as the Convenor and Prof Zhou Shaopeng, Department of Economics, Chinese National School of Administration, Beijing, China. The Institute is grateful for the generous support and constant guidance from Chinese National School of Administration, Beijing, China.

Prof. R.K. Mishra
Prof. Zhou Shaopeng

List of Participants

CHINA

Hang Kang	Vice President & Professor, China National School of Administration
Wang Jian	Director-General & Professor, Department of Economics, China National School of Administration
Cui Jungang	Deputy Director-General, Department of International Affairs, China National School of Administration
Wang Haibo	Professor & Academician, Chinese Academy of Social Sciences
Huang Hengxue	Professor, School of Government Management, Peking University
Li Xuefeng	Professor, Department of Economics, China National School of Administration
Xu Zhengzhong	Professor, Department of Economics, China National School of Administration
Zhang Zhanbin	Professor, Department of Economics, China National School of Administration
Dong Xiaojun	Professor, Department of Economics, China National School of Administration
Zhang Xiaode	Professor, Department of Economics, China National School of Administration
Zhang Qing	Professor, Department of Economics, China National School of Administration
Shi Hongxiu	Professor, Department of Economics, China National School of Administration

Xu Jie	Associate Professor, Department of Economics, China National School of Administration
Li Jiangtao	Associate Professor, Department of Economics, China National School of Administration
CaiChunhong	Associate Professor, Department of Economics, China National School of Administration
Xiaofang	Associate Professor, Department of Economics, China National School of Administration
Lui Shuangmin	Lecturer, Department of Economics, China National School of Administration
Fan Jida	Lecturer, Department of Economics, China National School of Administration

INDIA

Ram Kumar Mishra	Director & Professor, IPE (On the invitation of Govt. of China)
Suri Subrahmanayam Suribohtla	Associate Professor, IPE
Naresh Kumar Sharma	Professor, Department of Economics, University of Hyderabad
Lakshmi Kumari Chintalapudi	Assistant Professor, IPE
Kiranmai Janaswamy	Assistant Professor, IPE
Seeta Mishra	Assistant Professor, Post Graduate A.V. College (On the invitation of Govt. of China)
Venkateswara Rao Devarakonda	Principal Secretary, Department of Public Enterprise, Government of Kamataka, Bangalore
Lalitha Shanth Kumar	Senior Administrative Officer (Research), IPE

List of Contributors

INDIA

Ram Kumar Mishra	Director & Professor, IPE
Suri Subrahmanayam Suribohtla	Associate Professor, IPE
Lakshmi Kumari Chintalapudi	Assistant Professor, IPE
Lalitha Shanth Kumar	Senior Administrative Officer (Research), IPE
Kiranmai Janaswamy	Assistant Professor, IPE
Seeta Mishra	Assistant Professor, Post Graduate A.V. College
Venkateswara Rao Devarakonda	Principal Secretary, Department of Public Enterprise, Government of Kamataka, Bangalore
Naresh Kumar Sharma	Professor, Department of Economics, University of Hyderabad
Geeta Rani	Faculty, Waikato University, New Zealand

CHINA

Li Xuefeng	Professor, Department of Economics, China National School of Administration
Zhang Zhanbin	Professor, Department of Economics, China National School of Administration
Zhou Shaopeng	Professor, Department of Economics, China National School of Administration

Wang Haibo   Professor & Academician,
                                      Chinese Academy of Social Sciences

Li Jiangtao   Associate Professor,
                                      Department of Economics,
                                      China National School of Administration

Zhang Xiaode   Professor, Department of Economics,
                                      China National School of Administration

Dong Xiaojun   Professor, Department of Economics,
                                      China National School of Administration

Contents

Performance of Public Enterprises in the Era of Economic Liberalisation

R.K. Mishra and J. Kiranmai

This paper proposes to analyse the performance of the Public Enterprises (PEs) in the era of economic liberalisation against the backdrop of trenchant criticism of their non-performance and argument about their folding up in the wake of the development of private sector and private initiative. In doing so, the paper portrays the Government policy on PEs, performance of PEs during the era of economic liberalisation, salient features of functioning of PEs, and the scope for improvement in their future performance.

1. PE POLICY

PE policy in India has changed from time to time. The economic liberalisation has brought about a radical transformation in PE policy which is explained as below:

- Portfolio of public sector investments will be reviewed with a view to focus on the public sector in strategic, high-tech and essential infrastructure fields.

- Public enterprises which are chronically sick and which are unlikely to be turned around will, for the formulation of revival/rehabilitation schemes, be referred to the Board for Industrial and Financial Reconstruction (BIFR), or other similar high level institutions created for the purpose. A social security mechanism will be created to protect the interests of workers likely to be affected by such packages.

- In order to raise resources and encourage wider public participation, a part of the government's shareholding in the public sector would be offered to mutual funds, financial institutions, general public and workers.

- Boards of public sector companies would be made more professional and given greater powers.

- There will be a greater thrust on performance improvement through the mechanism of Memorandum of Understanding (MoU) with a view to give greater autonomy to management and hold them.

- To facilitate a fuller discussion on performance, the MoU signed between Government and the public enterprises would be placed in Parliament. While focusing on major management issues, this would also help place day-to-day operations of public enterprises in their correct perspective.
- The Government will commit itself:
  (i) To devolve full managerial and commercial autonomy to successful, profit-making companies operating in a competitive environment
  (ii) Not to generally privatize
  (iii) To modernise and restructure sick public sector companies and revive sick industries
  (iv) To sell/close down chronically loss-making companies
  (v) To induct private industry to turn-around companies that have potential for revival
  (vi) To use privatisation revenues for designated social sector schemes
  (vii) To encourage public sector companies and nationalised banks to enter the capital markets to raise resources and offer new investment avenues to retail investors.

Although, the PE policy leans towards a balanced approach, the behaviour of the Government at times has been inconsistent with the professed policy.[2] During the period 1999–2004, PE privatisation and disinvestment was attempted on an imprudent basis. The sale of Bharat Aluminium Company Limited (BALCO) and the transfer of property of the Hotel Airport, Mumbai are the cases in point. The sales were transacted at un-remunerative prices to the Government without a proper social safety net to the employees and disregarding the well established principles of preventing the creation of monopoly. The Airport privatisation has been opposed not only by the labour unions and the Left but also by a bidder on the ground of administrative sanctity. During the period of economic liberalisation, the Government has shown a bias in favour of reducing the involvement of PEs through their sale/ disposal/disinvestment – partial or full, based not on a rational basis but under the pressure of the ideology that markets are efficient, and such efficiency is greater when PE element is minimal. There have been suggestions on the setting up of a general asset fund on the pattern of China, which has a State Asset Holding Ministry. As an alternative, the Government has been toying with the idea of setting up a Special Purpose Vehicle (SPV). A general consensus about the PE policy has been sadly lacking even in the United Progressive Alliance (UPA) Government. The Left is completely opposed to the idea of removing the profitable PEs from the portfolio of PEs of the Central Government. This is supported by their stand against disinvestment of the BHEL and the sale of the leftover stake of the Government in BALCO.

2. PERFORMANCE

As the public enterprises are expected to run on commercial lines, the financial appraisal continues to be an important yardstick to measure the performance of these enterprises. An analysis of the performance of these enterprises with reference to some important ratios such as profit before interest and tax to capital employed, sales to capital employed, etc has been attempted. Considering the fact that the public sector has to discharge a number of socio-economic obligations, the performance appraisal also covers items like internal resources generation for financing the Plan outlay, contribution to the public exchequer, skill development, development of backward regions, employment generation, employees welfare measures, foreign exchange earnings, import substitute and such other related matters, so as to present a comprehensive picture.

Table 1: Trend Analysis

(₹ In crore*)

Particulars	1995-96	2004-05	2005-06	2006-07
No. of operating Enterprises	239	227	226	217
Capital employed	173948	504826	585484	665124
Profit before dep, int, tax & EP (PBDITEP)	40161	142606	150262	178083
Depreciation	12574	33132	34848	33138
Interest	27587	108491	23708	27069
Profit before Tax & EP (PBTEP)	13966	22428	90714	112033
Tax provisions	13621	86063	24370	34330
Net Profit before EP	4047	21661	66344	77702
No. of Profit making CPSEs	134	143	160	156
No. of Loss incurring CPSEs	100	73	63	59
Dividend	-	20718	22886	26805
Dividend tax	2205	2852	3215	4105
Retained profit	-	2851		
Financial Ratio %	7369	41394	43435	50640
PBDITEP to Capital employed	23.1	28.25	25.66	26.77
PBITEP to Capital employed	15.9	21.49	19.54	20.91
Dividend payout	23	31.66	32.91	32.87

* *US $ I billion = Rs.4500 crore as on June 1, 2006.*

Source: Government of India (Department of Public Enterprises, Ministry of Heavy Industries & Public Enterprises), Public Enterprises Survey: 2006-07, Vol-1, New Delhi

Table 1 depicts many brighter aspects of the financial performance of PEs:

  (i) The various profitability indicators are on the rise

 (ii) The number of loss making enterprises is on the decline

(iii) The relative ratio of profits of profit making enterprises is increasing faster than the losses of the loss making enterprises

(iv) There has been an appreciable increase in the dividend cover

 (v) The retained profits have sky rocketed.

The character of financing in PEs has undergone a complete transformation. Under the liberalised economic regime, these enterprises have followed the 'ABC' dictum. They started with complete assistance from the Central Government in the form of grants taking the route of equity or debt. Then they moved to the budgetary support under which the equity or debt had to come on the basis of project justification. However, with the onset of economic liberalisation since 1985, they moved to capital markets for mobilising resources. Table 2 shows the resource mobilisation by PEs in relation to plan investment. The budgetary support declined from a high of 50.57% in 1985-86 to 19.14% in 1991-92, and dropped to a low of 12.75% in 2006-07. PEs achieved this by exploiting new financial instruments such as commercial paper, bonds, public deposits, Global Depository Receipts and American Depositary Receipts. The European Commercial Borrowings also played an important role. The suppliers' credit assumed an important proportion. The foreign bonds raised in the Japanese capital market and the Luxemburg capital market helped these enterprises substantially. Some enterprises accessed funds successfully through floating rate debentures. The State Bank of India is a case in point. Public deposits have also yielded adequate finances to these enterprises especially in the present era when the interest rates are heading southwards. The working capital financing from the Government of India has drastically declined and the dependence of PEs on the commercial banks and capital markets has substantially increased. It may be noted that PEs have established themselves so firmly in the capital markets that they have been able to raise resources through taxable bonds. The proportion between taxable bonds to tax-free bonds is increasing in favour of the former. This is not to say that PEs did not resort to the traditional sources of financing such as the inter-corporate deposits. These were of vast magnitude amounting to ₹ 10986.29 crore during 2003-04 which turned out to be 12.94% of the total financing of these enterprises in that year.

Table 2: Resources Mobilisation and Plan Investment

(₹ in Crore)

Year	Net internal resources	Extra budgetary resources	Budgetary support	Plan outlay
1985-86	3333.05 (33.68)	1559.19 (15.75)	5005.38 (50.57)	9897.62 (100.00)
1990-91	6180.57 (33.68)	7696.74 (41.94)	4474.17 (24.38)	18351.48 (100.00)
2004-05	32222.46 (50.89)	26006.52 (41.07)	5090.24 (8.04)	63319.22 (100)
2005-06	42143.53 (51.31)	35723 (43.49)	4271.70 (5.20)	82138.53 (100)
2006-07	58981 (60.85)	32676.47 (33.71)	5263.76 (5.43)	96921.80 (100)

Source: Government of India (Department of Public Enterprises, Ministry of Heavy Industries & Public Enterprises), Public Enterprises Surveys for the years 1985-86 to 2006-07, Vol-1, New Delhi

The economic liberalisation much against the professed belief has not resulted in the decline of the contribution of the PEs to total industrial production. Public sector's contribution to the quantum of production of Coal, Lignite, Crude Oil, Natural Gas, Refinery Crude, Finished Steel and Aluminium has increased significantly over the period 1968-69 to 2006-07.

Table 3: Public Sector's Contribution in Total Industrial Production

Item	National production (NP)		Public sector's production (PSP)		PSP to NP (%)	
	1968-69	2002-03	1968-69	2002-03	1968-69	2002-03
Fuel (Million Tonnes)						
Coal	71.40	341.25	12.61	325.40	17.66	95.36
Lignite	3.98	26.02	3.98	26.02	100.00	100.00
Petroleum (Million Tonnes)						
Crude Oil	6.06	32.04	3.08	28.95	50.83	87.62
Natural Gas	NA	31.40	NA	25.99	NA	83.73
Refinery Crude	16.55	112.56	8.09	74.76	48.88	66.42
Basic Metal Industries (Million Tonnes)						
Finished Steel	4.58	33.63	2.55	10.97	55.68	32.62
Non Ferrous Metals (000 Tonnes)						
Aluminium	125.3	689.19	Nil	244.71	Nil	35.51

Source: Public Enterprises Survey, (Government of India, New Delhi) 2002-03: Volume 1, 2006

The contribution of PEs to the Central Exchequer has been rising year after year. The contribution can be in the form of dividends, interests, excise duty, custom duty, corporate tax, dividend tax, sales tax and other duties and taxes. During 2004-05 the contribution stood at ₹ 61037.48 crore which was ₹ 62865.53 in 2003-04.

3. SALIENT FEATURES OF PE FUNCTIONING

During the period of economic liberalisation, PEs have had certain special features of their functioning which were mostly the result of their own initiatives.

4. MEMORANDUM OF UNDERSTANDING (MoU)

The MoU was patterned on the French model of evaluating the performance of an enterprise based on the vision and mission, objectives, targets and performance score on the part of enterprise and the obligations of the Government to the enterprise. During 1991-92, as a part of economic liberalisation policy, the Government decided to extend the system to as many PEs as possible which resulted in 99 PEs signing MoUs with the Government during 2004-05 as opposed to 4 PEs signing MoUs in 1987-88. The introduction of MoU has given a rare opportunity both to the Government and PEs to negotiate certain measure of performance and compare the ex-post performance with the ex ante performance. Most of the MoU signing enterprises have shown a great deal of appreciation for the MoU system which distinguishes the managerial performance in PEs with the enterprise performance. The MoU system also presents an objective solution to the problem of conflicting interests of principals with the agent. The Arjun Sengupta generation of MoUs has undergone a drastic change with the current generation of MoUs based on the scrutiny of the Cabinet Secretariat of the expert committee report prepared by the National Council of Applied Economic Research. The revised system relies more on dynamic indicators as compared to the static indicators that formed the base of the first generation MoUs.

5. NAVRATNAS/MINIRATNAS

Taking a cue from the Korean concept of Chaebols, Government of India decided to elevate some highly successfull enterprises to the special status of Navratnas wherein they were delegated enhanced financial powers in relation to committing capital expenditure, starting joint ventures and providing incentives to their employees. Comparatively smaller enterprises that did not meet the stringent norms for qualifying as Navratnas but were way above the rest of the enterprises were accorded the status of Miniratnas which also benefited from the Government policy with regard to Navratna, albeit on a smaller scale. The concept has been applauded by PEs who have consistently shown better results year after year. The Navratna/Miniratna enterprises have proved that given sufficient freedom of operation and non-interference from the Government, they could not only excel in their field in India but also take on the multinationals and could snatch the market share from private sector enterprises in India and their competitors abroad. It is said that the extension of this concept would enable the rest of the successful enterprises in unlocking previous value by way of investment in physical and financial assets. The positive aspects of the Navratna concept have forced the Government to consider conferring this status upon the Coal India Ltd and Rashtriya Ispat Nigam Ltd. The Navratna / Miniratna concept has received a shot in the arm from the Arjun Sengupta Committee Report on Autonomy of PEs set up by the Government of India. The report advocates for greater autonomy to Navratnas in the matters of policy and day-to-day functioning.

6. PEs IN MARKET

Mr R Venkataraman, the then Finance Minister, Government of India, renewed the plea for the PE interface with the capital market strong case in favour of autonomous PEs was made as early as in 1959 by the Krishna Menon Committee. Economic liberalisation of 1990s is taking this interface forward immensely. As a result, a large number of PEs and banks have entered the capital markets. More than 50% of the market capitalisation belongs to PEs which also added a great deal of liquidity and credibility to the capital markets. The Oil and Natural Gas Corporation leads 33 Indian companies on Forbes list of top 2000 corporate titans across the world.

Table 4: Percentage of Investments by Institutional Investors during 2006-07

(In Percentage)

	2006-07
Bharat Petroleum Corporation	29.49
Chennai Petroleum	24.86
Hindustan Petroleum Corporation	39.96
IBP Limited	31.32
Kochin Refineries	20.92
Naveli Lignite Corporation	8.12
National Mineral Development Corporation	9.10
Bharat Earth Movers Limited	21.40
Bharat Electronics Limited	17.20
Bharat Heavy Electricals Limited	30.29
Cement Corporation of India	34.08
Shipping Corporation of India	13.57
ITI Limited	39.21
Hindustan Organics & Chemicals Limited	5.16
Life Insurance Corporation	48.94
State Trading Corporation	3.00
Tamil Nadu Newsprints Limited	44.62

Source: Institute of Public Enterprise database on Public Enterprises

The wealth engines of PEs had a market capitalisation of ₹ 5,79,242 crores as on March 31, 2006.[3] The market capitalisation of these wealth engines was ₹ 3,78,922 crores as on March 31, 2005. The wealth engines included Oil and Natural Gas Corporation Ltd, NTPC Ltd, Indian Oil Corporation Ltd, Bharat Heavy Electricals Ltd, State Bank of India, Steel Authority of India Ltd, Gail (India) Ltd, National Aluminium Company Ltd, Punjab National Bank and Bharat Petroleum Corporation Ltd. The capital market interface through Institutional investors has made a big dent and is a precursor to the future success of PEs as seen in Table 4.

Table 5 gives the percentages of investments in PEs by general public during 1998-99 to 2004-05. A perusal of the table shows that the general public has started finding in PEs to be a good investment channel. It is expected that PEs would be favoured a great deal more by general public in future.

Table 5: Percentage of Investments by General Public during 2006-07

(In Percentage)

S. No.	Name of the enterprise	2006-07
1.	Bharat Petroleum Corporation	2.86
2.	Chennai Petroleum	5.43
3.	Hindustan Petroleum Corporation	6.66
4.	IBP Limited	12.34
5.	Kochin Refineries	13.24
6.	Naveli Lignite Corporation	1.53
7.	National Mineral Development Corporation	3.81
8.	Bharat Earth Movers Limited	12.31
9.	Bharat Electronics Limited	4.3
10.	Bharat Heavy Electricals Limited	0.89
11.	Cement Corporation of India	1.83
12.	Shipping Corporation of India	4.43
13.	ITI Limited	3.22
14.	Hindustan Organics & Chemicals Limited	28.6
15.	Life Insurance Corporation	9.93
16.	State Trading Corporation	4.69
17.	Tamil Nadu Newsprints Limited	13.1

Source: Institute of Public Enterprise database on Public Enterprises

Encouraged by the market interface, more PEs proposed to benefit from it. The Government on its part is considering to make listing of PEs on stock exchanges[4] compulsory – may be in the initial run only for the enterprises which have consistently a good record of profit making and are also competitive in nature.

7. DISINVESTMENT

One of the major elements of the PE policy in the economic liberalisation era relates disinvestment therein through the sale of equity and trade sale. The policy has lacked consistency, continuity and well thought out rationale.

Table 6 provides the quantum of actual disinvestment in PEs and methodologies adopted during the era of economic liberalisation. The targets barely exceeded 50% mark in the planned exercise. The methodologies had a wide swing from bundling of shares to bidding, strategic sale and wholesale transfer of assets. There has been a trenchant criticism of the disinvestment moves during 1991-92 to 1999; between 2000 and 2004; and during the period 2004-06. Although many administrative innovations were effected to make disinvestment a logical exercise, the doctrinaire approach could not deliver the goods as it lacked pragmatism. Two of the oft raised questions against the disinvestment in India have been as to what was the motivation of the Government in neglecting the restructuring exercise earlier especially when it was a globally accepted practice and why the bias against IPOs as a method of sale of shares despite high ranking of many PEs in capital market in India as assessed by the credit rating agencies?

Table 6: *Actual Disinvestment and Methodologies Adopted*

(Rupees in crore)

Year	Target receipt	Actual receipts	Methodology
1991-92	2,500	3,038	Minority shares sold by auction method
1992-93	2,500	1,913	Shares sold separately for each company by auction method
1993-94	3,500	Nil	Equity of 7 companies sold by open auction
1994-95	4,000	4,843	Sale through auction method
1995-96	7,000	168	Equities of 4 companies auctioned
1996-97	5,000	380	Global Depository Receipt (GDR)
1997-98	4,800	910	GDR
1998-99	5,000	5,371	GDR and Domestic Cross purchase
1999-00	10,000	1,860	GDR
2000-01	10,000	1,871	Strategic sale
2001-02	12,000	5,632	Strategic sale
2002-03	12,000	3,348	Strategic sale
2003-04	14,500	15,547	Public offer of shares to retail investors
2004-05	4,000	2,765	Public offer of shares to retail investors
2005-06	5,000	1,567	Sale of stake to development banks
2006-07	–	–	–
Total	96,800	49,213	

Source: DPE Survey (GoI, New Delhi) and Ministry of Finance, GOI, Economic Survey, 2007

8. RECONSTRUCTION OF PEs AND SOCIAL SAFETY NET PROGRAMME (SSNP)

The Washington Consensus of 1983 as reflected in the economic liberalisation programme of 1992 was based on the sole premise that the wellbeing of people could be increased by disposing of the public assets owned by PEs. The global experience of disinvestment has relied on the restructuring of PEs prior to their sale as also their reconstruction for their rehabilitation. The Common Minimum Programme (CMP) of the UPA Government makes a mention of rehabilitation of PEs through the Board for Reconstruction of Public Sector Enterprises (BRPSE). 20 cases have been referred to BRPSE of which it has considered 17 cases and is in the process of giving its mind regarding the remaining three cases. BRPSE is implementing the plans for the rehabilitation of seven PEs including Bridge & Roof Co Ltd, Hindustan Salts Ltd, BBJ Construction Co Ltd, Praga Tools Ltd, HMT (Bearings) Ltd, Heavy Engineering Corpn Ltd and Braithwaite & Co Ltd. It is interesting to mention that as a part of the restructuring exercise and to fight for successful existence in the global market, merger of Air India and Indian Airlines, Rashtriya Ispat Nigam Ltd and Steel Authority of India Ltd and Oil Group Companies is being considered. The Indian Post is an excellent example of a Department undergoing restructuring to come back with a big bang to take on private sector couriers and foreign couriers like DHL. The Indian Railways are not lagging behind and giving a tough fight to the private sector Airlines. Many PEs are going for diverse types of restructuring such as manpower, operations, strategic, financial and organisational restructuring including setting up of joint ventures. Hindustan Machine Tools Ltd, State Bank of India, Hindustan Shipyard Ltd, Rashtriya Ispat Nigam Ltd are some of the cases in point.

To project the human face of the Government SSNP was started with a great fanfare during 1993-94. The programme was supported by the National Renewal Fund for five years. Thereafter a programme of counseling, retraining and redeployment was launched. The first five years of the programme covered by and large the surplus workers of the National Textiles Corporation. The subsequent programme had some financial support and also the organisational backup of a large number of well established institutes and centres. However, looking to the labour forces employed in PEs, it could be said that the SSNP did not cover a large chunk of the workers. Moreover, the stress of the programme is on only retraining and redeployment and that too partially. The insurance component of the SSNP has not received any attention at the hands of the Government. The SSNP abroad has insurance as the mainstay of the programme.

9. SCOPE FOR IMPROVEMENT

There are many areas where PEs could make a substantial headway and also have the potential of making these enterprises as the national jewels and market leaders.

10. INTER-CORPORATE COORDINATION

The inter-corporate coordination in PEs holds a great hope for their future. Such coordination could bring together the PEs to facilitate exchange of their strengths for eliminating their weaknesses. In each area e.g., marketing, finance, personnel, strategy, international business, customer relationship management, corporate social responsibility, productivity, value engineering, research and development, purchases and inventory management, public accountability, board practices, PEs could exchange their knowledge and strengths and learn from one another. This would provide them a rare opportunity to acquire a competitive edge to walk through the markets.

The toning up of the corporate governance function could help them a great deal in brand building and relating well to society, business, employees, legal institutions and accounting world. The application of Clause 49 of the Securities and Exchange Board of India (SEBI) Code is a point in reference. Although approved by SEBI in 2004, many PEs have not been able to appoint 50% of the board strength as independent directors. In turn, they have asked for relaxation to 33%. The corporate governance is not working well as could be seen from the operations of the Audit, Compensation and Appointments Committee report of many PEs. The Government directors continue to swell the ranks and block the progressive moves in these enterprises. There is no evaluation system in place for the independent directors and other directors including the Chairman-cum-Managing Director. In many PEs, the officers of the Indian Administrative Services swarm the Boards in the name of preserving the public-ness of the enterprise.

11. AUTONOMY

Autonomy is the key issue that lingers in a state of limbo. Government of India which has shied away from taking concrete decisions such as the removal of Article 12 from the Indian Constitution which hinders the autonomy of PEs in terms of recruitment, promotion and day to day business. Like in the private sector, there is a need to have a level playing field for PEs and going by this assertion we could easily make out a case for exempting PEs from Article 12 of the Indian Constitution. The Comptroller and Auditor General (CAG) audit is another thorn in the flesh. Till 1954, as pointed out by Ashok Chanda, there was no CAG audit for PEs. Later, in 1956 on the pretext of Government funding, the PEs were brought under the purview of the CAG. The business acumen of the CAG auditors' needs a pep up. In its absence they are not able to discern the difference between the action of the Government and the action of a commercial entity. The influence of the institution of the Chief Vigilance Commission (CVC) has not helped public sector in any way. The appointments at the

Board level get delayed because of too much time being taken by the CVC. Each time the same person is appointed, the CVC has to be approached afresh. The CVC takes about six months to one year in clearing the names for the consideration of the Cabinet Committee on Appointments. The Public Enterprise Selection Board (PESB) takes too long a time to put top managerial personnel in PEs in their respective positions. The salaries offered are not competitive and tagging the salaries to those of officers of the IAS would not take PEs anywhere as there is a severe shortage of good managers even in private sector. The Public Investment Board also impairs the autonomy of PEs, although to some extent the Navratanas and the Miniratnas do not come under its purview now. The investment decisions in PEs should be subjected to the same norms as those applied in private enterprises and, in addition, plus PEs should get an extra credit for the social content of their project appraisal.

12. REGULATION

In the marketised world when we talk of a new world economic order, the commanding heights could not be left to private institutions and business. Regulation could alone ensure a happy co-existence of public and private sectors; developed and developing world; and consumer and producer. Some examples of regulatory bodies in India include the Telephone Regulatory Authority of India (TRAI), Insurance Regulatory and Development Authority (IRDA) and Securities and Exchange Board of India (SEBI). PEs have been voicing their grievance against these regulatory authorities as private sector counterparts have been benefited more by their policies. The behaviour of private sector has been adverse to the interest of the consumer as proved by the power supply disaster during the Mumbai floods in 2005 and super-cyclone of Orissa, where private sector defaulted in fulfilling its obligations to the local consumers. It is the PEs which stood like the rock of Gibraltar in the service of the consumers. The Central Electricity Authority and the State Electricity Regulatory Authorities have found the behaviour of private sector power generation, transmission and distribution firms very inappropriate in terms of working out profits on capital employed, accounting systems, control on T&D losses, and modernisation of their functions.

13. CONCLUSION

To conclude, PEs in the era of economic liberalisation have done extremely well much against the prophesies of the prophets of doom who had expected them to wind up and disappear. They have performed well in the market based regime. They could have done better but for the waywardness of the Government in terms of the policy regime for these enterprises which has never been consistent and to some extent anti-PE. These enterprises are expected to perform better by superior inter-PE collaboration, Optima, lack of bias in regulation, improved corporate governance and strong interface with the national and the international capital markets.

REFERENCES

[1] Government of India (Department of Public Enterprises, Ministry of Heavy Industries & Public Enterprises), Public Enterprises Survey: 2006-07, Vol-1, New Delhi, pp. 2-3.

[2] Institute of Public Enterprise, Spot Light: Central and State Public Enterprises, May, 2006 p. 2.

[3] Standing Conference of Public Enterprises, *Keleidoscope*, New Delhi, April, 2006.

[4] Institute of Public Enterprise, Spot Light: Central and State Public Enterprises, May, 2006 p. 1.

The Reform of State-Owned Enterprises and the Non-Public Sector of the Economy in China

Zhou Shaopeng

At present China's reform of state-owned enterprises have entered a new stage in the modern enterprise system marked by the quickened development of public-listed companies (after experiencing the expansion of rights) and transfer of profits in the framework of planned economic system, and innovation of enterprise system in the environment of market economy. The non-public sector of the economy is booming while the reform of state-owned enterprises is consistently strengthened. In the new historical stage to follow the trend of combining development of state-owned economy and non-public sector of the economy, we shall further the strategic adjustment of state-owned economy, break down the irrational and simple structure of stock rights in state-owned enterprises (especially the large and middle state-owned enterprises), actively strengthen the corporate system and joint-stock reform of state-owned enterprises, facilitate holistic listing of state-owned enterprises, import domestic and foreign strategic investors to participate in the joint-stock reform of state-owned enterprises, and make great efforts to develop non-public sector to develop the economy of mixed ownership to a new level.

1. REFORM OF STATE-OWNED ENTERPRISES

China has been reforming and opening to the world for the last 30 years. Corresponding to the reform of economic system that has changed from planned economy, planned commodity economy, to socialist market economy, China's reform of state-owned enterprises have undergone the stages of expansion of rights and transfer of profits, substitution of tax payment for profit, contract management responsibility system, and establishment of modern enterprise system etc. At present China enterprises' property system and organisational mode are in conformity with international standard by way of strengthening corporate system and reform of companies joint-stock and the State-owned Assets Operation Budget System.

The expansion of rights and transfer of profits to state-owned enterprises is the basic framework of the planned economic system (1979-1992). From the beginning of

China's reforms and opening up of the economy to the beginning of 1990s, China had implemented the state-owned enterprise reforms staged by allowing enterprises to retain a portion of profits, contracting with enterprises for operations on a profit baseline, substituting of tax payment for profit delivery, and contract operation management responsibility system. By these reforms China gradually adjusted the relations of responsibilities, rights, and profits between the state and the enterprises, endowing the state-owned enterprises with more power for independent operations. The initially defined position of leading role of stakeholder in the enterprises is the foundation for the innovation of the enterprises later.

Expanding the self-managing rights of enterprises with approaches by allowing enterprises to retain a portion of profits or have contract based on profits. (1979–1982)

- Experiments for expanding enterprises' self-managing rights by allowing enterprises to retain a portion of profits.

The experiment for expanding enterprises' self-managing rights firstly began in Sichuan Province. In the fourth quarter of 1978, Sichuan Province began the experiment in 6 local state-owned industrial enterprises. The experiment mainly is to allow enterprises to retain a proportion of profits based on the increased output of the enterprises; employees may get certain amount of dividends. This experiment stimulated the enterprises and their employees to work hard, resulting in better performance. Later, the experiments for expanding enterprises' self-managing rights were carried out in many other places. At the end of 1980, the experiment of state-owned industrial enterprises in provinces, municipalities, and autonomous regions (except for Tibet) had reached more than 6,000, occupying 15% of 42,000 industrial enterprises in national budget, 60% of total gross production value, and 70% of gross profits.

The experiment of allowing enterprises to retain a proportion of profits has enhanced the profits of the state, the enterprises, and the employees. This approach is positively good for enterprises to care for production and amend operations and mend management defects by determining the enterprises' income and the employees' dividends based on the performance and profits of the enterprises. However, the experiment to expand enterprises' self-managing rights has certain defects; a major defect is that enterprises may retain certain proportion of profits when they have surplus, but they are not liable for losses. Meanwhile it is hard to determine the proportion of profits to be retained by enterprises. Those enterprises having higher profits often suffered more deduction in profits.

- The industrial economy responsibility system focusing on profit-based contracts of 1981 to 1982.

In April 1981, the industry and traffic conference convened by the State Council deduced from the experience of the experiment allowing enterprises to retain a proportion of profits in Shandong Province, and clearly demanded the building and implementation of industrial economic responsibility system. The economic responsibility system is for the management of production and operations to increase the economic benefits of enterprises by coordinated relationship of responsibilities, rights, and profits under the direction of national planning. The national economic responsibility system for enterprises allows the enterprises to retain the profits deducted by a profit baseline specified in contract, or to retain a proportion of profits after the gross profits are deducted by a profit baseline in contract. In enterprises the economic responsibility system carries out overall economic auditing for determining employees' income by employees' post responsibility, assessment criteria, and economic performance.

To an extent the implementation of industrial economic responsibility system has eliminated the situation that enterprises live on the fund allocated by the state and the employees live on salaries furnished by the enterprise, and activated the enthusiasm of enterprises and employees, resulting in increased output and income of enterprises. Meanwhile the industrial economic responsibility system has changed to some extent the stale mechanism by which the state strictly controls the enterprises' expenditures and incomes, endowing enterprises with certain current fund. Besides, the industrial economic responsibility system not only has defined clearly the economic responsibility of workshop workers, but has gradually furnished assessment criteria and measures for leaders, technicians, clerks, and assistants by defining clearly their economic responsibilities, effectively pushing higher the enterprises' management performance. However, by the economic responsibility system often enterprises will seek their own profits more than that of the state. Argy-bargy was a severe problem when to determine the profit baseline and the proportion of profit to be retained by enterprises. Meanwhile in some enterprises the economic responsibility system is not put into effect that equalitarianism of distribution prevails in these enterprises.

Substitution of tax payment for profit delivery featuring the maximisation of taxation (1983 – 1985)

• First step of substitution of tax payment for profit delivery

The first step of substitution of tax payment for profit delivery is to charge certain proportion of income tax from the profits earned by an enterprise at first. This substitution method has three following defects. This approach failed to manage the distribution between state and enterprises properly. The enterprise's profits deducted by paid-in income taxes shall be re-distributed between state and enterprises in the form of contract or proportion retaining. So an enterprise has no true responsibility for gains or losses. Meanwhile profits vary between different industries and between different enterprises for the existence of an irrational pricing system. This step is not enough to encourage high performance and punish low performance.

- Second step of substitution of tax payment for profit delivery

From Oct.1 the government began to experiment with the second step of substitution of tax payment for profit delivery. By this step the state-owned enterprises turn in taxes to the state while retaining all its profits or suffering all its losses. This had moderated the conflicts brought by irrational prices, resulting in competition among enterprises in an approximately fair environment. This step is useful for encouraging high performance and punishing low performance. However, taxes charged by the second step of substitution of tax payment for profit delivery include income regulation tax charged on enterprises with certain degree of profits. So enterprises with high performance are restrained. Essentially the first step and second step of substitution of tax payment for profit delivery cannot make enterprises become self-managing players responsible for gains or losses in the market.

- Contracted operation based on substitution of tax payment for profit delivery (1985 - 1992)

The contracted operation for large and middle state-owned industrial enterprises is different from the approach allowing enterprises to retain profits deducted by a profit baseline specified in contract that had never been implemented. Enterprises shall meet the contracted requirements on output, varieties, and quality etc. in addition to profits. For small state-owned industrial enterprises the lease operation responsibility system is experimented, and for a few large and middle joint-stock system is experimented.

- Contract system for most large and middle state-owned industrial enterprises

In May 1987 the State Council determined to popularise the contract operation responsibility system throughout the country on the basis of the experiment carried out in 1986. To the end of 1987, 8,843 enterprises out of 11,402 large and middle state-owned industrial enterprises used the contract operation responsibility system, a percentage of 77.6%.

The contract operation system has its constraints, although it has energised enterprises and made the economic benefits generally higher than those enterprises that are without it. It failed to make enterprises become self-managing players responsible for their own gains and losses in the market. So the operational system of enterprises may be essentially changed. Especially profits retained by an enterprise may see reduction when they have to share them with the state. Enterprises fail to expand their self-managing rights.

- Lease system for small state-owned industrial enterprises.

Enterprises using lease operation responsibility system have higher independence, which energises a small state-owned enterprise. In fact, the lease operation responsibility system was experimented in some small enterprises before the popularisation of this system in 1987. Later, the lease operation responsibility system is used for most small state-owned enterprises, except for some of them using the contract operation responsibility system and some being transferred to a collectivity or an individual. The application of the lease operation responsibility system moved forward. To the end of 1988, enterprises using lease system and other operational forms are 24,660, 56.1% of the total number. Enterprises using lease system have more flexible operational mechanism. So most of them achieved high economic benefits. Enterprises with lease system are to compete in the market with their hard work and equipment.

- Experiment of joint-stock enterprises

The experiment of joint-stock system began after 1984, under the guidance of the Third Plenary Session of the Twelfth Central Committee of CPC to separate ownership and operation rights, making enterprises relatively independent economic entities. Incomplete statistics on 34 provinces, autonomous regions, municipalities under the direct administration of the Central Government, and cities specially designated in the state plan showed that to the end of 1991, the total number of enterprises experimented with joint-stock system was 3,220 (excluding township enterprises, joint ventures, and domestic joint enterprises). Of these enterprises 380 are of corporate shareholding, 12% of the total number; 2,751 are of internal staff shareholding, 85% of the total number; public-listed companies are 89, a percentage of 3%.

The joint-stock experiment is beneficial to the enterprise's operational system in many ways: making enterprises self-managing players responsible for their own gains and losses in the market; beneficial for energising enterprises and realising the value retaining and increment of state-owned assets; beneficial for enterprises' collecting fund and improving enterprises' assets-liability structure to facilitate the adjustment of economic structure. The existing major problems are: Some experimented enterprises had no assets assessment, or had under-assessment of state-owned assets. Some experimented enterprises had disorderly managing system violating the joint-stock rules; the related administration used the original and stale style for the management of joint-stock experiments, causing choosing the operations of experimented enterprise; the severely unbalanced supply and demand caused over-arbitrage in stock and trade market.

- The stage of enterprise innovation in market economy, i.e., the building and consummating modern enterprise system (1993 – today)

China's state-owned enterprises began the reform of a new stage featuring innovations and changes of systems and mechanisms from 1990s marked by the target of building socialist market economic system.

The building and consummating of modern enterprise system is to establish and consummate the modern company system with "distinct property rights, clear rights and responsibilities, separated government and enterprises, and scientific management". A series of tasks have been carried out in theory and practice to adjust and consummate ownership structure, and to make strategic adjustment in national domestic context. Significant progress is made.

In the new century China's state-owned enterprises, aiming at development through structural adjustment, have made material progress towards the socialist market economic system under the conduct of the principle of "Decision Concerning Some Major Issues for State-owned Enterprise Reform and Development" and in the strategic planning of national "Tenth Five-year". At the National People's Congress The Report on the Work of the Government made an excellent report on high achievements obtained by the reform of state-owned enterprises: "State-owned economy has quickened the adjustment steps and greatly reinforced control and competitiveness. State-owned enterprises have basically reached the target to realise surplus through three years of reform. Most large and middle state-owned enterprises have initially established modern enterprise system. A number of competent enterprises with enormous strength and competitiveness appeared. Middle and small state-owned enterprises have been further freed and energised. The reform of monopolised industries has made material progress". After the Sixteenth Congress of CPC, the reform of state-owned enterprises entered a new stage for building and consummating the state-owned assets investor system. The integral quality of state-owned economy is consistently increasing and its activity and competitiveness is getting reinforced.

In November 2002 the Sixteenth Congress of CPC issued integral planning for the reform of state-owned assets management system, pointing out that a major task for strengthening the reform of economic system is to continue the adjustment of the context and structure. The Government shall make laws and regulations to control state-owned assets. The Central Government and local governments shall be the investors on behalf of the state to perform functions and enjoy profits and interests. Bound by certain duties and obligations, the state-owned assets management system shall manage assets, personnel, and affairs. The Central Government shall be the investor for large state-owned enterprises, infrastructure, and important natural resources that concern the vital part the domestic economy and state security. For other state-owned assets local governments shall be the investors on behalf of the state. The Central Government and provincial and municipal (prefecture) governments shall set state-owned assets management institutes to study effective state-owned assets, operation systems and style. At present China has established the basic framework of state-owned assets management system thereby strengthening of the reform of state-owned enterprises further.

The Seventeenth Congress of CPC further demanded the quickened corporate-system and joint-stock reform for state-owned enterprises. The state-owned assets are growing due to the progress in reforming state-owned enterprises and the consistently energising them. To the end of 2006, the total amount of the assets owned by state-owned enterprises was 29-trillion-Yuan, increasing by 45.7% than the end of 2003, average annual increase ratio 13.4%. In 2006 China's state-owned enterprises harvested sales income 16.2-trillion Yuan, increasing by 50.9% than 2003, average annual increase ratio 14.7%; gains 1.2-trillion-Yuan, increasing by 147.3% than 2003, average annual increase ratio 35.2%; turned in 1.4-trillion-Yuan of taxes, increasing by 72% than 2003, average annual increase ratio 19.8%.

China has not established complete socialist market economic system as of now, although the reform of state-owned enterprises have obtained breakthroughs and remarkable achievements. For example, the government still plays a role in operations of enterprises and capital. The efficiency of the state-owned assets management system should be further improved. There are many problems in the diversification, decentralisation, and rationalisation of stock rights. It is a common knowledge that the government is the single shareholder of an enterprise, or controls the majority of shares. Moreover, the corporate governance structure is not standardised yet.

2. THE DEVELOPMENT OF NON-PUBLIC SECTOR OF THE ECONOMY

China's non-public sector is booming due to the consistently strengthened reform of state-owned enterprises. CPC and the government have affirmed and made some favourable policies for the development of non-public sector of the economy to encourage and support the development of non-public sector of the economy. Early in August 1980 the document To Promote Employment of Urban Labours issued by the Central Committee of CPC pointed out that individual economy is "an individual's labour permitted by the law; it does not exploit others. This individual economy is a necessary complement to the socialist public ownership, and shall play an important role in a long period of the coming future." In June 1981 the Decision on Some Historical Issues After the Foundation of PRC by the Central Committee of CPC clearly stated: "The state-owned and collective economy is the basic economic form of China. The citizens' individual economy within certain confinement is the necessary complement to public-owned economy." Article 11 of The Constitution of the People's Republic of China passed by the fifth session of the Fifth National People's Congress in December 1982 states: "The individual economy of urban and rural working people, operating within the limits prescribed by law, is a complement to the socialist public economy." In 1984 by systematic way The Decision by the Central Committee of CPC on the Reform of Economic System demonstrated the basic guidelines for the development of individual economy, pointing out "to insist on the common development of multiple economic forms and operational styles is the policy guiding us in a long period, and a prerequisite for the progress of socialism." In November 1987 the Thirteenth Congress of CPC clearly issued the policy to encourage the development of individual economy and private economy. In April 1988 the first session of the Seventh National People's Congress passed the Amendments to the Constitution of PRC that defines the legal status and economic status of private economy. Article 11 of the Constitution adds a new paragraph which reads: "The state permits the private sector of the economy to exist and develop within the limits prescribed by law. The private sector of the economy is a complement to the socialist public economy. The state protects the lawful rights and interests of the private sector of the economy, and exercises guidance, supervision and control over the private sector of the economy."

In October 1992 the Fourteenth Congress of CPC defined the target of China's reform is to build the socialist market economic system featuring the long-term and common development of multiple economic forms wherein the public ownership (including ownership by the whole people and the collective ownership) plays a leading role, and the individual economy, private economy, and foreign capital economy are complementary. In September 1997 the Fifteenth Congress of CPC published: "The common development featuring the leading public ownership complemented by multiple ownerships is a basic economic policy for the primary stage of socialism in China." And "The non-public sector of the economy is an important part of China's socialist market economy. The non-public economies such as individual economy and private economy shall be encouraged and conducted continuously to promote their healthy development." In March 1999 the second session of the Ninth National People's Congress passed the Amendments to the Constitution of PRC, stating clearly "the non-public economies such as individual economy and private economy developing within the limits prescribed by law are important part of the socialist market economy." By these Amendments the government affirmed the rational existence and contribution of the non-public sector of the economy in its 20 years' development plan.

In November 2002, the Sixteenth Congress of CPC clearly published: "The government shall firmly support, encourage, and conduct the development of non-public sector of the economy." In 2005 the State Council issued the Several Opinions on Encouraging, Supporting and Conducting Non-public Ownership Economic Development, providing a policy environment favourable for the development of non-public sector of the economy. Enterprisers of non-public sector of the economy have higher social status in a new period for the comprehensive development of non-public sector of the economy.

Compared to the end of 2006, by the third quarter 2007 China has 5,387-thousand registered private enterprises, increasing by 8.2%; the total amount of their registered capital reached 8.8-trillion-Yuan, increasing by 16.5%; they employed 70,586-thousand people, increasing by 9.8%; investors 13,621-thousand, increasing by 7.1%. Compared to the same period of last year, the total amount of the fixed assets in non-public sector of the economy in urban areas reached 5.67-trillion-Yuan, increasing by 36.3%; the added-value of large-scale private industry increased by 26.5%; the total amount of import& export of private enterprises was 313.4-billion dollars, increasing by 43.7%, of which the export amount was 223.63-billion dollars, increasing by 46.5%; all the increase ratios are higher than the average national level.

From January to November 2007, the large-scale private industrial enterprises harvested gross profits of 400-billion-Yuan, increasing by 50.9% than the same period of last year. Meanwhile taxes from individual and private economies have seen great increase. Based on the statistics of the State Administration of Taxation, in 2007 the total amount of taxes paid by private enterprises was 477.15-billion-Yuan, increasing by 36.5% when compared to the same period of last year. The total amount of taxes paid by individual businessmen was 148.42-billion-Yuan, increasing by 24.2% when compared to the same period of last year.

3. THE COMBINED DEVELOPMENT OF STATE-OWNED ECONOMY AND NON-PUBLIC SECTOR OF THE ECONOMY

The Decision of the Central Committee of CPC on Some Issues Concerning the Improvement of the Socialist Market Economy passed by the third plenary session of the Sixteenth Central Committee of CPC pointed out: The government shall further the development of mixed-ownership economy and permit diversified investors, following the change of the market-oriented economy. The Seventeenth Congress of CPC again called for the firm encouragement and support to the development of non-public sector of the economy and pointed out: China shall develop mixed-ownership economy based on the modern property system, i.e., by modern property forms such as joint-stock cooperation and strategic investment to strengthen the interconnection among various ownership economies.

At present China has entered a new stage for the mixed development of state-owned economy and non-public sector of the economy, that the state-owned economy and the non-public sector of the economy became their cooperation and harmonious development from their original development in separate ways. More and more non-public enterprises and state-owned enterprises, collective enterprises have through joint-stock system, especially by public-listed company, achieved mutual promotion and mutual development at higher level.

Experiments have been carried out throughout China for the development of mixed ownership economy, resulting in high economic results. Major approaches for the mixed development are: Quicken the development of non-public sector of the economy and reinforce the foundation for the development of mixed ownership economy; facilitate the reform of state-owned property system and accelerate the development of mixed ownership economy; import foreign capital to improve the stock structure of the mixed ownership enterprises; exert the government's efforts to strengthen the construction of the capital market to further the development of the mixed ownership economy.

Following the trend of mixed development of state-owned economy and non-public sector of the economy, in this new historical stage China shall further the strategic adjustment of the state-owned economy. The simple structure and irrational context of state-owned enterprises (including enterprises owned or controlled by the state), especially of large and middle state-owned enterprises, should be broken down. To develop the mixed ownership economy to a new level we shall strengthen corporate-system and joint-stock reform of state-owned enterprises, push forward state-owned enterprises to go to public-listed as a whole, and invite domestic and foreign strategic investors to participate the joint-stock alteration of state-owned enterprises.

An Analysis of Mainland China's Economic Growth and Policy during 1992-2006

Li Xuefeng

In 1992, China announced its aim of building up a socialist market economy. From then on, its economic growth became an unprecedented scenery in its history and aroused the attention of the world. What really happened in the last fifteen years? What should the Chinese government do to sustain its economic growth in the future? This paper analyses the key issues of China' economic growth: the initial circumstances, the economic growth performance, the economic policy, the institutional reforms, and the related cultural and political evolution. The last part of the paper raises suggestions for future growth policies

1. INTRODUCTION

1.1 What 1992 Means?

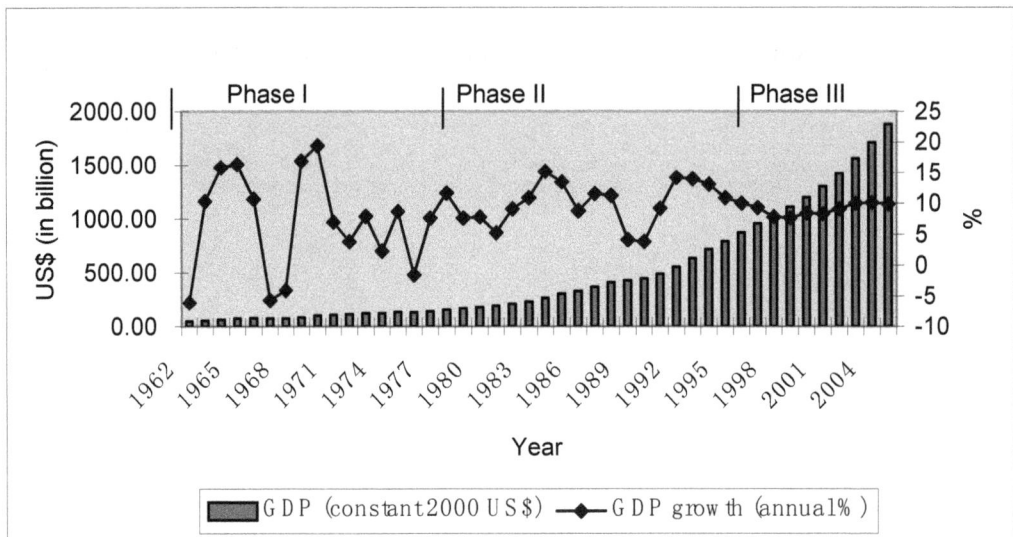

Fig. 1: China GDP Growth Rate (1962-2005)

Source: Data Derived from World Bank: World Development Indicator, 2007.

The year of 1992 is a turning point in the history of the country. The evidences of which includes:

It is the starting point of a new economic development stage. Figure 1 shows that China's growth has experienced three distinct periods since 1960's. (1) From 1962 to 1977, the rate of growth varied greatly. This was mainly affected by political-economical policies, plus the international environment. (2) From 1978 to 1991, the gap between growth rate changes was smaller than previous ones. This is a period when central planning dominate, while the market factors played an increasingly important role year after year. (3) From 1992 to 2005, the curve of growth rates was smooth. This shows the growth policy was getting stabilised and more mature.

The trigger for the third phase was the famous Southern Talks of the late senior leader Deng Xiaoping. Though having stepped down for three years from 1989, Deng could not help putting forward a series of talks to promote a bolder reform and growth, when he saw the economic growth to be slow and the related policies were conservative at that time. Deng asserted that market economy is not necessarily a capitalist one. Socialist countries could choose market economy too. Under his guidance, the Communist Party of China set up the fundamental direction of building up a socialist market economy in 1993. And inspired by Deng's brilliant thoughts, China's growth rate reached to 14.2% in 1992. The leadeing reason for the fifteen years of growth after 1992 was that the CPC arrived at coherence in the general direction of economic growth and institutional reforms. The Party itself became mature in dealing with growth, reforms and social stability.

Yet the fifteen years period was also a historical time that was full of exciting and complicated developments. Without understanding them, people outside China cannot understand China's today and tomorrow correctly. Without studying them, people inside China cannot understand the lessons of growth and reforms properly.

1.2 Aims of This Paper

The paper has two aims. One is to find the essence of China's economic growth in the past fifteenth years. Another is to study of sustainable growth in the future.

1.3 Could China be a Model of Growth?

This is an interesting, fashionable and challenging question. Nowadays, the world begins to recognise China's immense role in global economy and the achievements of its economic growth. Many people believe that China will sustain its economic growth in future. Yet, many others do not share such optimism on the economic front. Both assessments seem reasonable and sensible. To the utmost sense, this is concern about the re-evaluating of communism, Confucian and the Chinese people's capability of creativity. This paper will discuss about this at the last session.

2. CHINA'S CONDITION UNTIL 1992

The stating point of China's economic growth are its natural and social conditions. The initial conditions discussed here are neutral and important with respect to the country's further growth. They are the pre-requisites for understanding China's growth.

2.1 Geographical Conditions – Big territory

The first image of China is its big size. With a total land area of 9.6 million square kilometres, China is the largest country in Asia and the third largest in the world, next to Russia and Canada. The advantage of a big territory is it could take the advantage of a 'nation wide economy of scale and scope'. The country is a 'world' in itself. There is no tariff between provinces. People use the same official language; use the same money; live under the same political and legal system, and work and live under the same production and life system.

The disadvantage of the big territory is obvious too. A big country with large varieties poses severe challenges to the Government in controlling its economic and social life. The biggest dilemma in recent years of reform is as follows:

If a uniform policy is imposed, vibrancy is loot. If the policy is too loose, it will lead to disorder.

2.2 Complicated Natural Conditions

The terrain in China descends from west to east like a staircase with four steps. The highest step of the staircase is the Qinghai-Tibet Plateau ('roof of the world'), while the lowest land consists of the vast continental shelf formed by the shallows together with the islands on the rim of the mainland.[1] On climate, most of China has a continental monsoon climate. In terms of temperature, the nation can be sectored from south to north into equatorial, tropical, subtropical, warm-temperate, temperate, and cold-temperate zones. Precipitation gradually declines from the southeastern to the northwestern inland area, and the average annual precipitation varies greatly from place to place. In southeastern coastal areas, it reaches over 1,500 mm, while in northwestern areas, it drops to below 200 mm. As a whole, China is always subjected to extreme weather condition due to seasonal changes throughout the year.[2]

The advantage of such a natural condition is that at least, some of the places in the country could enjoy a pro-growth location, like the eastern regions. In fact, the eastern regions have been the most prosperous places since ancient times. But for

---

[1] Edited from www.china.org.cn
[2] *Ibid.*

other places, typically the west, are facing a worse national condition and are relatively backward regions from ancient to modern time. As a whole, this variety of natural condition makes very difficult for the Government to undertake a unified effective growth policy.

2.3 A Huge Amount of National Resources

China's cultivated lands, forests and grasslands are among the world's largest in terms of sheer area. China is rich in mineral resources, and all of the world's known minerals can be found in the country. The reserves of the major mineral resources, such as coal, iron, copper, aluminum, molybdenum, manganese, tin, lead, zinc and mercury, are in the world's front rank. These are great advantages for China's economic growth. It is one of the most important reasons for China to set up its all sectors of industry in the past decades. The disadvantage is that the 'natural resource curse' did occur to some extent. Waste of raw materials happens common. The mindset of resource and environment protection is difficult to inculcate.

Taking the above geographical conditions as a whole, some of the disadvantages are being overcome with the evolution of technological progress and globalisation. Television and internet make information delivery and public education easier; upgrading of transportation conditions makes the flow of people easier; and globalisation makes the country easier to access foreign resources.

2.4 Historical and Social Cultural Conditions

Until the year of 1992, China has gone through three historical and social cultural streams. The first is the 5000 years of traditional culture. The principles of Confucius permeate social life everywhere. The cultural accumulation is quite thick. The traditional literatures, arts, customs and medicine service the Chinese people well. Ordinary people's lives are full of meaning. It is basically a healthy culture. Frankly, however, it is not a culture that could promote rapid economic growth. The value of Golden Mean encourages a balanced life style, not pursuit of wealth.

The second stream is the culture of Marxism since 1949. Unlike Eastern European countries, the Chinese' acceptance of Marxism was not imposed by foreign forces. To a great extent, it chooses this ideology by itself. The Marxist Materialism and Dialectics help the Chinese take an objective mindset in dealing with difficulties. Yet, the traditional ideology of socialism, i.e., centrally planned command economy, also binds the Chinese's mindset too.

The third stream is the capitalist culture since 1978. With CPC's the guidelines of learning from all the excellent civilisations of mankind, the notions of efficiency, of money and market are widely recognized in the Chinese society. The advantage of the mixture of cultures is that it gives the Chinese a chance to take advantage of all of them. A new culture is in shaping quickly during the next fifteen years. The disadvantage of the mixture of cultures is that the Chinese are puzzled by what they should follow as guidance for life in general. The three streams are so different in their roots. The rebuilding of core value is a hard job.

2.5 Population Condition

Could a population of 1.3 billion be an opportunity or a threat to economic growth? The answer is both China takes advantage of the huge domestic market caused by the vast population and the abundant human resource and human capital. For example, there will be over a million students graduating from universities every year. It is a large of human capital pool for economic growth.

On the side of disadvantages, China suffered on every economic indicator in per capita terms. For example, due to China's large population, the areas of cultivated land, forest and grassland per capita are small, especially in the case of cultivated land - only one-third of the world's average level. A large proportion of people did not enjoy basic living condition (living in the mountains for example) and basic education, the disadvantage is really a big hindering factor to economic growth. The huge number of people that are absolutely poor indicates that China would be a developing country for quite a long time.

2.6 Political and Institutional Conditions

The 20th century saw great changes in China's political and institutional revolution and evolution. Till the end of 1980's, it showed both great opportunities and great challenges to China's economic growth.

The political and institutional advantages are mainly twofold. Firstly, a stable and powerful political framework is in place. The Chinese Communist Party exerted a powerful control over the country. At both central and local levels, were always the party committees in the lead; the Peoples Congress and its standing committees operate like Western parliaments; the governments lead daily operating; and the Chinese Peoples' Political Consultant Conferences (these are representatives from all political parties and social layers) operate like Western Houses of Representatives or Senates. The CPC, with a seventy-million membership all over the country, made it easy to implement the national strategy. Secondly, the institutional reform is on the way. Deng's theory of 'no matter black or white cat, it is a good cat as long as it could catch rats' rested deeply in peoples' minds. People took reform as the most powerful engine for economic development.

On the other hand, the political and institutional disadvantages were also obvious. The inefficiency and structural problems were widespread. The government system was low in efficientcy the market oriented institutional reform system was just at its beginning. The late senior leader Deng Xiaoping said 'reform is also a revolution'. It means China would experience lot of painful changes from then on.

2.7 Economic Conditions

On the economic front, China was faced with the advantages of central planning since 1949 and the advantage of reform since 1978. Yet it also was faced with the disadvantage of central planning and the undeveloped country. The advantages in economic conditions were mainly threefold. Firstly, the over four decades of construction from 1949 to 1991 left China a relatively highly industrialised. China had developed its own industries in almost every sector. Its raw material industry, manufacturing industry, heavy chemical industry, construction industry and so on were able to satisfy a large proportion of growth needs. Its technological achievements, like in astronomical and electronic industries, showed great potential for further economic growth. Secondly, the economic strength had largely enhanced through the thirteen years of reform and opening up since 1978 as compared with the earlier period. In 1992, the nation's economy was not plagued by shortages any more. The buyers' dominant market is shaping up. Thirdly, the foreign direct investment in the 1980's brought in investment, new technology, new business and management techniques.

The disadvantages were obvious too. The economic competitiveness of the country was relatively weak comparing industrialised countries. Many of the state owned enterprises were inefficient. The management system in all organisations, basically followed the former Soviet Union, which could not adapt to the market-oriented economy. The structural imbalances between urban and rural sectors and between deferent provinces were widespread. In fact, China's economy faces great challenges.

3. ANALYSIS OF CHINA'S ECONOMIC GROWTH

China experienced a high level of quangitative economic growth in the past fifteen years. The average GDP annual growth rate was at 10.19% during 1992-2005. With the average population annual growth of 0.896%, per capita GDP increased by an annual average of 9.2% on average each during this period.

The quality of economic growth was more complicated. The rate of growth as a whole is positive. The growth rate was basically constant, and seems to converge to an average of 10%. The first three years (1992-1994) were higher than average, due to Deng's assertion of accelerating the economic growth. Then, affected by the Asian crisis, the years after 1997 it was little lower. In recent years, the rates were basically the same, which shows that China has become a dept in controling the economy at a stable rate of growth.

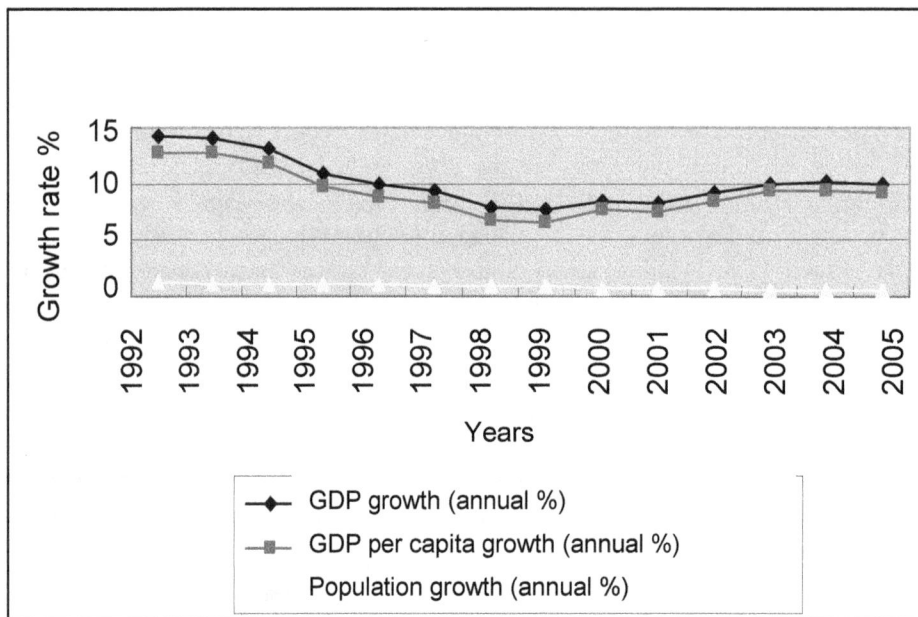

Fig. 2: China GDP: Growth Rate (1992-2005)

Source: Derived from World Bank: World Development Indicator, 2007

The outcome of growth was enjoyed by most of the Chinese people, but at the same time, the inequality was enlarged too. The Gini co-coefficienct was getting larger year by year. According to Chinese State Statistic Bureau, in 1990, it was 0.343; in 1995, 0.389; in 2000, 0.417[3]. The income differences between urban and rural areas, and between east and west have grown. This is inevitable for a country in its process of fast growth, though at the same time, it is a serious problem.

According to a Chinese government white paper, the number of poverty-stricken people in rural areas with problems obtaining sufficient food and clothing decreased from 250 million in 1978 to 30 million in 2000; and the impoverishment rate there decreased from 30.7 percent to about three percent. Of this, the number of poverty-stricken people in the impoverished counties to which the Chinese Government gave priority in its poverty alleviation efforts decreased from 58.58 million in 1994 to

---

[3] National Statistics Bureau web site.

17.1 million in 2000.[4] The 2004 International Aid-the-Poor Conference spoke highly of the achievements China had made in helping the poor, as 'a good example'.[5]

The environmental problems were serious. China has in fact followed the Western countries' model during industrialisation period. Fortunately, the central government had realised the importance of protecting environment. The amount of industrial waste water, oxygen for industrial chemicals, industrial sulfur dioxide, industrial smoke and industrial dust discharged in generating one unit of GDP in China in 2004 dropped by 58%, 72%, 42%, 55% and 39%, respectively, from 1995.[6]

China's minority people enjoy their special life style. The state respects the folkways and customs of minority peoples in such aspects as diet, burial, festivals and marriage. Minority peoples also enjoy freedom of religious belief, supported by specific state policies. To date, there are more than 18 million believers in Islam among ethnic minorities, over 30,000 mosques and 40,000 imams and ahungs. Just taking Tibet, there are more than 1,700 places for Tibetan Buddhist activities, and 46,000 lamas and monks.[7]

3.1 Deconstructing and Accounting Economic Growth

If we take the period of 1990-2000 as a presentation of recent years of growth, China's growth exhibits the following features:

Firstly, factor productivity account for nearly half of China's growth (see Table 1). It is extremely high in the world compared with other regions. This could be due to several reasons. (1) Institutional reform greatly liberated productivity. With the legal system in place, more efficience in governance, incentives reaching all levels of government and the whole society, the economic machine got speed up. The historical comparison in Table 2 verifies this, in which both the 1980's and 1990's showed high contribution of factor productivity to growth after the start of reforms in 1978. (2) Modern management techniques promoted productivity by learning from the west and by the diffusing of technology through FDI. (3) The vast scale of the economy contributed the productivity too. One example is, with the investment getting hot, there appeared several dozens of iron and steel conglomerates that had a production capacity of over one million tons of steel. (4) FDI contributes to the productivity greatly.

Secondly, physical capital accounts for one third of growth approximately. This rate is similar to that of industrial countries and East Asian countries, but much higher

---

[4] White Paper of the Government: The Development-oriented Poverty Reduction Program for Rural China, Chapter 1.
[5] White Paper of the Government: China's Progress in Human Rights in 2004, Chapter 1.
[6] White Paper of the Government: Environmental Protection in China (1996-2005), Chapter 2.
[7] White Paper of the Government: Fifty Years of Progress in China's Human Rights, Chapter 5.

than that of Latin American, South Asian and African countries. This rate is also higher than earlier times, i.e., in comparison with its own history from 1960's. What this implies is that the faster the growth, a higher proportion of investment contributes to growth. China's own experience and that of East Asian countries verify this.

Thirdly, labour force and education both account for lower proportions of growth. This may mean that relative importance of these two factors is lower than that of productivity and physical capital. The low contribution of labour force under the back ground of a large pool of labour may mean the potential of labour force to growth is low. The higher record of it in previous decades shows its highest period of functioning is over. The low contribution of education may mean that China needs to enhance its education. Its relatively high proportion in industrial countries is a good example to China.

Table 1: Sources of Growth 1990-2000

Regions	Output	Output per worker	Contribute of			
			Physical capital	Labour force	Education	Factor productivity
China	10.1	8.8	3.2	1.3	0.3	5.1
Industrial countries	2.5	1.5	0.8	1.0	0.2	0.5
East Asia (less China)	5.7	3.4	2.3	2.3	0.5	0.5
Latin America	4.0	1.1	0.6	2.9	0.4	0.2
South Asia	5.3	2.8	1.2	2.5	0.4	1.2
Africa	2.3	–0.2	–0.1	2.5	0.4	–0.5
Middle East	3.6	0.8	0.3	2.8	0.5	0.0
World	3.3	1.9	0.9	1.4	0.3	0.8

Source: Bosworth and Collins, extract and calculate from statistics of www.brookings.edu

Table 2: China's Sources of Growth 1960-2000

Period	Output	Output per worker	Contribute of			
			Physical capital	Labour force	Education	Factor productivity
1960-1970	2.8	0.9	0.0	1.9	0.3	0.5
1970-1980	5.3	2.8	1.6	2.5	0.4	0.7
1980-1990	9.2	6.8	2.1	2.4	0.4	4.2
1990-2000	10.1	8.8	3.2	1.3	0.3	5.1
1960-2000	6.8	4.8	1.7	2.0	0.4	2.6

Source: Bosworth and Collins, extract and calculate from statistics of www.brookings.edu

3.2 Savings and Investment

Figure 3 shows a basically high investment level. During the past fifteen years, China's net investment was extremely high. The gross capital formation was 36.88% of GDP. From Table 3 we could see: The high investment was first due to high FDI and high private sector investment (investments were approximately twice that of savings). Secondly, it was contributed by government (investments were approximately half of its savings). And thirdly, it was contributed by households (investments were approximately one-third of its savings).

The high investment level could be explained as: (1) Market oriented reforms had attracted investment from FDI and private sectors. (2) Taxation reform promoted government savings, which in turn increased investment. (3) Households saved for housing, children' education and medical care. Some of these savings were invested in the stock market. Savings were averaged at 39.13% of GDP during 1992-2004. This is high, compared with most other countries. Current account balance of payment was basically a small surplus, except for the year of 1993, when investment, climate was too hot. As a whole, the state of China's savings and investment was healthy, only with slightly vibrate, and saving were always slightly higher than investment.

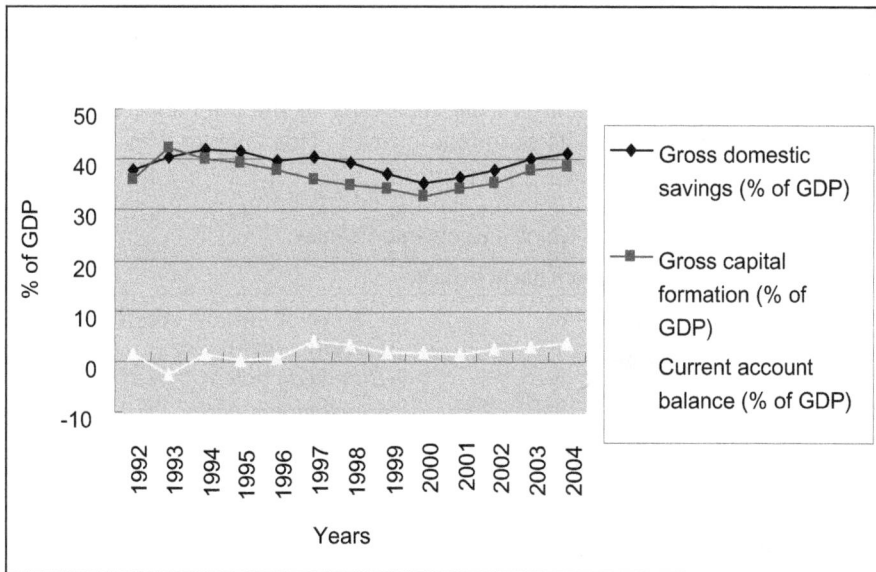

Fig. 3: Saving and Investment (1992-2004)

Source: Derived from World Bank: World Development Indicator, 2007.

Table 3: Savings and Investment in Several Important Years (percentage of GDP)

	1996	2000	2004	2005
Households				
S	20	15	16	16
S-I	14	10	10	10
Entreprises				
S	13	15	19	20
S-I	−16	−11	−13	−11
Government				
S	5	6	6	6
S-I	3	3	3	2
China				
GNS (above the line)	37	35	41	44
Gross capital formation	38	34	41	40
Current account (bop data)	1	2	4	7

Source: Louis Kuijs, How will China's Saving-Investment Balance Evolve? Workshop on The international financial integration of China and India, May 26, 2006, New Delhi.

4. ECONOMIC POLICIES: A PERSPECTIVE

As a big developing country, there is demand for various policies to deal with the many 'big' problems in China's economic social life. Even if the government does not want to intervene in the economy and society, the situations demand it. So the scope of economic policies in China is wide and many of the policies could not be ignored if we want to understand its economic growth. This chapter tries to discuss the following issues.

Table 4: China's Economic Policies

Fiscal policies: Pro-investment fiscal policies	
Pro-growth economic policies	Pro-human capital policies
Open-up Policy	*Poverty relief policy*
Grain policy	*Education policy*
Industrial policy	*Employment policy*
Environment protection policy	*Social security policy*
Policy designing	

4.1 Pro-investment Fiscal Policies

From the figures above, the Chinese fiscal policies have the following features:

Firstly, the revenue is optimal. Figure 4 show three indicators grow steadily. Government revenue as a whole grows steadily. The increase rate of government revenue after 1992 is always higher than that of GDP growth, at the rate of 18.4%.

The later is basically at around 10%. The percentage of government revenue to GDP has been growing after 1995. This may be due to the reform of tax system. Although the cancellation of agriculture tax has caused a little decline in tax revenue during 2002-2003, the steady growth of GDP and the rise of revenue from SOEs would still keep the trend of government revenue growth in the future.

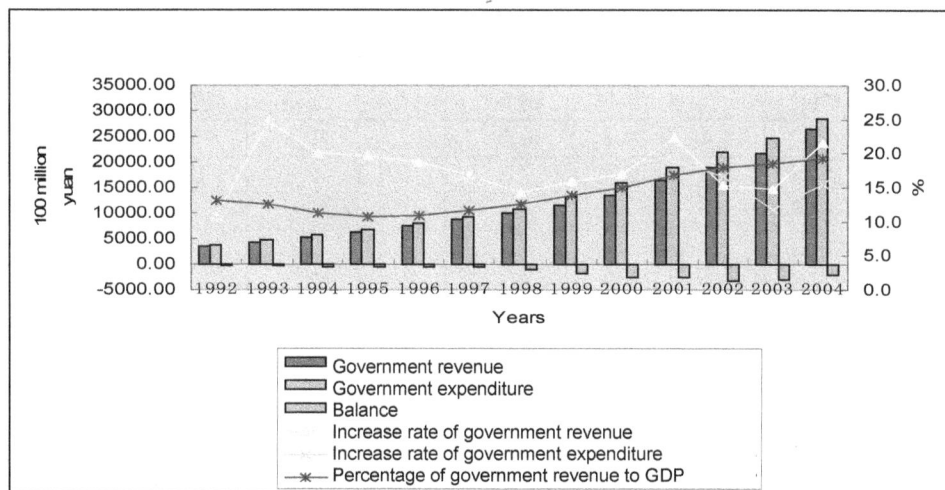

Fig. 4: China's Government Revenue and Expenditure

Source: China National Statistics Bureau web site.

Secondly, the non-tax revenue is too low (see Table 5). China's non-tax revenue was only 1.5% of GDP, compared with Singapore 10.4%, OECD 2.7%, etc. It is below that of most developed countries. If the large proportion of state owned enterprises are taken into account, the revenue from the assets is really low. Thirdly, Chinese fiscal policy is a proactive. This could be seen from the capital expenditure. The rate of capital expenditure to GDP is 3.9%, nearer to those of the fast developing countries, like Singapore (5.1%), Malaysia (5.1%), and Thailand (6.0%), but higher than the OECD countries (2.2%). Government investment in infrastructure is indeed an important source of growth. Fourthly, the Chinese government fiscal is an 'eating' fiscal (salaries' expenditure is high). The rate of current expenditure to GDP (14.7%) is similar to other Asian countries, like Singapore (14.0%), Korea (13.5%), and Philippines (16.4%). But if one takes the large number of employees in the Chinese public sector, the expenditure would mostly go to salary and basic operation fees. This is why the Peoples' Congress Annual Conference every year would call for increasing the development budget for education and R&D. Fifthly, the Chinese government fiscal is a prudent fiscal too. The overall deficit in 2006 is −1.9% of GDP, which is lower than the OECD countries (−3.6% of GDP). So, despite the debt is high in absolute terms, the total situation is basically safe. This is just as the IMF reported, 'the budget deficit could rise overtime, but fiscal consolidation over the past few years would allow this without jeopardizing longer-term fiscal sustainability'[8].

Table 5: Comparative Central Government Revenue and Expenditure

	China 2002-06	OECD 1990-2001	Singapore 1990-2001	Korea 1990-97	Malaysia 1990-97	Thailand 1990-2001	Philippines 1990-2001
Total revenue	16.9	33.3	33.5	18.2	26.1	17.8	17.5
Current revenue		33.3	26.5	17.8	26.0	17.8	17.1
Tax revenue	15.4	30.7	16.5	15.7	19.8	15.9	15.3
Tax on income, profit and capital gains	3.0	9.1	7.3	5.5	8.9	5.1	5.8
Social security contributions		8.4	0.0	1.3	0.3	0.3	0.0
Domestic taxes on goods and services	9.7	10.6	4.7	6.0	5.9	7.5	4.7
Taxes on international trade		0.2	0.4	1.3	3.7	2.6	4.1
Other taxes	1.7	2.5	3.7	1.6	1.0	0.4	0.7
Non-tax revenue	1.5	2.7	10.4	2.2	6.2	1.9	1.8
Capital revenue		0.1	7.1	0.4	0.1	0.0	0.4
Total expenditure and net lending	18.8	36.9	23.0	18.5	25.0	18.3	19.3
Current expenditure	14.7	34.6	14.0	13.5	19.7	11.8	16.4
Of which: interest payment		3.5	1.3	0.5	4.0	0.8	4.6
Capital expenditure	3.9	2.2	5.1	2.8	5.1	6.0	2.6
Net lending		0.0	3.9	2.3	0.3	0.5	0.3
Overall surplus/deficit	−1.9	−3.6	10.6	−0.3	1.1	−0.5	−1.8

Sources: China's data calculated from the data represented on 2006 IMF Staff Report on P.R. China, page 36; other data copied from 'Singapore Success' page 56.

---

[8] 2006 IMF Staff Report on P.R. China, p.20.

Besides the above, the fiscal reform, especially the adjustment of Central-Local relationship would make it possible to get more government revenue, because this could further encourage the government to get more revenue and better utilisation of expenditure. As a whole, as long as China's economy could keep growth in the future, the fiscal situation would surely be better year after year.

On the other hand, due to the lax control over lower level local government budgets, the accumulation of deficit at the county level and township level could be a big problem. Together with the burden coming from the state commercial banks, the gross burden to fiscal is quite heavy.

4.2 Pro-Growth Economic Policies

Open-up Policy

After launching open-up policy in 1978, the 1980's saw the setting up of four Special economic zones and fourteen economic and technological development zones. The open-up policy has proved to be an important engine to economic growth. After Deng's Southern talk, the open-up policy was implemented in the following aspects:

Firstly, the scope of open-up is enlarged. More than 800 economic development zones were set up. These economic zones, trying to absorb investment with low tax rate and other supporting policies, are the main avenues to absorb FDI during the past fifteen years. These economic zones also led to problems at the same time. Much cultivable land was wasted. Environment was getting worse in some of these places. These problems were realised by the central government and took control of the situation to some extent. Besides these, Pudong New District in Shanghai was developed and achieved great success in the 1990's. Encouraged by this success, the development of Binhai New District in Tianjin (another large city after Shanghai) was started last year. The diversity of open-up is increased. Other sorts of open-up models were in place too. The tax-free export-oriented manufacturing districts were setup in 15 cities. More inland places were opened up. Many inland border cities were opened up to the neighbour countries.

Thirdly, the depth of openness is extended. After joining the WTO, a fully open-up strategy was begun. More and more Chinese enterprises were encouraged to go out to invest in other countries. As a whole, the Chinese took a proactive pragmatic policy in opening up the economy. The action to get on the international track in regulation, management, technology and even terminology is steadily pushing China to be a modern society.

Grain Policy

The Chinese government believes that, 'grain production plays an important role in maintaining social stability. Otherwise, it will not be able to maintain its national economy's sustained, rapid and healthy development.'[9] The grain policy has evolved as[10]:

Firstly, strategically adjust agricultural institutions to raise the productivity. To stabilise the land policy, in 1993 the government made a decision that upon the expiration of a land contract[11] the term could be extended for another 30 years and that during the contract term farmers could freely transfer the land use right with compensation, on condition that the way of its use remain unchanged. In 2003, China exempted agriculture from taxation, which shows that utmost effort is being made to promote agricultural production.

Secondly, try to deal with the grain issue through market mechanism.

- To set up a full fledged grain market, the Chinese government abolished the state monopoly of purchase and marketing of grain in 1995. Now the following four methods are used to purchase grain: The state purchases grain through quotas; the state purchases grain through negotiations with producers; grain-processing enterprises purchase grain from the wholesale markets; and farmers sell their grain at fairs. In 1993 grain rationing was abolished in cities and towns throughout the country.

- Strengthened the regulation and control of grain markets. To protect grain producers and stabilize grain markets the Chinese government started in 1990 to set up the minimum grain price protection system and the special grain reserve system for regulating supply and demand and the prices in grain markets. In 1994 a grain market risk fund system at the central and provincial levels was set up.

- Made use of international market. The Chinese government believes that making timely and appropriate use of the international grain market and regulating the relationship between the domestic grain supply and demand through import and export trade are also necessary for stabilising grain markets. In recent years the grain prices on the domestic market have been approaching step by step those on the international market.

Thirdly, made use of technology for the grain issues. Chinese government launched the 'Seed Project'. China will perfect the breeding, import, processing, marketing and extension system of improved varieties. By 2000 seeds of all main grain crops will be

---

[9] Government white paper: the Grain Issue in China, 1996.

[10] *Ibid.*

[11] In 1983 the Chinese government declared clearly that the existing rural basic management systems would remain unchanged for quite a long time to come, and the public land contracted out by the collectives to peasant households could be used by the latter for as long as 15 years.

renewed; 50 percent of commodity seeds will be coated; and the unified seed supply rate and the coverage rate of improved varieties of rice, corn and wheat will be raised.

Despite for these achievements, the Chinese are facing big challenges too. The diminishing of cultivatable land is serious. The raising of farmers' income is still a Herculean task. Government should be alert to these problems for ever.

Industrial Policy

Industrial policy had been the major feature of centrally planned economy of China after 1949. It was reinforced by the learning of the Japanese style of industrial policy after 1978. In the last fifteen years, the industrial policy has acquired the following features:

Firstly, the government tried hard to enhance the economic competitiveness through industrial policy. The five-year plans, and the investment approval system played an important role in the economic activities. Secondly, the industrial policies in fundamental industries, like energy, steel, material, etc have been successful as a whole, but failed in consumer industries like home electronics. In service industries, the policies did not succeed till now. Thirdly, the industrial policies are closely connected with the state owned enterprises, and with institutional reforms. Under this circumstance, the policy tends to be even more complex and difficult to figure out performance. This is a policy area that is both important and difficult in China.

Environment Protection Policy

With the rapid economic growth in the last fifteen years, the conflict between environment and development is becoming ever more serious. Relative shortage of resources, a fragile ecological environment and insufficient environmental capacity are becoming critical problems hindering China's development. According to the government white paper, the environment policy has the following features:[12]

Firstly, the Chinese government established environmental protection as a basic national policy and sustainable development as an important strategy, and has adhered to a new type of industrialisation. But from the result, the Chinese government has adopted a basic policy of growth first and environment secondly policy. Especially for the local government, growth rate is their number one performance indicator. Secondly, the last decade has seen the largest increase ever in China's investment in its environmental protection. Since 1998, the State has focused treasury bond investment on environmental infrastructure construction, bringing along a large amount of social investment. In 2006, expenditure on environmental

---

[12] Government white paper: the Environmental Protection in China, 2003.

protection has been formally itemised in the State's financial budget. Yet this is far from enough in reality.

Thirdly, the government tries to make full use of market mechanism to control pollution. A mechanism to share fees for renewable energy resources has been established. Tax reduction or exemption are extended to enterprises engaged in reclaiming renewable resources, making comprehensive use of resources and producing equipment for environmental protection, as well as enterprises using waste water, gas and residues as the raw materials of production. The policy of collecting tax on the occupation of cultivated land is observed strictly, so as to promote the rational use of land resources, strengthen land management and protect arable land. Fourthly, the development of the environmental protection industry has been fostered. Preferential policies are given to investment, prices, taxes, etc., to encourage the development of the environmental protection industry.

As a whole, the performance of environment protection policy is getting better. The innovative policy factor of using market mechanism has contributed to this a lot. Yet this is still a difficult policy area. Local governments still prefer growth, rather than environment protection in practice.

Pro-human Capital Policies

Pro-human capital policy has four features. They are: poverty relief policy, which deals with the basic living issue; education policy, which deals with the quality of labour force; employment policy, which deals with participation of labour, and social security policy, which deal with the maintenance of labour force.

Poverty Relief Policy[13]

The Chinese government had tried its best to solve the poverty problem.

Firstly, the government dominates the task by central plans and programmes. Marked by the promulgation and implementation of the Seven-Year Priority Poverty Alleviation Program (a program designed to lift 80 million people out of absolute poverty in seven years from 1994 to 2000) in 1994, China's development-oriented poverty-relief work entered the stage of tackling the key problems. The Programme clearly stipulated that China should concentrate human, material and financial resources, mobilise the forces of all walks of life in society and work hard to basically solve the problem of food and clothing of the rural needy by the end of 2000. It was the first action program for development-oriented poverty reduction with

---

[13] Government white paper: The Development-oriented Poverty Reduction Program for Rural China, 2001.

clear and definite objectives, targets, measures and a time limit. By the end of 2000, the objectives of the Program had been basically realised.

Secondly, the administrative forces dominate the implementation of government programmes. To effectively implement the development-oriented aid-the-poor work, the Chinese Government established a Leading Group of the State Council for Development-oriented Poverty Relief, to be responsible for the organisation, direction, coordination, supervision and examination of the work in this regard. China practices the level-by-level responsibility system. The provinces with large numbers of poverty-stricken areas, have put development oriented poverty relief high on their agendas, and formulated concrete local implementation plans in line with the state's poverty relief programme.

Thirdly, government increased capital input for poverty reduction. Over the past 15 years, the special aid-the-poor funds arranged by the Chinese Government have constantly increased. In 2000, such funds totalled 24.8 billion Yuan, or 31 times that of the provision in 1980. Local governments have also increased to the aid-the-poor funds according to the proportion of supportive funds set by the Central Government (30-50 percent since 1996). Fourthly, governments try to formulate preferential a series of policies to support the development of the poverty-stricken areas and peasant households.

As a whole, the policy and strategy to provide poverty relief is a success. The development- oriented policy is an innovative one. Yet China's poverty relief task will still be heavy in the future due to the imbalances nature of the economy.

Education Policy

Firstly, in the fundamental education area, there are both achievements and inadequate investments. Since the promulgation of the 'Compulsory Education Law of the People's Republic of China' in 1986, the 9-year compulsory education has been implemented by governments at various levels and made significant progress. According to the statistics of 2002, the net enrolment rate of primary school age children attained 98.58%, and the proportion of primary school graduates continuing their study in junior secondary schools (including vocational ones) reached 97.02%.[14] In the urban areas of large cities and economically developed coast areas, the universalisation of senior secondary education has been launched. But at the same time, the government urged the society to contribute all kinds of donations to support rural education.

---

[14] Cited from the Ministry of Education website

Secondly, the reform and development of higher education have made significant achievements. A higher education system with various forms, which encompasses basically all branches of learning, combines both degree-education and non-degree education and integrates college education, undergraduate education and graduate education, has taken shape. Yet, at the same time, the fees charged raised rapidly, which makes the students from poor family face great difficulties.

The vocational education was emphasised. In 1996, the 'Vocational Education Law' was formally promulgated and implemented, providing legal protection for the development and perfection of vocational education. Yet mainly due to the bad tradition of looking down on technical jobs and their low wage level in reality, vocational education was not taken as important in the whole society and the quality is not satisfactory as well.

Employment Policy

Employment is a big issue for China and the government has to make every effort to deal with it. Firstly, China exercises a proactive employment policy by expanding employment through developing the economy. The Chinese government has always regarded promoting employment as a strategic task for socio-economic development. It involves controlling unemployment and increasing job opportunities as its principal macro targets and incorporates it in its plan for economic and social development. The policies include: Expanding the capacity of employment by developing tertiary industry; encouraging the development of an economy with diverse forms of ownership, and broadening avenues for employment; developing flexible and diverse forms and increasing avenues of employment.

Secondly, China tried to develop and improve the public employment service system. Since the late 1990s, the Chinese government has made great efforts tobuild scientific, standardised and modernised labour market, and established a public employment service system. Currently, at both city and district levels in large and medium cities and some small cities that have the necessary conditions, comprehensive service premises with public job agencies as their key service have been established widely. Government also encourages and has standardised the development of job agencies run by non-governmental entities.

Thirdly, China tries to promote the reemployment. In recent years, the Chinese government has formulated a set of policies for promoting reemployment of laid-off persons. The related activities include: Establishing reemployment service centers; instituting the supportive policies of reducing and exempting taxes and administrative charges; extending small security-backed loans; implementing policies of social insurance subsidies; tax reduction and exemption to encourage enterprises to recruit more of the laid-off persons and helping those who have difficulties finding jobs through reemployment assistance.

Social Security Policy

Under the central by planned economy, social security was totally covered by the government to urban workforce, and was partially covered by the government in the rural areas. The last fifteen years saw fundamental change in this respect. Here again there were successes and failures. Firstly, an institutionalised social security system is in the process of forming.[15] (1) For the pension system, the Chinese government has made great efforts to build a multi-level old-age insurance system. In addition to participating in the compulsory basic old-age insurance, enterprises with suitable conditions may set up annuities for their employees. (2) In the area of unemployment insurance, Chinese government standardised and improved the unemployment insurance system. For the army of SOE employees, government created the basic livelihood guarantee system for people laid off from state-owned enterprises. (3) In the area of medical insurance, the Chinese government launched a national reform scheme for urban employees. The state also encourages enterprises to establish supplementary medical insurance for their employees, mainly for settling medical expenses not covered by the enterprise employees' basic medical insurance. (4) In the area of work-related injury insurance the state stipulates that all enterprises and all individual businesses engaged in industry and commerce must participate in work-related injury insurance, and pay insurance premiums for all their employees, permanent as well as temporary. (5) Proceeding from the situation of national development, the Chinese government has made great efforts to provide the minimum standard of living for the urban and rural poor, to provide relief to natural disaster victims and to urban vagrants and beggars, while promoting and encouraging all kinds of social mutual help activities.

Secondly, funds are raised through multiple channels. For pension, China practises joint premium payment by both enterprises and employees; increasing the subsidy outlay from the government financial budget for basic old-age insurance. In 2000, a national social security fund was established. The Chinese government also actively promotes social welfare by raising funds through various channels to provide benefits for the elderly, orphans and the disabled.

Thirdly, serious shortcomings still persist in the social security area. For example, although the Chinese government actively promotes the development of an urban housing security system through affordable and functional housing, and the low-rent housing, in reality, the low-rent system is lags behind and many residents are under

---

[15] Government white paper: China's social security policy, 2003; China's human rights, 2005.

high pressure in face of high market prices in the housing sector. The market oriented medical system reform raised the cost of medical service dramatically, this also bring great burden that the progress in social medical insurance reform could not cover.

Besides, the rural social security system is still at its preliminary stage. Under the influence of China's traditional culture, there is a time-honoured tradition of provision by the family, security coming from self-reliance and help from the clan. The good news is, Chinese government began to set up a new rural cooperative medical service system based mainly on a financial-pool-against-serious-disease scheme. Farmers can participate freely in such a cooperative medical system, which is organized, led and supported by the government with funds coming from the government, collectives and the beneficiaries.

Policy Designing

Fifteen years of high rate of growth partly shows China's efficiency in policy making. While criticisms will be taken in the next section, three features of successful policy designing could be summarized here:

Firstly, policies are based on pragmatism and with Chinese characteristics. There were very few ideological obstacles in the last fifteen years. Except for the red-light districts or gambling industry are not officially permitted, everything else existing in the Western world is to be found in China. At the same time, China insists on its own way in policy-making. China's exchange rate has been criticized by the United States for several years. Yet China is very cautious to change the Renminbi exchange mechanism. Even when it is suffering losses today the issue is still under the control of the central government.

Secondly, policies are progressing with time, and policies are focused on binding constraints:

- In the early 1990's, China gave priority to the speed of growth in order to catch up with the West. So it emphasised on investment pulling growth policy. Governments, including local governments, made every effort to absorb foreign investment.
- In the late 1990's, when comprehensive competitiveness and knowledge economy became the new trend in Western countries, innovation and building knowledge economy was taken as the national strategy in China. At the same period, with the extent of globalisation increasing, the strategy of going abroad was also raised as a national strategy.
- In the early 2000's, China's development was more and more bounded by environmental issues. Sustainable development capability became a serious challenge and its new and important national economic strategy.

Thirdly, the government tried to make policy sustainable. The basic strategy of taking economic development as the national core strategy has not been changed in the last fifteen years. The policy of market oriented reform is steadily pushed forward.

5. MARKET-ORIENTED INSTITUTIONAL REFORM

5.1 Milestone in General Guidance

Institutional reform is one of the most important guidelines promoting China's high speed in economic growth (the other is openness). From the year of 1992, an important change in general guidance in China's history was put forward, which would deeply influence China's institutional reforms. This is the finally established notion of building socialist market economy. After Deng Xiaoping's famous South China Talk in 1992, the Fourteenth Congress of the CPC of October 1992 summarised the main contents of the socialist economy with Chinese characteristics. Setting-up the "socialist market economic system" became the clear national goal. From then on, the aim of institutional reform was clearer than before and really in place. In other words, China's fundamental economic institutions should be similar to that of successful market economies. From then on, benchmarking and learning was the order of the day.

Yet, confusion is still exists. People like to ask what is the difference between socialist market economy and capitalist market economy. Wise people in authority in China would say that it is the result of practice and not a predetermined one.

5.2 Governing by Law

Rule of law is the basic aim of institutional reforms. From 1992 onwards, the governing by law made great progress. Yet many problems exist.

The great progress was first reflected in the making of laws. Constitution was amended, important laws, like Property Law, reality. Right to private property is fully recognised. A lot of new laws or regulations became were put in place (see Table 6). This is a great leap forward. As a whole the basic legal system to suit market economy is set up.

However, the situation of executing of laws is still complex and weak during the last fifteen years. More and more citizens are consulting the legal system when their rights are offended by others, be they private or by public forces. The problem is the quality of judicature is low and corruption in the judicature still exists. Local government and local CPC branches' intervene from time to time. These problems show the path to the rule of low is still far.

The social foundation of rule of law was still weak. The government has implemented the universal knowledge education for many years. In the year of 1986, Chinese government launched its first five year law education plan. Now it is in the fifth five-year cycle. There has been lots of progress since then. But still, events caused by not realizing of illegal behaviors often happen.

Generally speaking, the institutional reform in the field of governing by law was exerting a positive function of market legitimation and market creating. Private property right was widely recognised by the society. The concept of contracts was also accepted by the society. Both producers and consumers now know well that the law is their best protective mechanism.

On the other hand, progress in rule of law shows it is difficult and complex process, and a long way to go. The process of learning is very difficult to accelerate. It must be a gradual process, where tough efforts are needed still.

Table 6: State Council's Work on Law

Government	Legislative proposals	Administrative statutes
LI Peng Period (1993-1997)	66	197
Zhu Rongji Period (1998-2002)	50	150
Wen Jiabao Period (2002-2006)	26	111

Source: Figures collected from Government Reports of 1998, 2003, 2004, 2005, 2006, 2007.

5.3 Market Economical Institutions

The last fifteen years saw a process of China setting up of its market-oriented macro-economic controlling system. This includes:

- A new fiscal and taxation system was setup. The National Taxation Bureau and its branches all over the country were separated from the local Taxation Bureaus in mid 1990's. This separation demarcated clearly the rights and duties between the central and local governments. This enabled both to be positive in enlarging their tax sources and using the government revenues effectively.

- A new banking system was brought into being. In the mid-1990's, China for the first time separated its banking and commercial banking policies; in the late-1990's, the People's Bank of China (the central bank authority) was restructured. In 2006, three state owned commercial banks were privatised, which was a step forward to build a healthy banking system.

- For regulating the financial system, three national regulatory committees were set up for commercial banks, stock markets and insurance markets respectively. The foreign currency management system was also restructured too.

- The foreign commercial regulation system and the domestic commercial regulation system were united during late 1990's and early 2000's for the first time in China.

From the progress described above, two observations could be made:

Firstly, the functions of institutions are realised through the institutional reforms. (1) A market regulating system which could cope with the market economy was in shape. The Chinese for the first time in history have a modern market mechanism. (2) The market stabilizing mechanism was in shape too. Figure 1 in Part I of this paper has shown that in the last fifteen years, China's economic growth was in a steady mode. This was partly because the institutions discussed above were in place.

Secondly, the institutional reform history in the last fifteen years also shows that the process of reform must be a gradual one. Nobody could do everything overnight. This is why many enlightened Chinese are optimistic about the future. They believe that every thing will be getting better over time. Deng Xiaoping's opinion of 'we need several decades to set up the basic socialist market economic system' enjoins people be patient in this regard.

5.4 Government and Administrative Reforms

Government and administrative reforms have been a continuing process since 1978. Yet in the last fifteen years, the reforms acquired three main features:

Firstly, the progress in administration by law is obvious. The Act of Administrative Procedure, the Act of Administrative Permission, the Act of Civil Servants and others pushed public administration onto the track of governing by law.

Secondly, the government sector's organisational reforms were also taken forward. In the last ten years, the ministries for industrial sectors were gradually revoked. The number of sectors and public servants reduced greatly in both central and local governments.

Thirdly, efficiency of governance and service were greatly enhanced. In every local government level, public administration and service centres (one-stop service centres) were set up on a large scale. With China becoming a full member of the WTO, progress on the deregulation front was accelerated. For example, during Zhu Rongji government (1998-2002), 2300 pieces of foreign related regulatory documents were re-investigated. 830 of which were abolished and 325 were revised.[16]

Besides these achievement, the government as a whole still lacked of accountability, still not confined to its own budget, still filled with too many people. The reasons for

---

[16] Zhu Rongji: Government Report, 2003.

these phenomena are complex, some owing to the political system, some owing to the historical burdens, and some owing to the under development of the economy.

5.5 The Wheel of Institutional Reforms

Till now, three important economic related institutional aspects are discussed. Among the three, governing by law is at the centre, market economic institutions are the active part to promote the economic growth, and the government administrative aspect of government is the supporting part. Their inter-relationship could be expressed as follows:

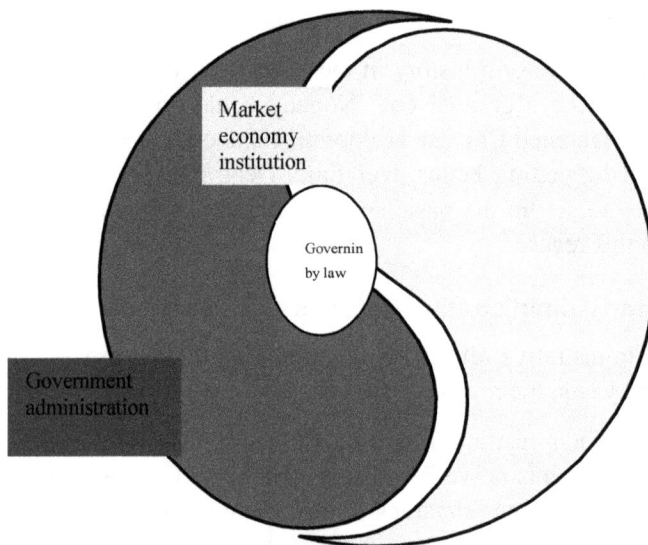

Market economy institution

Governin by law

Government administration

Fig. 5: The Wheel of Institutional Reform

6. CULTURAL AND POLITICAL FACTORS UNDERLINING THE INSTITUTIONAL REFORM–TE, TAO AND SHU

If we take the institutional aspect as the objective aspect that determines the pro-growth policy, the cultural and political aspect is the subjective part that ensures the objective operation of institutions in reality.

To illustrate the reason why the author put cultural and political aspects together, the ancient Chinese notion of Te, Tao and Shu could be brought in here. Te is the moral state. It is the mindset among the people or leader. De is a subjective strength that controls human behaviour. It determines Tao. Here De refers to the cultural mindset of the Chinese people. Tao, or the Way, is the basic strategy or methodology that people follow. It determines the Shu to be taken. Here Tao refers to the strategy of

CPC. Shu, is the tactics that people follow to implement the Tao. Here Shu refers to the government tactics. The relationship of the three could be summarized:

De   → *Tao*   → *Shu*

Cultural evolution   → Political   → Government tactics
                                                 strategy

Fig. 6: The Logic of Cultural, Political and Tactic Factors

6.1 Cultural Evolution

The period of last fifteen years is a of great change period. Besides dramatic change in the economy, the culture change of the nation could also be identified. The economic related mindset changes are:

6.2 Entrepreneurship, Pragmatics and Extensive Learning

The Chinese government, especially the local governments have taken governance innovation for granted. Experimenting new ways of development, setting new models and trying every effort to promote the local economic growth became a new fashion among officials. After Deng's southern talk and the set up of market economy notion, nothing seems to contain restrain the minds of active leaders. Usually, even the less innovative officials, would try to piece together some 'innovation' to show that their 'upward minded' and falling in line.

For private enterprises, innovation in production and especially in marketing became the most essential factor to survive in the market competition. For example, there is no such tradition like the Christmas festival or Valentine's Day in China, but the businessmen and department stores have made them to be shopping festivals, especially in cities. Advertisement has become an integral part of Chinese daily life. The degree of dramatisation in these promotional and advertising activities is not any less than most open societies in the West.

These economic and political driven activities are accepted as pragmatic. Ideology is forgotten by many practitioners. Closely related to this, people take learning from the West as a fashion too. Western management gurus find China a quite big and easy marketing target. Their skin colour itself is the best advertisement. Learning organisation theory, business process reengineering, decentralisation, horizontal organisation, and other 'frontier vocabularies' are all familiar words to many leaders. Numerous people claim that they are the followers of Peter Drucker, Michael Portor, Peter Senge or some other gurus in the West. Surely, not everybody accepts the necessity of entrepreneurship, pragmatism and extensive learning, nor the accepters' ways of the West totally correct or effective. But, at the least, they have become part of China's main stream ideology.

6.3 Middle Class Lifestyle and Work Ethic

When incomes are raising steadily, people's mindset are also changing marked by. Making money is now seen as good, not to-be-cursed as in the past. To lead a comfortable life became the universal pursuit among the masses. The Chinese people take three pursuits as their more favourite part of life, if enough money was available. One is decorating their apartment. Five star hotel guest houses become many people's decorating standard. The other is travelling to resorts or even abroad. If the first two are satisfied or not satisfied at all because of tight family budget, they will go to restaurants often. In the world, Chinese are believed to enjoy their delicious food most.

In order to enjoy life, people try every effort to make money. 'Playing' in the stock market or buying-selling mutual funds bonds have become part of daily life many people. Just think that the Chinese stock market in Shanghai and Shenzhen were opened only in 1990 and 1991. These sort of life is really new to the Chinese. Besides this, some people joined the chain marketing, like Anway's. A common joke going around is as follows: Among the one billion people 900 million people are doing business, while the rest 100 million were just getting ready to jump in.

To cope with the new life style in vogue, effective working, hard working and individual achievement are widely accepted among the work force. Training programs and books for successful life are popular. 'The seven habits of successful individuals' and other books are the bestsellers for quite a long time. The number one criterion of making friends (boys or girls) is usually their capacity to make big money.

6.4 Long Term Perspective

The long-term perspective has always been an integral part of Chinese culture from time immemorial. For example, all the emperors liked to make their dynasty last long and forever. Another factor Chinese philosophers regarded long-term view to be the wisest view because it follows the way of nature. One such teaching is, ten years is needed to bring a tree, but a hundred years are needed to build up elite. The ancient story of 'Yu Gong's moving of mountains' was well known among the Chinese. In that story, Yu Gong was determined to move away the two mountains before his house by the effort of generation after generation. The long-term planning notion of today is in the same traction as the centrally planned command economy market.

In the last fifteen years, the Chinese government has exerted three five year plans, the Eighth (1990-1995), the Ninth (1996-2000) and the Tenth (2001-2005). And the Eleventh (2006-2010) is just on the way. Besides these, long term plan scenarios and various other plans were made by the government too. Similarly, local governments and all kinds of organisations are used to make their own long-term plans. For the state owned ones, the plan would follow the government's planning period. For other organisations, they just make plans as they like.

Chinese families also have the tradition of long term view. Parents would plan for funding of their children's education even when the babies are just born. Young couple would plan to buy a second house just for the accumulation of assets for their future retired life. Surely, this is not to say that every government official or all families planning on a long term basis or good at it. Some officials would like to make exaggerate show of local resources to inflate their own performance figures, which could make the local development plans unsustainable.

6.5 Discipline

Discipline is both a tradition and a necessity in Chinese society. The notion of Li which means courtesy in Confucian tradition means behaviour must be follow what the social order for. The communist party also emphasised strict discipline. History tells that, if there no discipline, China would be in a mess or might even break up.

In the last fifteen years, the discipline of lower rank to obey the higher rank and the whole Party to obey the Central Committee has been a form of discipline to the seventy million Party members. This has ensured their implantation of governments. The ordinary people are also used to a disciplinary thinking. If they could have a basic life guarantee, they would never starve on the streets. The majority of the Chinese people are really kind-hearted, broadminded and hardworking.

6.6 Pursuing Harmony

There is a long ideological tradition of pursuing harmony. To Confucianism, self cultivating, managing the family, governing the country and make peace with the world are the four missions of gentlemen. The way to these is to keep harmony in mind, in family, in the country and in the world.

In the last fifteen years pursuing a balance life, not going to extremes, and to make the working place a happy place are the wishes of the ordinary people. The revolutionary class struggle was never mentioned. The aim of building a harmonious society and a harmonious world was emphasised in recent years. This leaves the Chinese society in a state of relative calm, which partly contributes to a relatively stable investment environment. Surely, due to the conflicts of benefit here and there,

there are lots of inharmonious phenomena. But if taking the large population and a transit period into account, the real situation is not as bad as is commonly imagined.

Besides the above observations, two aspects of cultural evolution could also be identified.

Firstly, the Chinese have enjoyed the advantages of different cultures. Traditional culture is still influential and deep in people's 'blood'. The traditional culture acts as a mechanism of social stability in time of great change. Marxism makes the Chinese accept the notion of 'seeking truth from fact', 'liberating the mind' and 'make progress with time', which are the foundation of reform and open door policy. Since 1992, capitalist culture is enabling the Chinese to be at home with market mechanism.

Secondly, the disadvantage of the cultural evolution is that backward aspects of each culture are still hindering modernisation. The traditional ones follow the principle of Golden Mean, which prohibits innovation and creativity. Some people take Marxism as doctrines and try to stop some further reforms. Young people love the notion of liberalisation in daily life and the inherited culture of discipline is ignored by them.

6.7 Political Strategy

If we compare the stage of 1992-2006 with the earlier stages, we could see that economic growth is smooth, which partly shows the success of the Communist Party's strategy. The new features of these years are:

Firstly, the Communist Party of China (CPC) enforced the general strategy successfully. The guideline of 'taking the economic construction at the centre' is not disobeyed in the last fifteen years. This is partly because the experience of the earlier years, especially from 1978-1991. Senior leaders saw clearly that whenever the direction was a little loose, growth would be harmed. After 1992, even though some 'left' people criticised the road taken was away from socialist principles, some 'right' people criticised the slow progress in democracy, the Central Committee did not waver in its mind at all. The notion of 'do not dispute' and put the 'whole-heart in promoting development' was the real motto of the CPC leaders.

Secondly, the CPC redefined its ideology, i.e., the setting up of the Principle of Three Representations for the Communist Party of China. According to this principle, the Party represents the most advanced economic forces, the most advanced elements of culture and the basic interests of a wide range of people. This is significant for it is in fact marked the turning point or transitional point of the CPC from a revolutionary party to a constructional party. The new ideology put emphasis on pursuing enhanced productivity and benefit of the masses. This principle supports the first strategy firmly.

Thirdly, the CPC promoted the learning strategy. The basic guideline is to learn from all the good experiences from other countries in the world, no matter where they come from. The CPC tries to shape itself to be a learning party. The broad mindset ensures the Party could keep track of Three Representations. The learning strategy promotes the whole society to learn eagerly and quickly. For the party, the learning strategy enhanced its capacity in controlling the country.

Fourthly, the CPC insisted to explore its own way of spearheading development in China. In a world of filled with capitalist countries, filled with criticizes from abroad, and facing so many problems, it is difficult for CPC to keep its own ideology. But it managed. The long historical experience of CPC made it alert learning from any correct model elsewhere. To learn from others, OK; but to copy them, no way. The logic is quite simple to the CPC and the Chinese elites.

So, as a whole, the CPC's strategy in the last fifteen years was no doubt successful. This is not to say it has done perfect job. In fact, it could have done better on democracy. The biggest problem the Chinese people are worrying about is the quality of the party itself. Only when the Party is really a meritocracy, the country could make more rapid progress.

6.8 Government Tactics

The government and the CPC tactics in leading reforms and economic growth in the past fifteen years are basically successful.

Firstly, the CPC's leadership controls every important aspect of the society. The most talented people are absorbed in the Party. The party's education mechanism tries to keep the members to be excellent. There many good examples to show the powerful situation of the party's leadership. In 2003 SARS crisis, the party branches in villages and local organisations exerted powerful leadership. Recognising the essentials of the party members and organisations, some famous international corporations, like Motorola, supported the setting up of the CPC branches in their offices and factories in China.

Secondly, the graduality in the reform routine is insisted. This methodology is pragmatic and could help in managing reforms step by step with little resistance. Thirdly, the grassroots democracy is promoted. The CPC emphasises grassroots democracy at village level elections and of listening to the people's voice. This is a good way to exercise democracy and to get the support from the masses. Fourthly, keep the principle of 'stability as a superior task'. The CPC made every effort to keep social stability intact. This makes China's social environment favourable to investment.

The success is obvious too, but not excellent. The principle of keeping stability and gradual path of reform has accumulated many deep layer problems. How to balance the short term and long term goals is still a big challenge to the Chinese government.

7. CONCLUSIONS AND POLICY SUGGESTIONS FOR ECONOMIC GROWTH

Could China's rapid growth be sustainable in the future? We do not know what will happen exactly. But we do know there are huge challenges ahead. The issues of mass poverty, serious corruption, political stability and rationality, environmental, challenges or even Taiwan could fatefully damage China's growth if fails to deal with them properly. Here several important aspects would be discussed, both by way of conclusions and suggestions. In the end, a short discussion on what China would mean to the future world is put forward as the find comment to the paper on China's growth (1992-2006).

7.1 'Taichi' Mind-set

To the author's understanding, the number one achievement of the Chinese Communist Party and the Chinese government since 1992 is the final recognition of the need to strike balance between socialism and capitalism.

Westerners find it difficult to understand the official notion of 'socialist market economy'. In fact, market economy, as an economic regime, is equal to capitalism. Because it is capital, not labour that dominated the allocation of resources. China combines these two with many deep meanings which maybe even the Chinese policy makers could not see very clearly.

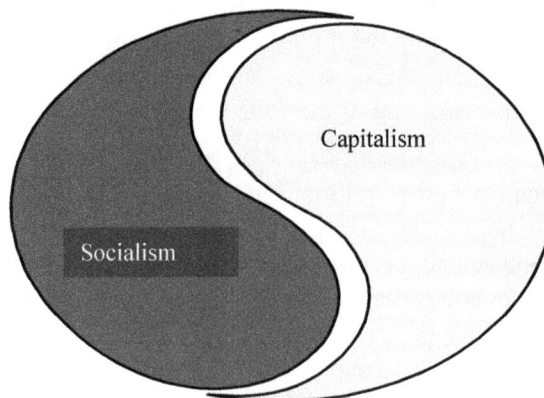

Fig. 7: The Taichi Mindset

Capitalism emphasises shareholder governance. The government policy should favourite the value adding of capital. The private organisation is purported to add value to the investors or owners. This is necessary for economic efficiency. The supporting policy to FDI and domestic private economy is the very essence of a pro capitalist policy.

Socialism emphasises stakeholder governance. It favours social parity. After over a hundred years of miserable life, the Chinese welcomed the CPC just because they needed social parity. Socialism has both short term and long term meanings. In the short run, it should support basic parity in economic life. In the long run, it is the ideology that is worthy of pursuit. If the CPC abandoned this ideology, it will be no more CPC nor could it survive.

China combines these two aspects and positions the relationship just as the ancient notion of Taichi does. The Taichi model believes that there are several aspects to the world and every layer is composed of the forces of Yin and Yang. The Yang is dominant and active factor, the Yin is adapting and supporting factor.

Capitalism is Yang. In the Chinese strategy, economic growth, i.e. to develop capitalist economy is taken as the number one national strategy. The government must make every effort to guarantee economic growth. Socialism is Yin, the social policy must serve the economic growth. The socialist leadership (CPC) and ideology must be upheld.

The two forces are contradictive with each other, people will say. Yes, the system of Yin and Yang is contradictive all the time. The contradiction is the true driving force to social progress. It is true in China. And we should say, in Singapore, in Europe, and in the United States. Contradict, but not conflict, is the very state of harmony. The new strategy of building a socialist harmonious society is thee new insight.

For suggestions, the author would say:

Firstly, China should insist on continuing with the Taichi mindset of socialism and capitalism. This is the true spiritual strength that pushes the rapid economic growth and social progress.

Secondly, the CPC should further develop this notion. Better to translate the philosophical notion into a set of detailed and clear guidelines. Among others, the indicators and borders of socialism and capitalism, the steps that lead to a better state of the harmonious society, must be clarified.

7.2 A Virtuous Circle of Improvement

The Singapore experience shows an integration of policies could form a virtuous circle that promotes growth. In China, the virtuous circle is in the process of shaping up, but not yet adequately.

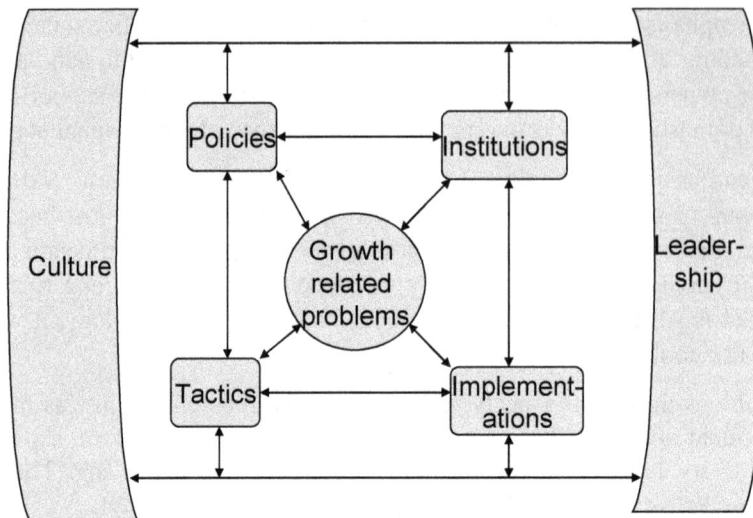

Fig. 8: The Virtue Circle of Governance

In the Chinese context, growth related problems, institutional reforms, policies, implementation of policies and tactics to deal with emergent problems are all used at the same time. The leadership and cultural factors are the leading forces. Gradually, all the six aspects get improved. This could be seen as an interpretation of the Chinese gradualism. If we take the anti corruption issue, we could see: (1) policy is getting more and more clear in detail; (2) institutions are improved gradually, especially in the CPC framework; (3) implementation is getting strict, for heavy penalty would surely be imposed, if the corruption is found; (4) tactics are so derived as to make the anti corruption drive serves the goals of economic growth and social satiability.

7.3 Suggestions for Future

Firstly, China should insist on the integrated and gradual way to deal with the growth related problems, not harsh, not lax. Secondly, China should learn more and in more detail from the success of other countries on how to promote virtuous circle in governance area.

7.4 Pragmatic and Innovative Policies

China's policy execution in the last fifteen years is a process of pragmatism and innovation at work. The complexity and difficulty of situations make it impossible to get to the policy goals directly. Tactics, pragmatism and innovative ways in executing are the only way to take. Here three ways could be observed. (1) To the bad phenomenon, to be tolerant and to fight at the same time. To corruption, China in fact is to somewhat tolerant, because it provides some sort of incentive to the local leaders to absorb FDI and / or to attract more investment. (2) To reform, more from easy issues to difficult ones. (3) To urgent problems, first deal with tactics, then take fundamental steps. For example, to the unemployed SOE workers, first provide urgent assist money when necessary, then gradually set up the social security system to cover them.

7.5 Suggestions are Obvious

Firstly, the pragmatic and innovative ways of dealing with difficult problems should be used in future when necessary. Secondly, the eternal aim should be to setup reasonable institutional arrangements. Institutions, not emerging ways are the best way to deal with problems in a modern society.

7.6 Chinese Style of Governance

China is a big, poor country with complex situation. With these features, China could only insist on its own way of governance. The author would like to emphases: (1) The leadership of CPC crucial. At present, any attempt of ignoring this reality could not work. CPC is the core leading force in the past fifteen years and it did well. (2) The decentralisation to local governments and competing relationship between local governments is important. The rapid growth is essentially due to the entrepreneurship of the thousands at various levels of local government. (3) The dual organisation system is unique and essential. In every public organisation, there are two controlling centres, one is the CPC branch, the other is the administrative authority. Basically, the CPC system is responsible for strategy and leadership building; the administrative system is responsible for achieving output and outcome. The first is like a board of management, the second is like the executing team.

The suggestions are:

Firstly, insist on these governance mechanisms. They have been proved and verified to be basically effective in for promoting development and reform.

Secondly, improve them until a best state or state of the art situation is achieved. In fact, the above mechanism is sometimes low on, efficiency. The improvement is a process of institutional reforms too.

7.7 China and the Rest of the World

Will there be a clash of civilisations? Will China change the world? Or would there be anything other countries could learn from China? Such 'big' questions are beyond the author's capability. But the author really believes:

Firstly, the western culture dominating world will surely be changed when the east raises inevitably. The Chinese culture, as part of the eastern one, will naturally affect the world cultural evolution. Here the Chinese culture is not only a Confucian one, but a modern socialist one with elements of ancient wisdom (surely, need to be verified).

Secondly, China will be a force to promote a harmonious international society. Both the cultural tradition and CPC foreign policy support such an outcome.

Thirdly, the institutional reforms should be emphasised and taken forward systematically.

Economic Reforms in Agriculture Sector in India

Naresh Kumar Sharma

An understanding of economic reforms with specific reference to a particular sector of economy such as agriculture must begin with an understanding of the nature of that activity as well as its historical context. Though the focus of the paper is on agriculture, it is important to look at economic reforms in their entirety as well as policies specifically directed at the agricultural sector. There has been a view that a pro-industry bias has in the past led to repression of agriculture.[1] Indeed, in India there were industrial policy resolutions soon after Independence (948 and 1956) as well as a Science Policy Resolution (1958). There have been subsequent statements of industrial policies from time to time. But, the first draft of a National Policy in Agriculture was presented before the public only in 1990 (but not adopted by the then government). Keeping this in view is important for a study of economic reforms with respect to agriculture. The paper is organised as follows. The remaining part of this section looks at two issues: (a) characteristic features of agricultural activity in brief; and (b) a brief comment on the theory of economic reforms. Section 2 provides a synoptic account of the historical context of Indian agriculture in pre-British and British period. This is followed by an overview of economic reforms as a liberalisation of the economy in section 3. Section 4 provides economic reforms in agriculture in the country after 1947 divided into three phases. Since July 1990 there have been several statements of national policy on agriculture.[2] Section 5 is devoted

---

[1] See Lipton (1977). In a provocatively titled article, "The The plundering of agriculture in developing countries", Schiff and Valdes (1995) say, "Industry long considered the engine of growth, has been the darling of development. Agriculture, by contrast, was believed to be unresponsive to economic incentives and did not lend itself to technical change. Thus, policy makers believed that promoting industry *at the expense* of agriculture would sacrifice little in output" (emphasis added).

[2] (a) National Agricultural Policy : Views of Standing Advisory Committee on Agriculture (July 1990) Chaired by Sharad Joshi, in 1991, (b) National Agriculture Policy, Department of Agriculture and Cooperation, Ministry of Agriculture, Government of India, in 2000, (c) Revised Draft National Policy for Farmers by National Commission on Farmers chaired by MS Swaminathan, in 2006, and (d) National Policy for Framers 2007, Department of Agriculture and Cooperation, Ministry of Agriculture, Government of India, in 2007.

to these statements of national agricultural policy. Next, a brief look at the agriculture scenario in the post reform period of 1990s and after is the subject of section 6. The paper concludes with some remarks in section 7.

1. CHARACTERISTIC FEATURES OF AGRICULTURE

Unlike industry or services, the production process itself is long in case of agriculture – an agriculture cycle can vary from a few months to a few years for particular crops. Thus agricultural events are discrete in time. Agriculture requires cooperation between nature and man and involves inherently biological processes. The remaining features of agriculture as an economic activity follow from this. One, knowledge is very important for agriculture.[3] Hence, R&D, dissemination and practice of evolving knowledge are basic to agriculture. Two, agricultural production is fraught with large uncertainties.

Production uncertainties are peculiar to agriculture, unlike industry or services. Three, labour and other inputs are required with varying intensity over the crop cycle. Thus, there are peaks and slacks of economic activity. This underlines the importance of allied economic activities. Four, the length of production time makes availability of credit an important issue for agriculture and intermediaries in credit market assume importance. Five, intermediaries in trade assume added importance in agriculture. Six, related to above, price received by produce can diverge widely from price paid by the consumer. This has several implications. Usual economic models fail unless they can incorporate intermediate trade (including storage by traders). Thus, terms of trade between agriculture and industry may fail to tell whether the farmers are actually gaining even if terms of trade based on wholesale prices appear to move in favour of agriculture. Seven, Indian agriculture is characterised by smallholder farming (over 100 million operational holding of average size of approximately 1.6 hectares). Eight, the individual producers are unable to directly trade – whether in domestic or in external market. All agricultural trade requires intermediaries. Nine, public investment is a critically important aspect of small farmer agriculture.

2. THEORY OF ECONOMIC REFORMS

Economic theory of reforms that are underway is disarmingly simple. It goes all the way back to the father of modern economics – Adam Smith. One, man has inherent propensity for "truck, barter and exchange". Two, division of labour and specialisation increase productive potential enormously. Thus, trade is both natural and beneficial for man. Expansion of market and free functioning of markets brings

---

[3] Agriculture pre-supposes a knowledge economy – and it happens to pre-date current talks of knowledge economy, knowledge society etc. by several centuries, nay millennia.

out Pareto optimal outcomes. Key to these outcomes is competition. The most important aspect of economic reforms advocating liberalisation of economic functioning (both in domestic sphere as well as in international arena) is "efficiency".

The proponents of market oriented economic reforms bring forward arguments which can be traced back to Adam Smith. Talking about the role of government Adam Smith in his celebrated book, ***An Enquiry into the Nature and Causes of Wealth of Nations***, says:

"According to the system of natural liberty, the sovereign has only *three* duties to attend to: three duties of great importance, indeed, but plain and intelligible to common understandings: *First*, the duty of protecting the society from the violence and invasion of other independent society; *secondly*, the duty of protecting, as far as possible, every member of the society from the injustice or oppression of every other member of it, or the duty of establishing an exact administration of justice; and, *thirdly*, the duty of erecting and maintaining certain public works and certain public institutions, which it can never be for the interest of any individual, or a small number of individuals, to erect and maintain; because the profit could never repay the expense to any individual or small number of individuals, though it may frequently do much more than repay it to a great society."

Almost 220 years later Joshi and Little (1995) have the following to say about a desirable economic regime. "The state should provide law and order, including definition and enforcement of contracts, the protection of property, and the outlawing and punishment of seriously anti-social behaviour. Where necessary it should promote or create other institutions required for operation of markets. …. It should provide public goods, such as defence and stable currency". One important thing added by these scholars is the role of Government in intervening for creation of markets. Adam Smith believed that good of society can be achieved by members of society pursuing their own interests:

"It is not, from the benevolence of the butcher, the brewer, or the baker, that we expect our dinner, but from their regard to their own interest. We address ourselves not to their humanity but to their *self-love*. …. The Individual is in this, as in many other cases, led by an *invisible* hand to promote and end which was no part of his intention … *I have never known much good done by those who affected to trade for the public good.* It is an affectation, indeed, not very common among merchants, and very few words need be employed in dissuading them from it."

It is clear from the above that de-centralised decision making in an economy is deemed to be superior as opposed centralised action for common good and market is seen as the mechanism to facilitate decentralised decision making in the economic sphere. This is also captured in what is called the Second Theorem of Welfare

Economics: "Any Pareto-optimal allocation can be realized as a competitive equilibrium in the presence of all round 'convexity' provided that suitable lump sum transfers can be arranged among all participants".

Allowing economic units to do what they can do best (specialisation and division of labour), creating condition under which they would do their best (competition), and allowing them to reap rewards of their efforts would bring about optimal economic welfare. It is also well known that these outcomes are predicated upon several strong assumptions, including existence of perfect competition, convexities and production and consumption, absence of externalities, non-satiatedness as a condition of human nature etc. Thus, there is ample ground for debate, difference and opposition between the protagonists of economic reforms (of above nature) and their opponents.

3. HISTORICAL CONTEXT: AGRICULTURE IN PRE-BRITISH AND BRITISH PERIODS: (A BROAD BRUSH PICTURE)

The ancient literature – which is not historical in the present sense – and other evidence does not give any indication that India was perceived by its inhabitants (in its several parts) a primarily as an agricultural society. One finds descriptions of a very large number of activities – bearing on economic as well as non-economic aspects of life. Till the British conquest of India brought about large scale changes, agriculture could be seen as a traditional way of life. This was largely independent of external (to itself) political and economic control which "was achieved through a social organisation that left the village largely autonomous." (Bajaj, 1982). The villages were connected with other autonomous villages through a web of social and economic relationships. This autonomy of village economy was also derived from the economic system which interconnected villagers with each other through a system of obligations and payments. Their external obligation ceased upon payment of a small proportion of their produce as revenue. It is estimated that the proportion of the produce payable to the *external authority* around 1750 was as small as 5 percent. A large part of the revenue was thus retained locally and paid to local functionaries (total revenue thus paid could be around 25 percent of the produce). Thus, kings and kingdoms changed, outside aggressors came and rulers changed but village economy continued more or less undisturbed with minor temporary perturbations.

However, it would be wrong to see this as a basically agricultural economy. "I do not agree that India is an agricultural country; India is as much a manufacturing country as agricultural; ... her manufactures of various descriptions have existed for ages, and have never been able to be competed with any nation wherever fair play has been given to them ..." (Dutt, 1940 as quoted in Bajaj, 1982). Agriculture and industry were intertwined in the village economy and complemented each other. Given the nature of agriculture, the peasant also took part in industry during slack in cultivation. However, there were numerous industrial and service occupations as well. It is important to understand this, since it implied that there was no excessive burden on agriculture.

This was to drastically changed with the British conquest. Early British accounts make it amply clear that the British regarded land to be ultimately vested in the Crown. They tried to bring support to this view from early Indian literature as well. Further, they believed in vesting of proprietary interest in land by the State. This was also conducive for the purpose of augmenting land revenue. Thus, the zamindars, taluqdars etc. who were essentially intermediaries between the then rulers (eg Mughals) and the cultivators and had been originally given only revenue collection rights were conferred proprietary rights in their zamindari etc land. This disrupted the village agricultural system. Revenue demands were increased manifold. Secondly, their quest for larger and larger markets for the British manufactures – then coming to grips with the industrial revolution and hence looking for ever expanding markets – resulted in an anti Indian industry policy. The account of "de-industrialisation" of India during about 200 years of British rule is well documented.

What is important for our purposes is the implication of this "de-industrialisation" for the functioning of the agricultural sector. Dependence on agriculture increased. Further, agriculture-industry relation within the village society came under severe strain. This process also led to a large number of artisans and crafts persons becoming landless labour – emergence of a new class in village India. Thus, agriculture suffered twin attacks: directly through increased collection of land revenues and indirectly through destruction of Indian industry, especially village industry. Further, village organisation, system of justice and administration further strained village management systems of common resources.

India found itself in a weakened state – both in industry and agriculture on the eve of her Independence.

4. ECONOMIC REFORMS: AN OVERVIEW

The new economic policy, heralded in India in 1991, has also been nicknamed as LPG, short for liberalisation, privatisation and globalisation, and is aptly expected to fuel a much faster economic growth. Many other expressions used for economic reforms include: unshackling the economy; freeing the market and economy; integration with the world economy; and, stabilisation and structural adjustment programme.

Economic reforms include all of the above and more. In essence, *economic reforms are concerned with the manner of circumscribing permissible domains of economic activity of different segments of society.* It is important to realise that this can be attempted and possibly achieved both directly and explicitly on the one hand, as well as indirectly and implicitly on the other hand. Licensing, reservation of areas of activity, restrictions on trade, restrictions on movement of commodities, compulsory levy of agricultural produce etc. are examples of the former. For obvious reasons, one needs to look more penetratingly to discover examples of the latter – which are no less important, indeed perhaps more important from the perspective of the rural poor. A very widely discussed and debated example is that of agricultural sector as a whole being implicitly discriminated against. Even though on surface, agriculture is given large subsidies, but it has been amply documented that agriculture has been *net taxed* on the whole. Indeed, restriction of economic activity in agriculture is seen to flow not so much on account of agricultural policy (there was no comprehensive agriculture policy document of the Government of India when these economic reforms were ushered in) but as a result of industrial and trade policies followed. Aggressive promotion of one sector can abridge space of activity available to another sector. This is implicit in restriction or delimitation of economic sphere of the latter sector. For example, active promotion of powerlooms has serious implications for the handloom sector, impacting on millions of weavers.

The basic philosophy of economic reforms is to rely on markets; remove bottlenecks, and infirmities that either completely block or distort functioning of markets; and hence market prices are taken as the most important signals in determining level of economic activity in different sectors. Post1991economic reforms have been sweeping in character, encompassing most sectors of economy – external sector, all sectors in the industry, financial sector, agriculture, and services – though extent of change and pace of reforms in different sectors has been uneven.

Thus, economic reforms aim at greatly reduced role for the government, as the World Development Report, 1991 says, ".. it is better not to ask governments to manage development in detail." It is suggested that, if at all, government must intervene reluctantly – and in areas like basic education, poverty alleviation, infrastructure and environment etc. In these cases, there must be systems of checks and balances, they must be put to the discipline of international and domestic markets and interventions must be open and transparent. Discretionary intervention must be avoided.

Elements of market friendly approach include the following. Invest in people. Create a climate of enterprise, by providing a regulatory framework to ensure competition, legal and property rights. Integrate with the global economy. The most important public good a government can provide is a stable macroeconomic foundation.

Stabilisation and structural adjustment are seen as distinct but twin components of economic reforms. Stabilisation is aimed at short term demand management whereas, structural adjustment programmes address supply side and they are long term in nature. Indeed, economic reforms proper are nothing other than structural adjustment.

Stabilisation means containing both internal and external imbalances in the economy. External imbalances basically refer to balance of payment imbalances, a component part of which can be external trade imbalance. Internal imbalance refers to imbalance arising out of fiscal management of the economy by the government and is reflected in increasing fiscal deficits, as well as to rising inflation, volatile outputs, and increasing unemployment. Stabilisation aims at correcting or containing these imbalances. Instability in the economic system is seen as giving rise to uncertainties in the minds of investors and hence retards the economic activity.

In a sense stabilisation is management of crises and not economic reforms proper. However, it is generally recommended that stabilisation should either precede structural adjustment programmes or preferably both programmes should be implemented at the same time. Stabilisation and structural adjustment programmes are interdependent. Without stabilisation, structural adjustment may not be achievable, and without structural adjustment, stabilisation is seen to be not sustainable. Stabilisation is sought to be achieved through adjustment of exchange rates, containing fiscal deficits at a low level which often calls for curtailment of government expenditure and a tight monetary policy. These generally cause hardships for the people at least in the short run. Structural adjustment programmes on the other hand are aimed at giving free play to the market.

The functioning of market may be curtailed by physical restrictions on the economic activity such as industrial licensing, quota restrictions on foreign trade, restrictions on investment by foreign entities, etc. as well as through fiscal policies such as differential taxation of different commodities. Restriction is also often in the form of limitations on the freedom of freely entering into contracts by two or more parties at mutually agreed terms. Freedom to employ a 'hire and fire' policy, as per mutually agreed terms of contracts between the employers and employees is one such example. Economic reforms require that these barriers in the functioning of market be reduced or dismantled in line with the spirit of free markets.

There have been moves towards delicensing in the industry sector, and also dereservation of the number of areas reserved for public sector in the domestic arena. Areas reserved for public sector have been reduced to three. Moves towards privatisation of the public sector units are also aimed at allowing markets to decide the level and manner of economic activity performed by these units. In the arena of fiscal policy, reforms have aimed at reducing and rationalizing tax structure, making them non-distortionary and now there is move towards further unification of domestic tax structure through introduction of goods and services tax (GST) throughout the economy. In foreign trade, similarly, India has moved towards reduction in number of custom duties as well as reduction of level of custom duties. There have been far reaching reforms in trade. Not only, tariffs have been brought down, most of Quantitative Restrictions (QRs) have been done away with.

Encouragement is being given to foreign investment and the restrictions on foreign investment are being lowered. It is also treated in a less discriminatory manner than before. Though full capital account convertibility of rupee has not yet materialised, there is greater permissibility of capital flows including investments by Indian entities abroad. In the financial sector, likewise, a greater role for market is being envisaged. For example, commercial banks are allowed greater flexibility regarding their lending policies. They enjoy greater autonomy in their functioning. As we shall see targeted lending policies have been liberalised. Even though there is no official change regarding priority sector lending by the scheduled commercial banks, scope for priority sector lending has been widened and targets for the priority sector lending are not being implemented for sub-sectors within the priority sectors. Insurance sector has been opened up for private sector participation.

With greater freedom to the private sector to operate in the market, it is considered essential that regulatory regime must be improved. It is pertinent that such freedom is not misused and abused against public purpose. This becomes particularly important when access to right information is limited. It has been pointed out, particularly in case of the financial sector, that regulatory regime has been very weak and systems of checks and balances have not been in place.

Economic reforms also encompass agriculture sector and services sector. Indeed, opening up of the economy in the industrial sector itself has implications for agriculture. In addition, there is greater liberalisation in trade in agriculture commodities. An area which is expected to have greater implications for agriculture sector is the operation of new intellectual property rights regime. India has been making changes in its legal framework in tune with WTO requirements on TRIPS. Further discussion on this follows in the next section.

There have been two schools of thought regarding the pace of implementation of economic reforms: an all-out approach as opposed to the graduated approach. The first approach, namely, replacing the centralised planning with rudiments of market economy in a single burst of reforms, was implemented in a number of countries which were formerly part of the Soviet Union. In these countries the task involved was much greater, namely, that of creating a market economy itself (once accepted as desirable), whereas, economic reforms in already existing market economies such as India are aimed basically at removing the distortions. *India has followed the latter, the graduated approach.*

The common consensus is that economic reforms in India started in 1991 in the face of a serious balance of payments crisis. It is alleged that they were not necessarily motivated by pure economic rationale per se. It is no great secret that reform package was implemented at the behest of Bretton Woods sisters, namely, the World Bank and the IMF. However, this is not the first attempt at economic reforms in India. Consider the following passage from Bhagwati and Desai (1970):

"The devaluation of the rupee in June 1966, quite apart from the contemporaneous measures taken to *liberalize import and industrial licensing, was perhaps* **the most dramatic episode** *in the shift of Indian economic policies towards a greater and more sophisticated reliance on the market mechanism*. On the other hand, this shift had begun *before* devaluation and had been ushered in via measures such as the decontrol (however limited) of steel distribution and exemption of a number of industries from industrial licensing." (p.477, emphasis added).

Note the use of expressions such as "liberalize", "the most dramatic shift in economic policy", "reliance on the market mechanism" – all the components of economic reforms we are talking about today. However, there is a sense in which it is justified to locate the beginning economic reforms in 1991. The crisis that was faced in 1991 was severe but so was the crisis faced in 1966 and indeed more so. However, in the earlier attempts there was no broad political consensus in accepting or inevitability of economic reforms or on the measures enunciated by Bhagawati and Desai (1970) above. Market is seen by the proponents of the market oriented economic reforms, such as the World Bank, to perform vital role in generation and transmission of economically relevant information among the producers and consumers, which is essential for decentralised decision making (The World Development Report, 1996). Similar view regarding Indian economy was put forth by Bhagwati and Desai (1970) towards the end of their study:

" … Indian planning for industrialisation suffered from excessive attention to targets down to product level, and a wasteful physical approach to setting and implementation thereof, along with a generally *inefficient framework of economic policies* designed to regulate growth of industrialisation, Towards the end of the period [i.e. late 1960s] …, India did begin to pull away from this type of planning, in the direction of *greater flexibility* and concern for the more important decisions (combined with a greater area of decision-making left outside the Government)."

Of course, another 25 years had to pass before this picture actually started to materialise in reality. In between, de-bureaucratisation and some liberalisation had begun by 1980s. The basic difference in earlier reforms and those ushered in 1991 onwards is that the latter reforms accepted the philosophy of market to guide economic activities and thus challenged the very basis of planning and policy making that guided economic development in India since its Independence (Vyas, 2003).

The contention that these reforms were not well grounded but a response in the face of economic crisis has been hotly challenged as well. Thus Bardhan and Srinivasan (1993) say, "These reforms in our, and in many other developing countries' policies, were being advocated from the early 1960s and the proponents, the pioneers included Indian economists …Indeed, these ideas have been recycled back to us by the staff of the multi-lateral institutions who learnt them from *our own pioneering economists.*" and further and more significantly, "conditionality played a role, for sure, … But the *seriousness and sweep* of the reforms, and the Rao government's explicit embrace of them as against the earlier 'reforms by stealth', demonstrated that the driving force behind the reforms was equally, even overwhelmingly, our own conviction that we had lost precious time and that the reforms were finally our only option" (emphasis added).

Indeed, by 1991 there was widespread feeling of frustration in the prevailing economic system and a perception of a great deadweight and sloth in existing system. There was wide acceptance that economic system needed an overhaul, though there was not such a consensus what the content of that change should be. The crisis was seen to be economy wide. Even the parties that were opposed *in principle* to the particular measures of economic reforms have brought in some components for these reforms *in practice* where they have been in power. An example of such wide ranging sharing of views on economic policies among the main political parties cutting across ideological moorings was witnessed in the passing of the budget for year 1999-2000 *even without a debate.*

Thus, a new era of economic reforms did indeed begin in India in 1991.

5. ECONOMIC REFORMS IN AGRICULTURE AFTER 1947

Three distinct phases can be discerned in a study of evolution of economic policy concerning agriculture in India after its Independence. These can be seen as an era of land reforms[4] (or alternatively, some like to call it pre-green revolution phase) from 1950 to 1965; era of green revolution from 1966 to 1991[5]; and finally era of economic reforms and globalisation from 1991 onwards.

---

[4] It may be argued that the land reform was neither completed nor implemented properly in this period. However, it will be hard to deny that abolition of intermediaries like zamindars etc. was a momentous change by itself which heralded a new era in Indian agriculture.

[5] It is not to say that 1991 marks end of green revolution technologies. !991 marks major changes in economic policies sweeping almost all sectors of economy and hence beginning of a new phase. The second phase itself may be seen as consisting of two sub-phases: the first from the start of green revolution till 1980 and second from the beginning of liberalisation from 1980s however haltingly.

The most important changes in the first phase concern waves of land reforms through out the country. This is significant, since land reforms were carried out at the level of individual states of the Indian Union. Intermediaries like zamindars, taluqdars, mirasdars etc. were abolished in one go. Cultivators were sought to be brought into direct relation with the State. Other institutional reforms include ceiling on land ownership, consolidation of scattered holdings, and bringing in of new tenancy laws, which severely restricted right to lease out agricultural land. There were major lacuna in land reform laws (in terms of retaining of land by erstwhile landlords, the level of ceiling, exemptions from ceiling etc); effectiveness in implementation of these laws and corruption. However, a new basis of agrarian relations had been laid. This period also saw development of some major irrigation projects (called "temples of modern India" by Jawahar Lal Nehru). Nehru also imagined cooperatisation of agriculture as a way forward, in view of smallness of holdings, to usher in modernisation in agriculture and many incentives were provided for forming land cooperatives. These dreams never could take root. In this period India also saw massive *bhoodan* (land gift) movement. There was also an attempt at increasing institutional credit to farmers through cooperatives, land development banks, farmers service societies etc.

To sum up, "the focus of agricultural policies in [this] phase remained on reforming agrarian structure, building up cooperatives, creation of extension network and improving rural infrastructures including irrigation" Rao (1996, p. A-55).[6] At the same time this was also the period which laid great emphasis on rapid industrialisation for India.

There was significant increase in foodgrain production in this era. The increase came both from expansion of area under cultivation but also significant productivity gains[7]. This can be seen from Table 1. Gross irrigated area under foodgrains also increased from 17.61 mha to 23.86 mha in this period. This achievement is quite impressive by all accounts. However, it was not enough from the point of view of low base, increasing population and needs of rapid industrialisation.

The period beginning 1966 heralds what has been called green revolution in India – basically referring to phenomenal increases in wheat production following introduction of high yielding varieties in package of HYV seeds, assured irrigation and relatively high application of chemical fertilisers. There was substantial increase

---

[6] See Rao (1996) for a more detailed account of agricultural policy in this and the second phase.

[7] Surprisingly, Vyas (2003) remarks that initial land reforms did not contribute to growth of agricultural productivity. Likewise Chand (n.d.) remarks that "[e]expansion of area was the main source of growth in the pre green revolution period." Indeed, growth in foodgrain production as well as growth in foodgrain productivity were both higher in the land reforms phase (pre-green revolution) than the same in the comparable period in the green revolution phase.

Table 1: Growth in Production, Yield and Area under Foodgrains

Period	CARG in output	CARG in yield per HA	CARG in area
1950-51 to 1964-65	4.11	2.69	1.39
1967-68 to 1981-82	2.45	1.99	0.44
1980-81 to 1990-91	3.13	3.03	0.09
1990-91 to 2000-01	1.10	1.65	− 0.54
1990-91 to 2003-04	1.43	1.65	− 0.22

Source: Calculated from Government of India (2004): Agricultural Statistics at a Glance. CARG = compound annual rate of growth in percent (%) per annum. 1965-66 and 1966-67 have been excluded due to severe depression in foodgrain production due to drought.

in yield as well as area under wheat in this period. However, as is evident from Table 1 above, productivity gain for foodgrains as a whole declined from 2.69 % per annum observed during 14 years preceding green revolution (excluding two severe drought years) to 1.99 % per annum in 14 years following green revolution. As area under plough was slower to expand, growth rate of foodgrains production declined from 4.11 % per annum to only 2.45 % in the later period.[8] There is a view that it was not so much slowness of growth in agricultural production, as the needs of fast industrialisation which depended on cheap food supplies for labour. Though output increased substantially, marketable surplus did not increase much. Thus, according to report of the National Commission on Agriculture (vol 1, p. 188, emphasis added), "the unique feature of the food situation during the Second Plan [1957-62] period were the increasing demand for foodgrains and a steady decline in market arrivals *despite higher production.*" It appears that the Green Revolution did serve an important purpose. It was focussed in the areas (present Punjab, Haryana and western UP) which had better irrigation, and which already had higher production levels and marketable surplus. This ensured that most of the increased production arising from Green Revolution crops will reach the markets. Concentrating efforts on limited area was already thought of as a strategy, under names of Intensive Area District

---

[8] Chand (n.d.) says about Green revolution that,"[T]he strategy produced quick results as there was quantum jump in yield. Consequently, wheat and rice production in a short span of 6 years between 1965/66 and 1971/72 witnessed an increase of 30 million tonnes which is 168 percent higher than the achievement of 15 years following 1950/51". Unfortunately, agricultural production can have such wide swings from year to year that it is easy to show a particular period favourably against another by selective choice of cut off years. In the above case, the cut off year chosen by the scholar happens to be an year of severe depression in foodgrain production (including production of wheat and rice). Thus, performance of the pervious period is artificially depressed and that of the succeeding period artificially boosted. After removing the two outlier years from calculations, the results are evident from Table 1.

Programme in the closing years of the Second Plan and subsequently as Intensive Agriculture Area Programme in 1964 (See Bajaj, 1982). This could be done since Green Revolution technology came as a package. Unless irrigation was made available, demand for green revolution technology will not arise soon.

There were other changes affecting agriculture – both positive and negative. Whereas two important institutions were established in 1965 – Agricultural Prices Commission and Food Corporation of India, agricultural sector was subject to compulsory levy on foodgrains, restrictions on foodgrain movements, restrictions on storage etc. To facilitate higher credit to agricultural sector, major bank nationalisation took place in 1969. Output of wheat and to a lesser extent rice increase substantially, but of pulses, oilseeds and coarse grains was sluggish or even declined.

The decade of 1980s saw substantial increases in foodgrain productivity and production – highest gains in productivity of food grains for any decade was achieved in 1980s. Further, higher gains were made in hitherto lagging states such as West Bengal and Bihar. Throughout this period credit to agriculture from institutional sources expanded.

In the third phase of economic reforms started in 1991, major reforms were in liberalizing internal trade, bringing down barriers to movement of foodgrains, bettering terms of trade in favour of agriculture, and disprotection of industry. At the same time this period has seen increase in prices of several agricultural inputs – particularly chemical fertilizers, and plant protection chemicals. This period has also seen slowing down of growth of agricultural sector, indeed highly fluctuating farm business incomes with a falling overall trend. Table 2 taken from Alagh (2003) captures these adverse movements of prices of agricultural commodities and their inputs.

Table 2: Relative Price Movements in Indian Agriculture

Year	Price index	
	Intermediate consumption purchased	*All commodities sold*
1989-90	401.4	393.5
1997-98	920.1	785.4
% increase in 1997-98 over 1989-90	229	199

Source: CACP, 2000, Table 4.2, p.302 (Taken from Alagh, 2003, p.xvi)

However, this period has also seen some diversification of agriculture. Over the entire period of six decades since 1947, there have been large changes in composition of agricultural sector (in terms of GDP from agriculture). Share of crop production has been declining, share of livestock including milk has been rising. Within crop sector, horticulture sector has seen higher growth compared to non-horticulture crops, thus the share of the former has risen relative to the latter.

Agreement on Agriculture in WTO negotiations has been a subject of much debate and controversy in India. It is ironic that inclusion of agriculture in the Uruguay Round of GATT discussions was seen as an important gain. Indeed, "India is one of the leading developing nations which initiated from the very beginning of the Uruguay Round of discussion at Punta Del Este in September, 1986, that "agriculture" should be brought within the purview of GATT" (Mishra, 2003, p.10). Mishra, who was Deputy Director, Ministry of Commerce, Government of India, further shows in his paper that the concerns on the three issues of (a) market access, (b) export subsidy and © domestic support are at present at least misplaced as far as India is concerned. In the given circumstances (Indian agriculture being either net disprotected or only marginally protected), India does not face constraints in following its domestic policies to suit its needs, Indian imports of agricultural commodities are generally small (with a few exceptions as we will see in section 6) and India's bound rates are in most cases much higher than existing duties.[9] We shall see later that there are indeed areas of concern where agricultural performance in the post reform period is concerned.

The new initiatives concerning agriculture also include contract farming on the one hand and micro-finance institutions and self-help groups on the other hand. Futures trading in agricultural commodities is another new development in the era of economic reforms.

6. NATIONAL AGRICULTURAL POLICY DOCUMENTS

India saw a turbulent decade of widespread farmers' movements from late 1970s onwards, then through out 1980s and sporadically during 1990s. Though these movements varied from state to state, they had some common elements. They were all mass movements and they uniformly focussed on remunerative prices for agriculture. They also used terms such as just prices, scientific prices alternatively. Though in individual cases other demands were added (eg dignity for farmers; crusades against corruption; movement against MNC seed companies etc), they believed that farmers needed a fair deal rather than doles and subsidy. They also

---

[9] Indeed, there has been an argument to the contrary by some scholars. Since India's bound rates are much higher than existing duties, and that for most of agricultural commodities, it is unlikely that India will ever raise its duties anywhere near bound rates, India can bargain in negotiations by offering to lower its bound rates on selected commodities.

believed that government policies have been anti-farmer and the mechanism for that has been unfair exchange (unfavourable pricing) rather than any direct extraction of agricultural surplus. Indeed, it will not be an exaggeration to say that many later economists sound no different from this (see section 1 above) though some economists did raise these issues in an earlier period.

A Standing Advisory Committee (SAC) on Agriculture was constituted under chairmanship of Sharad Joshi[10] by the Government of India in March 1989 to represent the views of the farming community. Department of Agriculture and Cooperation prepared a draft of the Agricultural Policy Resolution and referred it to the SAC. The SAC put its views in public domain in January 1991. Subsequently, three other such policy documents have emerged from Government of India. We take up these for a quick look.

6.1 National Agricultural Policy: Views of Standing Advisory Committee on Agriculture (July 1990)

The document consisting of 135 numbered paragraphs is divided into four chapters. After a long Introduction, the document describes programme of action in brief. The two major chapters enunciating what needs to be done are chapter three: Infrastructure Programme and chapter four: Economic programme. It is pointed out that no comprehensive policy or even a view of agriculture was ever formulated – agricultural policy remained centred on the notion of grow more food. It points to "A large armoury of instruments ... deployed to enforce the regime of low agricultural prices – restriction on movement, compulsory levy procurement, import-export manipulatios, dumping in domestic markets, artificially pegged exchange value of rupee." A large economic literature on the subject precisely echoes these very issues.

The document calls for expanding irrigation, improving utilisation of water resources, improving tools, machines, practices and "above all,.. creating amongst the agriculturists a high level of motivation. Further it calls for improvement of infrastructure like transport, communication, storage, marketing, processing and credit and strengthening of backward and forward linkages. (p.9)

The policy suggests the following grand: infrastructure and technology and economic viability including price policies. It proposes,

"...new approach to economic development would rely primarily on insaturation of cost effectiveness ... All grants of subsidies would be abolished at the level of production except in cases where the agricultural units are, by their very size and character, uneconomic." (p.18, emphasis added).

---

[10] One of the main leaders of farmers movement of 1980s.

Chapter on infrastructure programme, touches on issues of maintaining natural resources, promise of rainfed agriculture in horticulture, distribution and consolidation of land, development of human resources – particularly young farmers inducted into modular courses on stipend, seeds – ".. the New Seed Policy to enable the import of high quality seeds, to encourage competition, and to support private sector participation side by side with the public sector.. " (p.26), fertiliser and energy – including reliance on organic wastes, and diversification of products. It calls for giving further impetus to animal husbandry and dairying – including development of indigenous breeds, poultry development through better marketing, horticulture development through more efficient storage, marketing, grafting and price incentives, and fishing and farm forestry.

Chapter on economic programme calls for remunerative prices by removing lacunae in cost calculations. It suggests that "provision of warehousing.., easy availability of credit, modernisation of agriculture produce markets, improvement of transport and communication would ensure satisfactory returns ... most of these infrastructural facilities will be created by farmers themselves .. " if farming becomes profitable (p.34). It suggests gradually increasing support prices each month after the harvest to meet costs of storage. It calls for rationalised and trimmed public distribution system delivery with optimum efficiency to targeted class of people. Emphasizing need for insurance in the face of risk and uncertainty, it suggests that in the long run insurance scheme should not depend on any element of subsidy.

On agricultural research, the report requires that it be demand driven at least in a large part and such that farmers are willing to bear a major part of the cost. Lastly, it asks for government decision making to incorporate interaction with farmers' organisations. It asks for Panchayats to have powers for imposing taxes and to receive financial assistance from State as well as Central government and to perform functions including management of health, education, electricity and dividing irrigation water.

Apart from specific aspects, the document calls for a greater participation of the private sector, including farmers themselves, reducing dependence on the state, debureaucratisation and what later came under the rubric of liberalisation.

6.2 National Agriculture Policy, Department of Agriculture and Cooperation, Ministry of Agriculture, Government of India, in 2000

The 2000 national agricultural policy recognises that capital inadequacy, lack of infrastructural support and demand side constraints such as controls on movement, storage and sale of agricultural produce have affected the viability of agriculture sector. Chand (n.d.) suggests that "the challenges facing Indian agriculture can be grouped in four categories relating to (1) growth (2) sustainability (3) efficiency and (4) equity." The policy document under review here organised around the following themes: (a) sustainable agriculture; (b) food and nutrition security; (c) generation and transfer of technology; (d) inputs management; (e) incentive for agriculture; (f) investment in agriculture; (g) institutional structure; and (h) risk management.

The document projects a growth rate in excess of 4 % per annum and aims at growth in agriculture that is inclusive, equitable, and sustainable. Towards sustainable agriculture, it promises soil conservation, rational utilisation and conservation of country's "abundant water" including watershed development, conservation of bio-resources including conservation of indigenous breeds, promotion of integrated nutrient and pest management (INM & IPM), promotion of agro- and social-forestry and pooling, distilling and evaluating traditional practices, knowledge and wisdom to harness them for sustainable agricultural growth. For food and nutrition security, it talks of raising crop productivity; support for rainfed agriculture,employment generation; development of animal husbandry, poultry, fishing and dairying. Priority attention is to be given to processing, marketing and transport facilities. In technology, it lays emphasis on evolving new location-specific and economically viable improved varieties of agricultural and horticultural crops.

It promises creation of favourable economic environment for increasing capital formation and farmers' own investments by removal of distortions; formulating commodity-wise strategies to protect growers against adverse impact following from dismantling of QRs in external trade; and promotion of exports. It also promises stepping of public investment for narrowing regional imbalances, and accelerating development of supportive infrastructure in particular rural connectivity. Setting up of agro-processing units in producing areas will be encouraged.

In institutional reforms, besides redistribution of surplus land to the landless, it enunciates policy of tenancy reform recognising rights of tenants and developing lease markets for increasing the size of holdings, provision of giving private lands on lease for cultivation and agri-business. It envisages private sector participation through contract farming. Micro-credit is to be promoted and self-help group-bank linkage system to be developed as a supplementary mechanism to bring rural poor into the formal banking system.

For risk management, the policy promises development of insurance, drought and flood proofing and enlarging the overage of futures markets – the latter for minimizing the wide fluctuations in commodity prices and for hedging of risks.

6.3 Revised Draft National Policy for Farmers by National Commission on Farmers chaired by MS Swaminathan, in 2006 and National Policy for Framers 2007, Department of Agriculture and Cooperation, Ministry of Agriculture, Government of India

The National Policy for Farmers, 2007 ("National Policy" for short) is based on the Draft National Policy, 2006 ("Draft Policy" for short) submitted by Swaminathan. Hence these can be taken up together. However, not all recommendations in the Draft Policy were accepted by the government. We point out some major omissions from the National Policy document at the end of this section. The National Policy recognises that "there is a need to focus more on the *economic well-being* of the farmers, rather than just on production. Socio-economic well-being must be a prime consideration of agricultural policy, besides production and growth." (p.2). The major goals set by National Policy were:

(i) To improve economic viability of farming by substantially increasing the net income of farmers and to ensure that agricultural progress is measured by advances made in this income.

(ii) To protect and improve land, water, bio-diversity and genetic resources essential for sustained increase in the productivity, profitability and stability of major farming systems by creating an economic stake in conservation.

(iii) To develop support services including provision for seeds, irrigation, power, machinery and implements, fertilizers and credit at affordable prices in adequate quantity for farmers.

(iv) To strengthen the bio-security of crops, farm animals, fish and forest trees for safeguarding the livelihood and income security of farmer families and the health and trade security of the nation.

(v) To provide appropriate price and trade policy mechanisms to enhance farmers' income.

(vi) To provide for suitable risk management measures for adequate and timely compensation to farmers.

(vii) To complete the unfinished agenda in land reforms and to initiate comprehensive asset and aquarian reforms.

(viii) To mainstream the human and gender dimension in all farm policies and programmes.

(ix) To pay explicit attention to sustainable rural livelihoods.

(x) To foster community-centred food, water and energy security systems in rural India and to ensure nutrition security at the level of every child, woman and man.

(xi) To introduce measures which can help attract and retain youths in farming and processing of farm products for higher value addition by making it intellectually stimulating and economically rewarding.

(xii) To make India a global outsourcing hub in the production and supply of the inputs needed for sustainable agriculture, products and processes developed through biotechnology and Information and Communication Technology (ICT).

(xiii) To restructure the agricultural curriculum and pedagogic methodologies for enabling every farm and home science graduate to become an entrepreneur and to make agricultural education gender sensitive.

(xiv) To develop and introduce a social security system for farmers.

(xv) To provide appropriate opportunities in adequate measure for non-farm employment for the farm households."

The main points in the National Policy are recapitulated here. (a) It reiterates water harvesting, exhorts enhancement of water-use efficiency by appropriate choice of seeds, nutrients etc; and emphasises equity in water use. Drought Code is to be introduced in drought prone areas; (b) Livestock, fisheries draw its attention; (c) It incorporates several specific suggestions for conservation and development of bio-resources, incorporating participatory procedures; (d) In S&T, it proposes that NGOs and private sector R&D institutions would be included under NARS[11] umbrella. There is also a proposal for setting up of a National Bio-technology Regulatory Authority (obviously keeping in view increasing importance of GM crops); (e) Mutually beneficial farmer-seed company partnerships will be encouraged. Farmers will be issued soil health passbooks. Agro-forestry, IPM etc. will be implemented; (f) The policy assures that banking system will endeavour to meet credit needs; other avenues of provision of credit, e.g. Micro-credit, kisan credit cards be provided; National Agriculture Insurance Scheme to be revamped; (g) Cooperatives are exhorted to work as economic enterprises and not extension of the government; (h) KVKs (agriculture science centres) and ICT will be harnessed for extension and knowledge connectivity.

In terms of economic incentives the following are included in the National Policy: continuation of minimum support price mechanism; establishment of community foodgrain banks; developing single national market by relaxing internal restrictions; markets to be developed in public-private partnership; promotion of grading, branding, packaging and development of markets for local produce; infrastructure for enabling agro-processing and value addition at the village level itself. There is a small section on genetically modified (GM) crops, which does not tell us much. There are also two small sections on contract farming and Farmers' companies. The

---

[11] National Agricultural Research System.

policy recognizes the need for rural non-farm initiative but does not tell us much in terms of what is to be done.

Surprisingly, the policy document is silent on futures markets in agricultural commodities. Finally we take a look at the major omissions in the National Policy with reference to the Draft Policy. These include: (i) Issue of water pollution from use of chemical fertilizers; (ii) Most of recommendation concerning fisheries are not accepted; (iii) Suggestion of exempting farmers from certain provisions Wildlife Protection Act, 1972 under specified circumstances (threatening their livelihood) is not accepted; (iv) Proposal for setting up an India Trade Organisation (ITO) to safeguard interests of farmers by establishing a Livelihood Security Box to ensure fair trade. The Livelihood Security Box was to have provision to impose quantitative restrictions on imports and or/increases in import tariffs, under conditions where imports of certain commodities will be detrimental to the work and income security of large numbers of farming families. This suggestion is omitted; (v) Draft policy calls for reorientation of CACP (Commission on Agricultural Costs and Prices), so that "the 'net take home income' of farmers should be comparable to those of civil servants" is not accepted; (vi) Large parts of recommendations regarding tribal farmers and pastoralists are removed; (vii) Two whole sections entitled "Public policies for sustainable livelihoods" and Matching national policy with local diversity" containing about twenty recommendations are omitted.

7. INDIAN AGRICULTURE IN POST-REFORM PERIOD

This section takes a bird's eye view of the Indian agriculture in the post-reform period after 1991 in a comparative framework. We already had a broad picture of progress in foodgrain production and productivity in Table1. It is clearly seen that the growth rates of production as well as productivity have declined after 1991 – they are their lowest in this period. The agriculture contributes at present about 20 % to India's GDP and about 57 % of her workforce is employed in agriculture. Share of agriculture in the National Income has been falling sharply since 1990s. The reason is not far to seek. Agricultural growth rates have come down,whereas growth rates in industry and service sectors have accelerated in the same period. Further, growth in agricultural GDP remains highly volatile. This can be seen from Table 3.

In contrast a large number of sub-sectors in industry and services have grown very rapidly – industry and services growing at average rates near or above 6 % per annum during 1992-2006. Indeed the sub-sectors that have grown at 8 % or above in this period include: Beverages (11.9), Silk, wool textiles (8.1), Chemicals (7.8), Non-metallic minerals (8.3), Basic metals (9.3), Transport equipment (9.3) among Industry and road transport (8.3), Water transport (9.5), Telephone services (18.8),

Miscellaneous services (27.8), Business services (23.3), Community services (8.9), Education (8.8), Medical and health (9.4) among services. (See Nagaraj, 2008, p.56).

Table 3: Annual Growth Rate of GDP at Factor Cost in Agriculture during 1951-52 to 2002-03 (at 1993-94 prices)

Year	Growth rate	Year	Growth rate	Year	Growth rate
1951-52	1.6	1970-71	7.4	1989-90	0.7
1952-53	4.2	1971-72	−2.7	1990-91	4.4
1953-54	9.0	1972-73	−5.6	1991-92	−1.9
1954-55	2.8	1973-74	8.4	1992-93	6.2
1955-56	−1.5	1974-75	−2.8	1993-94	4.1
1956-57	6.0	1975-76	14.2	1994-95	5.1
1957-58	−5.1	1976-77	−6.1	1995-96	−1.1
1958-59	11.2	1977-78	12.5	1996-97	10.1
1959-60	−1.5	1978-79	2.0	1997-98	−2.8
1960-61	7.3	1979-80	−13.4	1998-99	6.9
1961-62	−0.3	1980-81	14.4	1999-2000	−0.1
1962-63	−2.1	1981-82	5.6	2000-01	−0.4
1963-64	1.9	1982-83	−0.5	2001-02	6.7
1964-65	10.3	1983-84	10.3	2002-03	−6.0
1965-66	−13.5	1984-85	1.4		
1966-67	−2.3	1985-86	0.7		
1967-68	17.1	1986-87	−0.6		
1968-69	−0.3	1987-88	−1.4		
1969-70	7.2	1988-89	16.8		

Source: Government of India (2004): Agricultural Statistics at a Glance.

At the same time share of agriculture in employment has also fallen but relatively slowly. Even now, ratio of GDP share of agriculture to employment share of agriculture is as low as 0.33. What are the key aspects of this growth performance? We look at some factors important for growth and also at disaggregated picture on some variables across Indian states.

7.1 Credit and Capital Formation

In Table 4 we take a look at growth rate of outstanding credit by Scheduled Commercial Banks (SCBs) for agriculture and for total credit for comparison. Table 5 provides share that agricultural credit has in total bank credit or in total bank deposits. It is clearly seen that in the 1990 rate of growth of agricultural credit from banks has fallen drastically, whereas total credit growth has increased. In terms of shares as well, share in total bank credit has fallen sharply from 18% to 12% and similarly there is fall in its ratio to bank deposits. Thus support of institutional finance from banks has declined quite sharply for agriculture during the reform period. More detailed data disaggregated at state level also shows growth of credit was very similar for agricultural credit and total credit across states in 1981-91 but it was lower for agricultural credit for every state in 1992-200. (see Sahu, 2007 for details)

Table 4: Growth of Outstanding Credit to SCBs (% per annum)

Period	Agriculture	Total
1981-91	15.2	15.7
1992-2000	10.9	16.0
1981-2000	12.0	15.3

Source: Sahu (2007), p. 667.

Table 5: Ratio of Credit to Agriculture to Total Bank Credit and Total Bank Deposits

Period	Agriculture credit to total net bank credit	Agriculture credit to total bank deposit
1981-85	17.9	11.7
1986-90	18.1	11.2
1991-95	14.7	8.6
1996-2000	11.7	6.8

Source: Sahu (2007), p. 668.

Now let us look at capital formation. It is provided in Table 6. It is seen that capital formation in public sector rose marginally in early part of the decade and then fell. Capital formation in the private sector has continued to grow in contrast. The declining trend in public investment in agriculture started in 1980s and has continued into 1990s. Inaugurating the annual conference of the Indian Society of Agricultural Economics in 1994, Dr. Manmohan Singh, then Finance Minister (and now Prime Minister) of India shared his concern over falling public investment in agriculture and emphasised the need for increasing public investment in agriculture. However, there does not appear to be any noticeable improvement in the situation.

Table 6: Capital Formation in Agriculture in 1993-94 Prices

Year	Public	Private	Total
1993-94	4467 (2.2)	9056	13523 (6.6)
1994-95	4947 (2.3)	10220	14969(7.0)
1995-96	4849 (2.3)	10841	15690 (7.4)
1996-97	4668 (2.0)	11508	16176 7.0)
1997-98	3979 (1.8)	11963	15942 (7.1)
1997-98	3870 (1.6)	11025	14895 (6.1)
1999-2000	4222 (1.7)	13082	17304 (7.2)
2000-2001	3919 (1.66)	12768	16687 (7.1)
Growth rate (%)	−1.8	5.03	3.05

Source: Awasthi (2004).

7.2 Profitability of Crop Production

We have already seen that there has been slow down in terms of foodgrain production and productivity as well as in terms of GDP from agriculture. These findings are further confirmed by the studies of farm business income. Clearly, earnings per hectare are growing rather slowly during 1990s. Not only that, it is found that farm business per household has been not only highly volatile but showing a declining trend in 1990s. (see Mishra, 2008, p. 40)

Table 7: Changes in Value of Output, Cost of Production and Farm Business Income in Crop Production, Deflated by CPIAL with 1993-94 base (all in rupees)

Year	Output/ha.	Cost A2 /ha.	Farm income/ha.
1981-82	7588	3472	4115
1982-83	7607	3471	4136
1983-84	7751	3457	4294
1984-85	8427	3608	4819
1985-86	8340	3580	4760
1986-87	8263	3746	4518
1987-88	8409	3781	4628
1988-89	8585	3811	4774
1989-90	9295	3984	5311
1990-91	9491	3923	5568
1991-92	9424	3906	5518
1992-93	9446	4214	5232
1993-94	10332	4338	5994
1994-95	10451	4256	6195

Contd...

Table 7 Contd...

Year	Output/ha.	Cost A2 /ha.	Farm income/ha.
1995-96	9953	4226	5727
1996-97	10530	4336	6194
1997-98	9818	4413	5406
1998-99	10123	4292	5830
1999-00	10344	4425	5919
Rate of growth:			
1981-82 to 1989-90	2.22	1.76	2.59
1990-91 to 1999-00	0.90	1.20	0.68

Note: Cost A2 includes all paid out expenses, own machine and bullock labour cost, depreciation and rent paid for leased in land.

Source: Sen Abhijit and Bhatia (2004). Cost of Production and Farm Income, Millennium Study on State of India's Farmers, Academic Foundation, New Delhi

Chand and Pandey (2007) take a look at rates of change of various farm inputs during 1980s and 1990s. Some of those results are extracted below in Table 8. It is quite apparent that not only rate of capital formation and hence growth in the net fixed capital stock (NFCS) has slowed down, but there has been slowdown in use of chemical fertilizer, electricity consumption, and gross irrigated area. They even find that rate of crop shift area too has declined – used as a measure of diversification this is also a negative trend. All these are in per unit area (per hectare) terms, No wonder there are negative signals in incomes, GDP, farm business income etc.

Table 8: Growth Rates (in %) of Selected Inputs in Agriculture

Item	1980-81 to 1989-90	1990-91 to 1996-97	1996-97 to 2004-05
NPK /ha	8.26	2.4	2.0
Public sector NFCS/ha NSA	3.94	1.87	1.98
Private sector NFCS/ha NSA	0.642	2.13	1.72
Total NFCS/ha NSA	2.09	2.01	1.83
Area witnessing crop shift	5.6	5.6	4.8
Electricity / ha NSA	14.2	9.4	–0.2
Gross cropped area	0.43	0.43	–0.48
Gross irrigated area	2.28	2.62	0.51
Terms of trade	0.19	0.95	–1.63

Source: Chand and Pandey (2007) Table 4.

7.3 A Disaggregated Picture

The changes in the agricultural sector are quite dynamic across states of India. Growth rates in production across states vary quite widely. Copping patterns are undergoing significant changes, though the aggregate picture is unable to capture these changes. Some states have greater incidence of contract farming, high value floriculture etc. than others. Tables 9 and 10 captures some of these aspects. It must be realised from this that consequences of policy changes are also uneven. For examples, over the past decade, the crisis in agriculture has manifested in a large increase in suicides by farmers. These have been reported largely from Andhra Pradesh, Maharashtra and Karnataka. However, states that are seen economically lagging behind by a wide margin, such as Uttar Pradesh and Bihar have not reported such increases. Could it be that certain kind of agriculture more prone to uncertainties than other kinds? Are the states devoting more of their resources for averting such crises?

Table 9: Agriculture Growth across Major States of India

State	Agricultural growth between 1993-96 and 2000-03 at 1993-94 prices	Growth in value of food grains between1993-96 and 2000-03 deflated by respective state agricultural deflators
Andhra Pradesh	19.6	11.6
Assam	2.9	--
Bihar	28.2	--
Gujarat	−6.0	−24.5
Haryana	11.9	18.4
Karnataka	25.1	−25
Kerala	−18.6	3.9
Madhya Pradesh	−7.9	−9.4
Maharashtra	14.3	−44
Orissa	−9.4	--
Punjab	15.8	16.9
Rajasthan	5.6	6.5
Tamilnadu	1.5	−11.3
Uttar Pradesh	14.1	14.0
West Bengal	28.3	16.9
All India	11.3	2.6

Source: Mathur, Das and Sircar (2006), extracted form figures 4 and 5, pp. 5329-30.

Table 10: Cropping Pattern of Area under Cultivation (% of gross cropped area)

State/Year	Cereals	Pulses	Oilseeds	Sugarcane	Cotton (Lint)	Plantation crops	G C A
India							
1980-81	60.37	13.01	10.20	1.55	4.53	1.34	100
1990-91	55.55	13.28	13.00	1.99	4.01	1.11	100
2001-02	52.80	11.53	11.94	2.31	4.78	1.17	100
Andhra Pradesh							
1980-81	59.53	11.77	15.15	1.07	3.41		100
1990-91	46.47	12.37	23.65	1.73	4.97		100
2001-02	40.27	14.96	19.13	1.71	8.69		100
West Bengal							
1980-81	73.16	6.87	4.12	0.19		1.23	100
1990-91	71.36	3.62	5.93	0.14		1.18	100
2000-01	64.92	3.01	6.83	0.24		2.20	100
Haryana							
1980-81	58.00	14.55	5.70	2.11	11.77		100
1990-91	56.36	12.44	7.92	2.50	19.51		100
2000-01	66.39	1.84	6.53	2.34	22.62		100
Karnataka							
1980-81	52.28	1.00	13.36	1.45	9.50	1.46	100
1990-91	46.02	1.00	21.68	2.32	5.07	1.25	100
2000-01	46.49	1.00	18.12	3.40	4.49	1.79	100
Maharashtra							
1980-81	55.88	13.82	8.78	1.32	12.98		100
1990-91	49.16	16.03	14.00	2.18	13.43		100
2000-01	43.70	15.90	11.29	2.66	13.77		100
Punjab							
1980-81	66.73	5.05	3.58	1.06	9.58		100
1990-91	73.60	1.95	1.54	1.34	9.33		100
2000-01	78.40	0.74	1.10	1.52	5.97		100
Tamilnadu							
1980-81	57.24	8.41	16.60	2.84	3.42	1.32	100
1990-91	45.80	13.02	17.32	3.51	3.61	1.33	100
2000-01	50.33	13.49	16.66	4.97	2.68	1.91	100
Kerala							
1980-81	28.23	1.18	1.06	0.30	0.18	11.55	
1990-91	18.83	1.14	0.74	0.25	0.28	17.26	
2000-01	11.71	0.73	0.30	0.11	0.13	19.72	
Madhya Pradesh							
1980-81	61.35	22.68	8.42	0.28	2.76		100
1990-91	56.71	19.77	17.38	0.20	2.64		100
2000-01	36.50	21.42	31.41	0.42	2.65		100
Uttar Pradesh							
1980-81	71.92	12.0	3.11	5.43	0.17		100
1990-91	68.56	11.93	4.28	6.86	0.06		100
2000-01	69.96	10.76	5.60	7.78	0.02		100

Source: Devi and Sharma (2008).

7.4 Trade and Volatility

There have been fears that with freeing of trade small farmer agriculture may not be able to withstand global forces. Of course, there is no inherent reason for such fears. There is no evidence to suggest that small farmers are less efficient. Fears emerge from their insignificant economic power in the market place. India's net imports of foodgrains since 1991 have been negative except for two years (see Government of India 2005, Table 1.18). Balance of trade in agricultural commodities has remained positive through since 1991. In fact agricultural export to GDP (ag) has gone up from 3.5 % in 1990-91 to 5.6 % in 2002-03, whereas imports as a proportion of GDP (ag) have gone up from 0.83 % in 1990-91to 3.4 % in 2002-03. Thus imports have grown faster than exports but balance of trade remains positive (Sathe and Deshpande, 2006). These aggregates do not tell us about specific crops. Whereas India has emerged as a significant exporter of rice, it has imported wheat occasionally. In either case imports in cereals have been a very small proportion of domestic production or domestic requirements. It is unlikely to have caused major perturbations in domestic prices. The case of oilseeds has been different. India has been importing large quantities of oilseeds and it has been created problem for oilseed growers in some of the years.

In this context it is interesting to note that the scholars have found conflicting evidence regarding price volatility in domestic prices in India compared to price volatility of the world prices of those commodities. (See Bhattacharya 2003, whose study indicates greater instability in world prices both in rice and wheat and Chand 1998, whose study indicates lower instability in world prices for all commodities reported, which include: wheat, rice, sugarcane, cotton, groundnut and tea). If it is true that domestic price instability is higher, then it is contended that opening India to external markets should have stabilizing effect on India's domestic prices in traded commodities – if anything India might transmit some of its price volatility to the world prices, since it will have major presence in world trade in agricultural commodities. One may also have to keep in mind that price movements are highly dynamic and the differing results could pertain to different time periods.

This quick overview of certain aspects of agriculture in the post reform period does put us on caution. There are certain vulnerabilities. It does not call for closing the markets or reversing liberalisation. But it does call for keeping the structure and diversity of Indian agriculture firmly before us while looking at policy responses.

8. LOOKING AHEAD

A large number of economists are agreed that for a long time industry was protected, that this amounted to effective disprotection of agriculture, that there were other restrictions placed on agriculture, and that agriculture was loosing large surplus to other sectors. Yet, economic reforms, under which hold of bureaucracy is being loosened to a large extent, which are providing greater flexibility in market operation, and which imply that protection to industry is being lowered, are also seen to be causing a sense of uncertainty and apprehension in the farm sector. We may need to develop new methods, and look at new variables to understand this paradoxical situation. We close this paper with some suggestions along these lines.

Most of the variables are at far too aggregate level. It would pay to look at the structure of those variables. We, for example always seem to be looking at capital formation – segregating into public and private, across smaller units such as states etc. But hardly any studies analyse the components of this capital formation. How it is broken into irrigation devices, into farm machinery, into tractors or into threshers? Does it lead to cost escalation in cultivation or cost reduction? These are important questions and suggest a line of enquiry.

Similarly, we are used to looking at terms of trade between agriculture and other sectors (particularly industry). Does favourable movement in terms of trade for agriculture as seen from price data necessarily imply that agriculture sector and the agriculturists are likely to benefit? What about intermediaries? Could it be that increased prices in agriculture may largely flow to the intermediaries?

Similarly, it may be useful to analyse what is relation of value added from agriculture (GDP) and total output in value from agriculture. Is value added shrinking as a proportion of total output and if so, are intermediate inputs being ploughed back into agriculture? This will be useful in telling us how value of rupee earned by selling a unit of agricultural output is disposed.

Further, linkages between agriculture and other village industries need to be studied deeply. Will greater industrial activity at the village level benefit agriculture itself. Could it provide an immediate solution to the problem of slack in agricultural activities? What infrastructure will induce such rural industrialisation? What is the role of quality testing and standardisation in bringing, say, agri-industries to the villages? It is interesting to note that in the index of industrial production, agriculture based industries have a weight of almost 25 %. (see Economic Survey, Government of India,2005, p. S-34). Could some of this industry be better situated in villages, which provide raw materials to these industries, provided appropriate quality and standard institutions are available? This will become even more significant with opening up of trade.

Research and development, creation of technology assumes importance both for agriculture and for village industries (on this issue for agriculture see, Kalirajan and

Shand, 1997). Creation of technologies and economic viability will be far more potent in helping agriculture than subsidies could have possibly ever done.

REFERENCES

[1] Alagh, Y.K. (ed. 2003): Globalisation and Agricultural Crisis in India, (New Delhi: Deep and Deep Publications (P) Ltd).

[2] Awasthi, Arvind (2007): "Production and Investment credit of scheduled commercial banks in India: Need for a systematic approach", *Indian Journal of Agricultural Economics*, 62, 3, July-September, pp.314-320.

[3] Bajaj, J.K. (1982): "Green revolution: A historical perspective", *PPST Bulletin*, Vol. 2, No. 2, March.

[4] Bhagwati, Jagadish N. and Padma Desai (1997): India: Planning for Industrialisation.

[5] Bhattacharya, B. (2003): "Trade liberalisation and agricultural price policy in India since Reform", *Indian Journal of Agricultural Economics*, 58, 3, July-September.

[6] Bhagwati, Jagadish N. and T.N. Srinivasan (1993): India's Economic Reforms (New Delhi: Oxford University Press).

[7] Chand, Ramesh (n.d.): "India's National Agricultural Policy: A critique", mimeo (from internet).

[8] Chand, Ramesh (1998): "Agriculture: The challenge and strategy" *Economic and Political Weekly*, XXIII, 15, 11 April, pp. 850-854.

[9] Chand, Ramesh and L.M. Pandey (2007): "Growth crisis in agriculture" *Economic and Political Weekly*, XLII, 26, June 30, pp.2528-2533.

[10] Devi, Reena and Naresh Kumar Sharma (2008): "An analysis of agricultural credit market and capital formation in agriculture", mimeo.

[11] Dutt, Rajani Palme (1940): *India Today*.

[12] Government of India (2000): National Agriculture Policy, Department of Agriculture and Cooperation, Ministry of Agriculture, Government of India.

[13] Government of India (2004): Agricultural Statistics at a Glance, (New Delhi: Government of India)

[14] Government of India (2005): Economic Survey, Ministry of Finance.

[15] Government of India (2006): Revised Draft National Policy for Farmers, National Commission on Farmers, Government of India

[16] Government of India (2006): National Policy for Framers 2007, Department of Agriculture and Cooperation, Ministry of Agriculture, Government of India.

[17] Joshi, Sharad (1991): National Agricultural Policy: Views of Standing Advisory Committee on Agriculture, July 1990.

[18] Joshi, Vijay and I.M.D. Little (1996): Economic Reforms in India, (New Delhi: Oxford University Press).

[19] Kalirajan, K.P. and R.T. Shand (1997): "Sources of output growth in Indian Agriculture", *Indian Journal of Agricultural Economics*, 52, 4, October-December, pp. 693-706.

[20] Krueger, Anne O., Maurice Schiff, and Alberto Valdes (ed. 1992): Political Economy of Agricultural Pricing Policy, (Baltimore: The John Hopkins University Press)

[21] Lipton M. (1977): Why Poor People Stay Poor: Urban bias in world development, (London: Temple Smith).

[22] Mathur, Archana S., Surajit Das, and Subhalakshmi Sircar (2006): "Status of Agriculture in India", *Economic and Political Weekly*, XLI, 52, 30 December.

[23] Mishra, R.S. (2003): "The WTO agreement on agriculture (AoA) and agricultural crisis in India", in Alagh (ed, 2003), pp. 3-12.

[24] Mishra, Srijit (2008): Risks, Farmers' Suicides and Agrarian crisis in India: Is there a way out?", *Indian Journal of Agricultural Economics*, 63, 1, July-September, pp.38-54.

[25] Nagaraj, K. (2008): "India's Recent Economic Growth: A closer look", *Economic and Political Weekly*, XLIII, 15, 12-18 April.

[26] Rao, V.M. (1996): "Agricultural Development with a Human Face", *Economic and Political Weekly*, XXXI, 26, pp. A-50 – A-62, June 29.

[27] Sahu, Gagan Bihari (2007): "Supply analysis of institutional credit to agriculture for major states in India", *Indian Journal of Agricultural Economics*, 62, 4, October-December, pp. 664-678.

[28] Sathe, Dhanmanjiri, and R.S. Deshpande (2006): "Sustaining Agricultural Trade", *Economic and Political Weekly*, XLI, 52, 30 December.

[29] Schiff, Maurice and Alberto Valdes (1995): "The plundering of agriculture in developing countries", *Finance and Development*, March, pp 44-47.

[30] Sharma, Naresh Kumar (1992): Land Tenures and Tenancy Law in India: A Historical Review and a Comparative Study, mimeo, April.

[31] Vyas, V.S. (2003): India's Agrarian Structure, Economic Policies and Sustainable Development, (New Delhi: Academic Foundation).

Second Generation Reforms in India: Looking to Future

Seeta Mishra

The 21ˢᵗ century belongs to Asia. India and China is the leading economy of Asia from many view points. It is a democratic country. The market forces, regulated through appropriate institutions and interventions, rule its economy. There is devolution of political power from the centre to the states, and the states to the local level administration. The executive, judiciary and press co-exist and work together for the advancement of the country. The armed forces of the country strive for peace and are engaged in nation building when the country is not at war. The development of science and technology is focused on innovation and change leading to the transformational progress of the country. After suppression of more than 350 years, the country has started marching on the path of development with the ambition to become the economic leader of the world. India is presently engaged in bridging the gap between growth and development through social equity, balanced regional development, removal of inequity in income distribution, and ensuring access to markets, products and services to all sections of the society.

Independence in 1947 ushered in a new era of growth and development for the nation. The first few years of the independence were devoted to rebuilding of the nation. The planned era started in 1951 during which year the 1ˢᵗ five year plan was launched. Now, we are in the 11ᵗʰ five year plan. The character of planning has undergone a fundamental change. The domination of public sector is giving way to the pre-eminence of private sector. The central concern of economic planning is no more 'machines to make machines'. The development of agriculture and social development have been identified as the goals of economic planning. Control of inflation and generation of employment have come to be identified as the prime goals of the economy. The structural economic imbalances compelled the country to opt for economic reforms and introduce macro and micro reforms at the national, central, local and firm levels. The stabilisation and structural adjustment policies brought about fundamental restructuring in agricultural, industrial, fiscal, financial, commercial, monetary and public enterprise policies. Globalisation has stirred the past assumptions of economic planning and forced the country to liberalize the trade in line with the thinking of the World Trade Organisation (WTO) resulting in decimation of its tariff wall. The dearth of foreign exchange no more constrains the economic reconstruction of the country. Not only huge foreign exchange reserves have been built up but there has been an unprecedented growth of capital flows inundating the country paving the way for taking on the challenges of developing socio-economic infrastructure, retiring the expensive debt, creating facilities for research and development, infusion of funds into agriculture, irrigation and industry, and modernising the State.

1. FIRST GENERATION ECONOMIC REFORMS

India is witnessing a new regime of high rate of economic growth. The minuscule Hindu rate of economic growth is a thing of the past. It is identified as the country distinguished by high rate of economic growth and the Hindu rate of inflation! This high rate of economic growth has been the outcome of introducing market reforms, eliminating licensing and controls, and exposing every player to competition. Liberalisation of the external sector has given a big push to economic growth. Trade was made free of controls and foreign direct investments were freed from economic and political shackles. Imports of goods and services have moderated price increases and forced domestic industry to become more efficient. Liberalisation of financial sector has played a key role in lifting the rate of economic growth. In particular, mention should be made of reforms in the insurance, banking, pension, provident fund and capital market sectors. Reforms in financial sector have led to more optimal allocation of resources, better price discovery, adoption of international disclosure norms and accounting standards, and more efficient management of risks. The enhanced public expenditure also contributed to a rise in the rate of economic growth. Expenditure on education, health care, rural and urban roads drinking water supply and rural employment have led to higher incomes in the hands of people resulting in higher consumption of goods and services and finally higher growth.

However, the path of high rate of economic growth is fraught with serious challenges. There is a challenge of increasing the tempo of present savings to the international benchmarks achieved by many developing countries. This would require the policy makers to bring more people into the fold of formal financial sector. Financial inclusion therefore becomes the central issue. The self help groups and micro finance institutions have to play a much bigger role. The concept of branchless banking needs to be promoted by these financial institutions. Financial sector has to rise up to the expectations. The rate of growth of credit should increase significantly. While the financial sector institutions increase the credit supply, they have to look for resources to meet the capital adequacy norms imposed by the regulator and the international organisations. Capital markets have to modernise itself and have suitable legal framework. New measures of risk management need to be introduced in our lackadaisical banking system. The challenge of infrastructure has to be met on utmost priority basis. We need humongous investment in infrastructure of Rs 10 lakh crores. Not only that such money is needed, there is a need also to hone the project management skills of managerial personnel handling the infrastructural projects. A majority of the infrastructure projects suffer from time and cost overruns. The rate of growth of agriculture has been causing anxiety. It has declined to a historical low. Country cannot afford to face wage good crisis which will dampen the entire cycle of economic growth. Public investments supplemented by adequate credit and suitable credit delivery mechanisms alone can help in resolving this crisis. The fiscal incentives, appropriately designed trade policies, measures to check dumping and over subsidisation, and removal of stagnation of very high work force ought to rescue agriculture from the present crisis. Country has to accept the challenge of removing non-merit subsidies. There is perennial challenge of eliminating opportunities for rent seeking and punishing the corrupt. The 'demographic dividend' is not an unmixed blessing as it has to match the demand from the growing labour force. In other words, the challenge is to sustain India's growth momentum by expanding employment opportunities and improved labour productivity. Improving service skill enhancement delivery is another crucial challenge which requires an increasing outlays on the twin merit goods: primary education and basic health. The country needs to spend not only more but also more efficiently. It is both the quantum and quality that decide the efficiency of the service delivery system. The fiscal consolidation, on track, has to gain a greater momentum. The administrative efficiency needs to undergo further improvements. In the globalised economy, this may appear a difficult task especially as one posed by the 'impossible trinity' – the problem of managing capital flows, exchange rate and interest rate all at the same time. The globalised economy has brought in train the problem of rate of exchange of rupee. The rise of Indian rupee has made a dent in India's exports and compelled the industry to re-examine its internal processes and systems.

1.1 Contextualising India's Economic Reforms in terms of Growth Strategies

Rethinking India's growth strategy initiates us to look afresh at the orthodox and unorthodox growth theories and then to comment whether India's growth model relates to either of them or it is a breakaway from the past. The unorthodox growth theories have been developed by Johansen, Meade, Phelps, Samuelson, Solow, Swan, Tobin, von Weizsacker, and Yaari, building on earlier ideas coming from Domar, Harrod, Hicks and Robinson. They have been applied in empirical studies to determine the magnitude of different factors explaining economic growth, or in various analyses of productivity growth for example by, Abramovitz, Denison, Kendrick, Salter, and Solow. The most important characteristic of orthodox theory (which distinguishes it from other theories of economic growth) is the assumption that technical progress is independent of investment. Vintage theory, a modification of orthodox theory, asserts that the assets created as a result of investment at any one time are superior to the assets created in earlier times, and inferior to those created later. The unorthodox theories do not make the assumption that technical progress is independent of investment. While the unorthodox growth theories usually retain orthodox concepts, they graft on to these an extra relation between investment and technical progress. These growth strategies are unsuited to explain the Indian growth 'phenomenon'. It is much better to jettison such concepts and start afresh with a simpler and direct analysis of growth in India.

2. SECOND GENERATION REFORMS

This section makes an attempt to unfold the challenges that were not addressed during the first phase of economic reforms extending between 1991-2001. The second generation of economic reforms need to concentrate issues such as a new thrust on savings, transformation of the financial sector, overhaul of infrastructure, bringing agriculture back on rails and social restructuring. These challenges have been discussed in detail below, as these are formidable challenges for the Indian economy.

3. NEW THRUST ON SAVINGS

The first, and obvious, challenge maintain such growth rate is not only to keep up the present rate of savings but further accelerate it to the levels of rate of savings of some highly developed countries. In order to sustain high growth and in order to finance such growth largely by domestic resources, it is necessary that domestic savings should be adequately high and also increase as the economy moves to a higher growth plane. It is a happy augury that domestic savings have improved from 23.7 per cent of GDP in 2000-01 to 34.7 per cent of GDP in 2006-07. What is of great significance is that public sector savings which were negative at 1.7 per cent of GDP in 2000-01 has become a positive 2.0 per cent of GDP in 2005-06. Private corporate savings (8.1 per cent) as well as household savings (22.3 per cent) continue to remain high. It is important to maintain this trend of rising domestic savings and, in my view, it would not be too ambitious to aim for domestic savings of 40 per cent of GDP by 2011-12, the terminal year of the Eleventh Plan. In fact, the draft Eleventh Plan envisages an average annual savings rate of 34.8 per cent through the Plan period, and that is neither too ambitious nor unattainable:

In order to promote savings—and for other reasons too—it is necessary to bring more people into the formal financial sector. The poor also save, except that their savings are not part of the formal financial sector. As a result; the poor are not able to leverage their savings or earn a reasonable return on such savings; their savings are not .secure; and those savings are not intermediated efficiently and turned into investment. Financial inclusion is therefore an important goal. Eventually, it is my hope that every household in this country will have a bank account. Meanwhile, we must experiment with new models of institutions. The self help group (SHG) movement has proved to be a phenomenal success. Public sector banks have financed 3 million self help groups so far, and the number is growing every year. SHGs have promoted thrift. We must replicate the success of the SHG movement in other bodies such as joint liability groups, chit funds; micro finance organisations, etc and bring them into the mainstream of the banking sector. We must also harness technology – and such technologies are available today – to spread the concept of "branchless banking". The possibilities are virtually unlimited: mobile banking, wireless banking and cell phone banking are among technologies that are proven and popular. The Indian banks have begun bold experiments with new technologies to expand the reach of the banking sector. However, financial inclusion should not become a 'public sector bank'-centric subject of discussion. This approach must be taken beyond public sector banks and promote greater competition in banking services among different service providers.

4. TRANSFORMATION OF FINANCIAL SECTOR

The second challenge is the challenge to the financial sector in general and the banking sector in particular. In order to sustain an average growth rate of 9 per cent a year, the economy would have to mobilise vast resources. Bank credit alone would need to grow at about 24 to 26 per cent a year. Besides, investors would need to raise equity and quasi-equity resources. Research and development would require resource support of a different kind from investors who are willing to take higher risks. Some investments would need funds with short tenures, others—especially infrastructure projects—with long tenures. Hence, all segments of the financial sector would have to be tuned to fire on all cylinders, be it the capital market, banking, insurance or pensions. Each one of them is important, and each one of them is crying out for more reforms. There is, however, one common need for all these segments, and that is capital. For example, it has been estimated that Indian banks would need to raise ₹ 1,00,000 crore as additional Tier-I capital over the next three years. Given the current life insurance penetration of 4.8 per cent and life insurance density of US$ 38.4, even to double those numbers over the next five years, the life insurance industry would need to increase its capital by about Rs 15,000 crore. The same arguments would apply to the health insurance and general (Le. Non-life) insurance industries as well. India is still at the first step towards creating a pension fund industry, and building such an industry would require a large amount of capital. We have a well-regulated capital market but modernisation of that market including technological up-gradation of different kinds of market participants would also require vast amounts of capital. These industries cannot raise the huge additional capital required unless they are perceived to be well governed and well regulated. Therefore, we need to pass new laws or amend existing ones. We need to introduce new measures for risk management. It may be pointed out that any further delay in addressing the unfinished agenda in the financial sector will severely constrain the growth of these industries and adversely affect the high growth rate to which we aspire.

5. OVERHAUL OF INFRASTRUCTURE

This takes me naturally to the third sectoral challenge, and that is the challenge to the infrastructure sector. They are two important aspects to the infrastructure challenge. The first is the financing of infrastructure. An assessment made by the Planning Commission for the Eleventh Plan indicates that investment (or gross capital formation) in infrastructure at 2006-07 prices would need to increase from 5.0 per cent of GDP in 2006-07 to 9.0 per cent of GDP in 2011-12. It means that the investment in infrastructure at 2006-07 prices would need to increase from ₹ 2,58,580 crore in 2007-08 to ₹ 5,71,315 crore in 2011-12. Simply adding the resources required annually will result in a humongous sum of ₹ 20,01,777 crore. A question crops up as to whether resources do intend to find these resources? Broadly, one-half would have to come from non-debt funds and one-half from debt funds. The estimate of debt funds is ₹ 9,96,291 crore. The banking sector alone would have to provide ₹ 4,23,691 crore. We have also estimated the amounts that could be raised from external commercial borrowing (ECB), non-bank finance companies (NBFCs), pension funds and insurance companies. Nevertheless, there is still a financial gap of ₹ 1,70,752 crore which is about 17 per cent of the debt resources required and about 8.5 per cent of the total resources required. If the price of growth is high the price of infrastructure is higher. It is only a world class financial sector that would be able to provide the resources for the infrastructure sector, and there is a considerable distance between the current architecture and the desired architecture.

Building infrastructure is a not a function of resources alone. It requires determination and skill that seems, sadly, absent in our system of governance. The United States built a world class national road network under the Eisenhower programme in the years immediately following the end of the Second World War. In recent years, Japan re-built the city of Kobe that had been literally razed to the ground following a devastating earthquake in 1995. China seems to have the capacity to build anything in record time—the tallest building, the largest stadium, the deepest port, the biggest dam and what not. It is worth noting the Indian system of governance—eminently suitable, no doubt, for a variety of purposes—is singularly unsuitable for executing large infrastructure projects within the estimated cost and time. According to data gathered by the Ministry of Statistics and Programme Implementation, as on March 2007, there are 301 projects, each costing Rs 20 crores or more, that are delayed for periods ranging from one month to 196 months and a cumulative cost overrun of Rs 49,867 crore. No purpose will be served by priding ourselves on the "checks and balances" that are in place. At the end of the day, a project that is incomplete and with no deliverables or a project that is no longer financially viable will be akin to issuing a cheque on an account with no balance. Hence the need to invent a new model for executing infrastructure projects. Public Private Partnership is the current favourite. India has had limited success with the *concessionaire* model in the case of roads and port berths. India is trying out a different model in the case of ultra mega power projects. Experimentation will continue, but what has to be ensured is to summon Japanese skills and Chinese determination.

6. BRINGING AGRICULTURE BACK ON RAILS

Agricultural growth is at the lowest ebb in the era of present economic reforms. There are a number of reasons responsible for this downturn. Firstly, agricultural workers do not have the skill sets to take up jobs in industry or services. Secondly, the rate of job creation in industry and services has not been sufficiently robust. It is therefore necessary to address both aspects of the issue. Policies must be redesigned to promote sectors that create a large number of jobs in the shortest possible time. These sectors would include small and medium enterprises (SMEs), trade, transport, construction, communication, entertainment and financial services such as micro finance and micro insurance. Simultaneously, we must launch an ambitious programme to impart new skills to agricultural workers. According to NSSO data, only 5 per cent of the population in the age group of 19 to 24 years has acquired some skills through vocational education. The corresponding figure for Korea is 96 per cent. Government has taken up upgradation of all Government Heavy Industries in the country. A new programme has been launched to provide vocational education involving 20,000 schools and with an intake of 25 lakh students by 2011-12. Another plan is being drawn up for an ambitious nationwide Skill Development Mission. However, the new initiatives can succeed only if there is close cooperation between Government and the private sector. At present, participation of the private sector is less than active and it remains to be seen how many will actually come forward to take over its management or to contribute to the proposed Skill Development Mission.

7. SOCIAL RESTRUCTURING

There is the challenge of higher education, improving the gross enrolment ratio (GER) and funding research and development. There is the challenge of fiscal policy, tax administration and ensuring tax compliance. There is the challenge of targeting subsidies to the poor and removing non-merit subsidies. There is the perennial challenge of eliminating opportunities for rent seeking and punishing the corrupt. The list is virtually endless. To effect social restructuring, there is a need to ensure an effective decentralisation of politico-economic powers in the States and at the level of local governance. The three Constitutional lists – central, state and concurrent – need to be redrawn. The devolution of political power and economic power will determine the success of second generation economic reforms. The Planning Commission and the Finance Commission have to play an active role. The sprit of the 73rd Amendment of the Indian Constitution has to be taken beyond what has been understood in common parlance.

8. CONCLUSION

The second generation reforms are acutely needed to intensify the impact of the first generation reforms. The second generation reforms are fraught with severe constraints. These include increasing the tempo of savings, removing bottlenecks of the shortage of infrastructure and its expansion, bringing monetary and fiscal stability and lifting the sagging morale of the agriculturalists in India.

REFERENCE

[1] Herrick, Bruce, and Kindleberger, P. Charles, (1993) 'Economic Development', Mc Graw Hill Book Company

[2] Maurice FitzGerald Scott (1989), A New View of Economic Growth, Oxford University Press.

Social Sector Reforms in India

Lakshmi Kumari and S.K. Lalitha

Economic reforms should be accompanied with human face and also social restructuring through educational, health and employment sector reforms. Economic reforms sans social sector reforms result in social inequity and unrest. In a democratic society, the populace expresses its disenchantment by a popular vote against such policy. This paper presents the poverty estimates in India, critically looks at the debate going on about the methods of measurement of poverty, analyses the programmes initiated to combat poverty and exclusion, and suggests finally, a broader framework for the elimination of the twin problems from the Indian society. Some broad features of poverty and exclusion in India such as rural and urban poverty, agricultural poverty, gender and poverty, and economic reforms and poverty have also been discussed in this paper. The paper begins by providing the backdrop of poverty and development policy in India. The concluding section of the paper sums up the major issues relating to poverty and exclusion in India.

1. INTRODUCTION

Poverty and Exclusion, the two key features of the Indian society, continue to dominate the socio-economic and political scenario of India even during the post-economic reforms period. Though the pro-poor policies have resulted in a considerable decline in the number of people below poverty line, the extent of such people is so large that the country could ill-afford to neglect the various dimensions of poverty. The problem of exclusion continues to haunt the Indian society since independence of the country. In terms of societal integration, the tribals have yet to integrate themselves with the Indian society. The scheduled castes, which form a considerable chunk of the Indian population despite having been accorded a special status, have not become the part of the main stream of the Indian society. Further, 1.9 percent of the total households face unavailability of two square meals a day.[1]

2. POVERTY AND DEVELOPMENT POLICY

The focus of development policy in India has shifted from the rate and pattern of growth, and on inequalities, distribution of income and wealth to the extent to which people are deprived of the minimum requirements for a long, healthy and fulfilling life. The policy makers have veered round to the idea that overall growth while necessary is not by itself adequate to take care of the needs of the poor. The pace of growth has not been uniform across regions, and a variety of sections of the population are not integrated into wider economy, and large sections are not equipped to take advantage of the opportunities arising from growth. Therefore, programmes that could attack direct on poverty have come to be recognised as the only desirable mechanism to reduce poverty. For the first time, assurance of basic minimum needs found an expected and prominent place in the Fifth Plan.[2] The basic minimum needs included not only an assurance of purchasing power sufficient to procure the collection of basic items of consumption, but also elementary education for all children up to 14 years of age; minimum public health facilities integrated with family planning and nutrition for children, protected water supply, amenities for landless labour, and slum improvement in larger towns; and rural roads and rural electrification. This gave rise to the formulation of targeted poverty alleviation programmes which could spread across the entire national spectrum. The governments at the central and the state levels have earmarked increasing allocations and devising new schemes to eliminate the targeted poverty. However, there has always remained a gap between so called motivations to remove poverty and the slogans made out in this regard.

3. EXTENT OF POVERTY

The quantification of poverty depends on how it is measured.[3] An important yardstick of quantifying poverty is the computation of food poverty. The basket of goods could be identified providing for the minimum of calorie consumption and those who do not have access to such basket of food products could be called as poor. On this basis, the Head Count Ratio (HCR) of poor could be calculated. However, this method suffers from ignoring the level and structure of prices differing between the states, between rural and urban area as well as the behaviour of prices over time during different states. This method does not take into consideration even the regional variations and social anomalies. The other method could be to price the basic minimum needs and ascertain the per capita income. The extent of poverty quantified as per this method is called as dollar/income poverty.

The most important and richest source of information concerning poverty and levels of living in India is the National Sample Survey (NSS) which has been in existence for nearly 50 years. NSS quotes information in this realm on quin-quennial basis. Large-scale sample of surveys on household incomes and consumption, education and health have also been done by National Council of Applied Economic Research though at a lower frequency. The National Nutrition Monitoring Board has been conducting for over 20 years detailed surveys of actual food intake and nutritional status of individuals on a sample basis in several states. The National Family Health Survey provides detailed information in this regard especially pertaining to children and women. The National Accounts Statistics (NAS) also captures data on various aspects of poverty during 1970s. The Planning Commission uses NAS estimates for consumption expenditure and NSS estimates of the distribution of population by level of consumption to estimate poverty incidence. The Lakdawala Committee suggested the estimation of poverty line on the basis of NSS data.[4] The Planning Commission accepted the recommendations and final estimates of poverty are based entirely on the NSS. However, it is appropriate to mention that during 1970s and 1980s the NAS and NSS showed similar, though not identical, time profiles of change in mean consumption at the national level. Both showed the declining trends in the head count ratio. However, the NSS, whose estimate of mean consumption was lower and it rise considerably slower than the NAS, showed poverty incidence to be higher and declining much more slowly than the official estimate. After 1987-88, the NSS began providing only estimates of mean consumption and per capita consumption. This showed no significant trend in either in inequality or mean per capita consumption in rural areas and therefore in the incidence of poverty. In urban areas according to NAS, poverty has declined largely because of increase in per capita real consumption. The overall poverty incidence has not changed significantly. The NAS data on the other hand show per capita consumption increase progressively at an overall rate of 2 per cent during 1990s and hence an overall decline of poverty incidence in the country. To clarify poverty divergence, it must be mentioned that except quinquennial surveys, whose primary focus is consumption and employment the sample size is large enough to provide state level estimate at an acceptable margin of sample error. The NSS in other years acquired consumption and employment data with a much smaller sample subsidiary to the main theme which varied each year. It is clear that this increases the scope for both sampling and non-sample errors. The changes in sampling reference policy with questionnaire design, and interview procedures have also made a difference. The reference periods have varied between one year to one month, one week to one day. The questionnaire designed has been alleged to be complex with 380 questions being asked from the respondents. The interview procedures have created distrust in the statistics collected as the interviewers were found to fill data on the basis of approximation of average consumption.

Table1 provides the estimates of incidence of poverty in India. The latest available large sample survey data on consumer expenditure collected for the 55th round covered the period July 1999 to June 2000. The poverty ratios indicated in Table 1 relates to period for 1972-74 to 1999-2000. The poverty at the national level is estimated as the weighted average of statewide poverty levels. The poverty ratio declined from 54.9 per cent in 1973-74 to 36 per cent in 1993-94. The poverty ratio declined by nearly 10 percentage points in the 6 years period, from 36.0 per cent in 1993-94 to 26.1 per cent in 1999-2000 while the proportion of the poor declined from 320.3 million to 260.3 million during this period. The table shows that the proportion of poor under reference in the rural areas declined from 37.3 percent in 1993-94 to 27.1 percent in 1999-2000. The percentage of urban poor declined from 49 per cent to 23.6 per cent during this period. In absolute terms, the number of poor declined to 260 million in 1999-2000, with about 75 per cent of this being in the rural areas. The table shows the poverty ratio is planned to be brought down to 19.3 percent by 2007. The rural and urban poverty ratios are expected to decline to 21.1 percent and 15.1 percent respectively by 2007. Table 2 shows the estimates of incidence of urban and rural poverty in the various states.

Table 1: Estimates of Incidence of Poverty in India

Year	Poverty ratio (%)			Number of poor (million)		
	Rural	Urban	Combined	Rural	Urban	Combined
1973-74	56.4	49.0	54.9	261.3	60.0	321.3
1977-78	53.1	45.2	51.3	264.3	64.6	328.9
1983	45.7	40.8	44.5	252.0	70.9	322.9
1987-88	39.1	38.2	38.9	231.9	75.2	307.1
1993-94	37.3	32.4	36.0	244.0	76.3	320.3
1999-00	27.1	23.6	26.1	193.2	67.1	260.3
2007*	21.1	15.1	19.3	170.5	49.6	220.1

* Poverty projection for 2007.

Source: Government of India, Ministry of Finance & Company Affairs Economic Survey 2002-2003, pp. 213.

Table 2: Headcount Poverty Ratios: Rural India and Urban India
(in Percentage)

State	55th Round Rural India	55th Round Urban India
Andhra Pradesh	11.1	26.6
Assam	40.0	7.5
Bihar	44.3	32.9
Gujarat	13.2	15.6
Haryana	8.3	10.0
Himachal Pradesh	7.9	4.6
Karnataka	17.4	25.3
Kerala	9.4	20.3
Madhya Pradesh	37.1	38.4
Orissa	48.0	42.8
Punjab	6.4	5.8
Rajasthan	13.7	19.9
Tamil Nadu	2-0.6	22.1
Uttar Pradesh	31.2	30.9
West Bengal	31.9	14.9
All-India	27.1	23.6

Source: Planning Commission, (Government of India, New Delhi) as published in Economic & Political Weekly, Bombay, January 25, 2003, pp. 323-324.

Table 2 shows that the incidence of rural poverty has been below the national average in the case of states such as Gujarat, Haryana, Himachal Pradesh, Karnataka, Maharashtra, Kerala, Punjab and Rajasthan. This incidence has been found higher in the states such as Assam, Bihar, M.P., Orissa, UP and West Bengal.

The incidence of urban poverty is found below the national average in the case of Assam, Gujarat, Haryana, Himachal Pradesh, Kerala, Punjab, Rajasthan, Tamilnadu, and Delhi. The level of urban poverty was higher as compared to the all India average in the case of A.P., Bihar, Kerala, Maharashtra, Orissa and Uttar Pradesh.

Alternative measures of poverty have been employed in India to discuss poverty trends in 1990s. Table 3 depicts the poverty trends in India between 1983 to 1999-00.

Table 3: Alternative Measures of Poverty in India: All-India Rural, Urban All-Areas: 1983-1999-2000

Segment/Measure	Measures on URP		Measures on MRP	
	1983	*1993-94*	*1993-94*	*1999-2000*
All-India rural				
Head-count ratio (per cent)	49.02	39.66	37.85	28.93
Poverty-gap index	0.1386	0.0928	0.0825	0.0579
*FGT**	0.0545	0.0315	0.0267	0.0173
Sen-index	0.1882	0.1278	0.1145	0.0806
Number of poor (000)	268.062	261.389	249.441	210.498
All-India urban				
Head-count ratio (per cent)	38.33	30.89	28.80	23.09
Poverty-gap index	0.0995	0.0749	0.0672	0.0504
*PGT**	0.0366	0.0265	0.0232	0.0160
Sen index	0.1362	0.1034	0.0932	0.0695
Number of poor (000)	65.720	72.586	67.675	63.827
All-India all areas				
Head count ratio (per cent)	46.47	37.35	35.47	27.32
Poverty-gap Index	0.1293	0.0881	0.0785	0.0558
*FGT**	0.0502	0.0302	0.0257	0.0170
Sen-index	0.1758	0.1214	0.1089	0.0775
Number of poor (000)	333.782	333.955	317.116	274.325
Memorandum item				
Total (all areas) population (000)	718.300	894.006	894.006	1004.086
Share of urban population (per cent)	23.87	26.28	26.28	27.53

Sources: Estimates HCR, PGI, FGT* and SI for 1983 are drawn from, Tendulkar *et al.* (1993), Parallel estimates for 1993-94 with uniform and mixed reference periods and with mixed reference period for 1999-2000 have been estimated from unit record data for the 50th rounds at consumer expenditure survey.

URP: Uniform Reference Period.

MRP: Mixed Reference Period.

The table shows that in both rural and urban India, and hence, also at the all India level, there is a clear reduction in the head count ratio, poverty gap index (PGI), Squared Poverty Gap (FGT) and SEN Index (SI). In rural India, the annual average decline in the head count ratio over the 10 ½ year period of July 1983 and January 1994 was 0.7 per cent points per year. For rural and urban areas taken together, the average decline in HCR was close to below 0.9 per cent per annum. While in rural India, the size of the poor population declined by little under 6.9 million over the 10 ½ years period, in urban India, the number of poor people increased by 6.9 million during the same period, despite the corresponding reduction in the head count ratio. However, it was during this period that there was a rapid growth in urban population of over 3 per cent per annum. During the period from January 1, 1994 to January 1, 2000, the head count ratio declined by close to 9 percentage point, translating to only average decline of 1.5 percentage points. This was significantly higher than the average annual decline in the head count ratio of 0.9 per cent points between 1983-1994. During the same period, a 5.7 per cent point decline in HCR corresponding to annual average decline of 0.95 percent, translates into a decline in the number of urban poor by a little over 3.8 million between January 9, 1994 and January 1, 2000. As noted earlier, the period 1988-89, witnessed an increase in the number of urban poor by close to 7 million. The PGI, FGT, as well as SEN Index show that the performance has been better in 1990s in urban India. It goes without saying that at all India level, the overall performance in all dimensions of poverty were far better between 1994 and 2000 than in the preceding 10 ½ years.

4. POVERTY ALLEVIATION PROGRAMMES

The programmes which are aimed at directly helping the poor are termed as poverty alleviation programmes. The main objective, of these programmes is to primarily help the poor and, thereby, improve their economic, financial and social conditions. These programmes directly target the poor and benefit them[5]. The programmes for the poor in India can be broadly categorised as wage employment programmes (for example, public works), credit-based self-employment programmes, (for example integrated rural development programmes–IRDP), general access programmes (for example, public distribution systems), and nutrition programmes (for example, Integrated Child Development Services - ICDS). It has been found that in terms of targeting success, self-targeting schemes like rural public works score over income based and general access schemes. The pro-poor schemes presently in currency are: Golden Village self-employment Scheme (Swarnajayanti Gram Swarojgar Yojana, Total Village Employment Scheme (Sampoorna Grameen Rozgar Yojana), Prime Minister's Village Development Scheme (Pradhan Mantri Gramodaya Yojana), Prime Minister's Village Development Rural Housing Scheme (Pradhan Mantri

Grameena Awas Yojana), Prime Minister's Village Rural Drinking Water Project (Pradhan Mantri Gramodaya Drinking Water Yojana),Food For Poorest Families Scheme (Antyodaya Anna Yojana), Food Security for Senior Citizen Scheme (Annapurna), Indira Dwelling Units Scheme (Indira Avas Yojana), Jayaprakash Employment Guarantee Scheme (Jayaprakash Rojgar Guarantee Yojana), Golden Jubilee Urban Employment Scheme (Swarna Jayanti Shahari Rojgar Yojana), Valmiki Ambedkar Slum Dwellers Scheme (Valmiki Ambedkar Avas Yojana). A study of the objectiveness of the schemes point out to the fact that the government is not cautious about effective targeting of the poor and continues to politicise poverty.

India being a federal set up, both the centre and the states have launched programmes for the eradication of poverty and social exclusion. The states have by and large supported the central programmes and added some new programmes on their own. The central government has initiated programmes such as Integrated Rural Development Programme, Training of Rural Youth for Self Employment, supply of improved tool kits to rural artisans, development of women and children in rural areas, Wage Employment Programme: Jawahar Rozgar Yojana, Employment Assurance Scheme, Million Wells Scheme, National Social Assistance Programme etc. Andhra Pradesh which is one of the most progressive states of India, has included in its gamut, programmes such as 'Podupulakshmi' (grow by savings), 'Velugu' (grow by literacy) "Neeru Meeru"(Water for all), "Janmabhoomi" (sustenance through motherland), "Phani Ahara Padakam" (food for work programme". The Government of Andhra Pradesh has developed a long term strategy to eradicate poverty by making it a part and parcel of its Vision-2020 document. It may be because of this reason that the official poverty ratios show very low levels of rural poverty in Andhra Pradesh. The Government at the centre, is still in the process of formulating such vision. The Central Government has set up a Ministry and the various state governments have followed suit. The National Institute of Rural Development has been set up to deal with rural poverty and the states have set up its counter part to tackle the problem at the state level. The key issue in this context is the effectiveness of the programmes and institutions. One thing, that needs to be ascertained is the fact as to whether 'people have accepted these programmes and institutions'. Both the programmes and institutions have to prove their relevance in the present times.

A comparison of public works programmes and the integrated rural development schemes in Maharashtra show that participation in public works programme is the highest for the poorest households and it tapers off with the rising expenditure levels. In recent years, comparisons have been made between employment guarantee schemes and the public distribution system[6]. The transfer efficiency is higher under the Employment Guarantee Scheme. The benefit cost ratio in the case of public distribution and general access schemes has turned out to be only half of that in the employment guarantee programmes. The wage employment programmes are considered superior to the other programmes as they result into additional benefits such as asset creation, increase in agriculture wages and insurance benefits. Regarding credit based self-employment programmes, group lending has been found to be more successful than lending to individuals. In general, government run programmes are less successful in targeting as compared to the Non-Government Organisation (NGO) programmes. The credit-based programmes include the integrated rural development programmes and allied programmes are the development of women and children in rural areas (DWCRA) programmes. The wage employment programmes include Training Scheme for Rural Youth Self-Employment (TSRYSM), Jawharlal Rojgar Yojana (JRY), Employment Assurance Scheme (EAS) and employment wealth schemes. The generic coverage programmes include, public distribution system, and land reforms programmes. As noted earlier, a large chunk of these programmes have not been very effective. The case of land reforms could be very well cited for this purpose. The ceiling surplus land has not been distributed among the landless poor expeditiously. In order to circumvent the ceiling laws, fictitious transfers have been affected. The detection and distribution of ceiling surplus land requires tremendous political and administrative will. The tenancy rules are outdated. Despite the legal provisions to abolish tenancy, it continues to flourish. In spite of the commitment that tribal lands must remain with the tribals, alienation of tribals, from their land continues in a large scale due to various legal loopholes and administrative lapses and lack of updation of land records which is crucial for effective implementation of land reforms. However, land records are in disarray in several states.

Anti-poor laws have over-shadowed the success of the various poverty alleviation programmes. The tribals are facing problems in gathering minor forest produce due to diversion of non-timber forest produce to the industry. Rural artisans who make products out of bamboo have shortage of raw-materials as the forest departments allot them bamboos in rationed quantities. In some cases, forest land is leased out to private industry for long periods. This too affects the poor. The cattle flayers in Uttar Pradesh have no legal control over their own produce. The real poor do not have a level playing field as the market for their finished products are dominated by either a single proprietor or a cartel of traders operating in the area.

5. POVERTY POLICY

India's poverty policy is based on millenium development goals to be achieved by 2015 as discussed in the Human Development Report 2002 of the United Nations Development Programme. This millenium development goals are as follows:

Millennium Development Goals to be achieved by 2015
Goals for development and poverty eradication set at the UN General Assembly in 2000:

1. Eradicate extreme poverty and hunger:
   - Halve the proportion of people living on less than $ 1 a day.
   - Halve the proportion of people suffering from hunger.
2. Achieve universal primary education
   - Ensure that children everywhere—boys and girls alike—complete a full course of primary education
3. Promote gender equally and empower women
   - Eliminate gender disparities in primary and secondary education, preferably by 2005, and in all levels of education by 2015
4. Reduce child mortality
   - Reduce infant and under-five mortality rates by two-thirds
5. Improve maternal health
   - Reduce maternal mortality ratios by three-quarters
6. Combat HIV/AIDS malaria and other diseases
   - Halt and begin to reverse the spread of HIVA/AIDS
   - Halt and begin to reverse the incidence of malaria and other major diseases
7. Ensure environmental sustainability
   - Integrate the principles of sustainable development into country policies and programmes and reverse the loss of environmental resources.
   - Halve the proportion of people without sustainable safe drinking water
   - Achieve by 2020, a significant improvement in the lives of at least 100 million slum dwellers
8. Develop a global partnership for development.

Source: Human Development Report 20002 of United Nations Development Programme.

Table 4 shows the Central Government expenditure on social services and rural development have gone up consistently over the years. The share of central government expenditure on social services, including rural development in total expenditure (plan and non-plan), has increased from 11 per cent in 2001-02 to 16.4 per cent in 2007-08 (BE). Central support for social programmes has continued to expand in various forms although most social sector areas fall within the purview of the states. Significant amount of programme specific funding is available to the states through the Centrally Sponsored Schemes. The pattern of funding for these schemes varies depending upon the priority laid on the sector. At the same time, the objective is to make states more and more self-reliant in supporting this scheme as is borne out by the funding pattern proposed for Sarva Shiksha Abhiyan.

Table 4: Central Government Expenditure (Plan and non-Plan)
on social services and rural development

(as percent of total expenditure)

Item	2001-02	2002-03	2003-04	2004-05	2005-06	2006-07	2007-08
1.Social Service							
a) Education, Sports, Youth affairs	2.39	2.39	2.32	2.81	3.48	4.04	4.58
b) Health & Family welfare	1.65	1.58	1.53	1.64	1.96	1.85	2.11
c) Water supply, housing etc.	1.65	1.65	1.67	1.81	1.88	1.68	1.95
d) Information & Broadcasting	0.35	0.34	0.28	0.26	0.30	0.27	0.23
e) Welfare of SC/ST and OBC	0.30	0.28	0.24	0.27	0.29	0.32	0.37
f) Labour & Employment	0.23	0.19	0.18	0.20	0.25	0.24	0.24
g) Social Welfare & Nutrition	0.72	0.57	0.50	0.52	0.73	0.80	0.82
h) North Eastern areas	0	0	0	0	1.52	1.77	1.91
i) Other Social services	0.55	0.11	0.15	0.34	0.40	0.24	0.13
Sub Total	7.86	7.10	6.86	7.85	10.81	11.21	12.35
2. Rural Development	1.72	2.89	2.59	1.91	2.75	2.69	2.46
3. i) Pradhan Mantri Gramodaya Yojana	0.70	0.63	0.51	0.56	0	0	0
ii) Pradhan Mantri Gram Sadak Yojana	0.69	0.60	0.49	0.49	0.83	0.94	1.62
4. Social Services, Rural Dev, PMGY and PMGSY	10.97	11.23	10.46	10.81	14.40	14.84	16.42
5. Total Central Government Exp	100	100	100	100	100	100	100

Source: Budget documents and Ministry of Rural Development.

India's ranking in HDI could possibly go up by increasing expenditure on poverty alleviation programmes and their effective implementation. Thus, proportion of expenditure on the total poverty alleviation programme as the percentage of Central Government total budget allocation increased marginally from 5.3 percent in 1991 5.9 percent in 2001-2002.

Table 5: Human Development Index 1981, 1991 and 2001
(arranged in rank order of 1991)

S.No.	States/ Union Territories	1981		1991		2001	
		Value	Rank	Value	Rank	Value	Rank
1	Chandigarh	0.550	1	0.674	1	n.e	
2	Delhi	0.495	3	0.624	2	n.e	
3.	Kerala	0.500	2	0.591	3	0.638	1
4.	Goa	0.445	5	0.575	4	n.e.	
5.	A & N Islands	0.394	11	0.574	5	n.e.	
6.	Pondicherry	0.386	12	0.571	6	n.e.	
7.	Mizoram	0.411	8	0.548	7	n.e.	
8.	Daman & Diu	0.438	6	0.544	8	n.e.	
9.	Manipur	0.461	4	0.536	9	n.e.	
10.	Lakshadweep	0.434	7	0.532	10	n.e.	
11.	Nagaland	0.328	20	0.486	11	n.e.	
12.	Punjab	0.411	9	0.475	12	0.537	2
13.	Himachal Pradesh	0.398	10	0.469	13	n.e.	
14.	Tamil Nadu	0.343	17	0.466	14	0.531	3

Contd…

Table 5 Contd...

15.	Maharashtra	0.363	13	0.452	15	0.523	4
16.	Haryana	0.360	15	0.443	16	0.509	5
17.	Gujarat	0.360	14	0.431	17	0.479	6
18.	Sikkim	0.342	18	0.425	18	n.e.	
19.	Karnataka	0.346	16	0.412	19	0.478	7
20.	West Bengal	0.305	22	0.404	20	0.472	8
21.	Jammu & Kashmir	0.337	19	0.402	21	n.e.	
22.	Tripura	0.287	24	0.389	22	n.e.	
23.	Andhra Pradesh	0.298	23	0.377	23	0.416	10
24.	Meghalaya	0.317	21	0.365	24	n.e.	
25.	Dadra & Nagar Haveli	0.276	25	0.361	25	n.e.	
26.	Assam	0.272	28	0.348	26	0.386	14
27.	Rajasthan	0.256	28	0.347	27	0.424	9
28.	Orissa	0.267	27	0.345	28	0.404	11
29.	Arunachal Pradesh	0.242	31	0.328	29	n.e.	
30.	Madhya Pradesh	0.242	31	0.328	29	n.e.	
31.	Uttar Pradesh	0.255	29	0.314	31	0.388	13
32.	Bihar	0.237	32	0.308	32	0.367	15
	All India	**0.302**		**0.381**		**0.472**	

Note: n.e. : No estimate was made for these States.
Source: Human Development Report 2001, Planning Commission.

6. SPECIAL FEATURES FOR POVERTY AND EXCLUSION

The agriculture growth in India has a great role to play in combating poverty and seclusion. The rate of growth of agriculture growth declined during the post-reform period. The rate of agricultural growth declined to 3.3 percent during the 1990s from 3.9 per cent during the preceding decade. The relative cereal prices as against the trend in 1970s and 1980s registered a rise in the 1990s amidst ever-increasing buffer stock. The intake of the food is positively related to cereal prices. As a result of increase in prices, the per capita intake of food has declined in 1990. There have been poor deprived of two square meals a day.

Table 6: Percentage Distribution of Households by Availability of Two Square Meals a Day at the National Level Households Getting Two Square Meals A Day

	Throughout the year	*Only in some months of the year*	*Not even in some months of the year*	*All*
Rural India				
Less than Rs. 120 MPCE	84.2	11.8	3.4	100
All Classes	98.5	4.2	0.9	100
Urban India				
Less than Rs.160 MPCE	91.9	4.5	3.3	100
All Classes	98.1	1.1	0.5	100

Source: NSS 50th Round (1993-94) Report No.415.

Table 6 shows that 1.9 percent of households did not have availability of two square meals a day. The investment growth in agriculture has also declined during this period. This has affected the wellbeing of agriculturist and also the agricultural workers who depend to a large extent on agricultural employment. The total credit to agriculture has declined. Innovations have hardly influenced the organisation and technology in agriculture.[7] The non-farm employment has also declined. The impact of the rulings of the World Trade Organisation has been adverse and made the agriculture scenario very bleak. The real wages of agricultural labour have not increased in the post-reform period because of increase in relative food prices. Effective measures have not been taken for raising agriculture labour productivity and reducing employment intensity of agriculture.

The literature is replete with evidence suggesting a close link between poverty, and education and income opportunity. The income poverty has been associated with lack of educational opportunities in India. The income poverty pulls children out of the school system thus denying the opportunity of participating in school education even at the basic level. In the case of India, the rates of education attainment at each grade or level of education are consistently at the bottom among the poorest 40 percent of the population and at the top among the richest 20 percent of the population.[8] It is also revealed that the deficit in reaching the goal of universal attainment of basic education is the highest in the case of the poor and the lowest in the case of rich. To add, it is worth mentioning that enrolment rates are low, dropout rates are high and correspondingly completion rates at the lowest among the poor income groups compared to middle and high-income groups. One of the of the strongest reasons of poverty among the school children is the presence of serious malnutritional deficiencies which is found to permanently impair mental capability of children in very early years.[9] To add, it is also seen that enrolment rates are low, dropout rates are high and correspondingly completion rates are the lowest among the poor income groups compared to middle and high income groups.

The growth helps in the reduction of poverty because it creates jobs which pull-up the poor into gainful employment by providing more economic opportunity. It provides the revenues to spend on social services for the poor and creates the incentives that enable the poor to access these facilities.[10] India left behind the era of the Hindu Rate of Growth of 3.5 percent existing between 1960s and 1980s and entered the period of high rate of growth of 6.5% in 1990s. The target for the rate of growth has been fixed at 8% during Eleventh Five-Year Plan (2002-2007). However, the rate of growth during the recent years has declined to 5.5 percent. India's self-reliance policy, heavy dependence on public sector, choice of capital intensive techniques and overwhelming expansion of direct/indirect controls kept the growth under limits earlier and continue to impede securing the high growth, currently.

The urban poverty eludes an effective remedy. The migration from the rural areas to urban areas is adding to the increase of slums, creating urban pollution, transport congestion and lack of availability of social facilities. The income poverty in urban areas denies the access to urban poor to adequate food, sanitation, education and health care and housing.

The gender discrimination continues to haunt the poverty scenario. The rate of literacy is very low among females. The female employment rates are very low. Their representation in political bodies is minimal. The bill to reserve 30 percent of the seats for women in Parliament and the state assemblies is hanging fire from 1996.

The conditions of the scheduled castes and scheduled tribes continue to remain critical. Together, they constitute about 30 percent of the Indian population. Though they have been provided reservations to this extent in the government jobs and political bodies, their socio-economic condition continues to remain lamentable. Between scheduled castes and scheduled tribes, the scheduled tribes have yet to integrate themselves with the main stream and have not attracted the attention of the policy makers. A large number of widows, the street children and old people face an abject poverty and political indifference.

7. COMBATING POVERTY AND EXCLUSION: A NEW FRAMEWORK

Poverty anywhere is danger to prosperity everywhere. Although the approaches followed to combat poverty and exclusion have resulted in the decline in the proportion of poor, there is a need to reformulate entirely the policy framework in this regard. In our view, the involvement of people in the formulation of public policy for the elimination of poverty and exclusion is the most vital pre-requisite. The amendment of Article 73rd and 74th of the Indian Constitution has empowered the local administration including Panchayats, Municipalities and Municipal Corporations to deal with 29 subjects directly. The state governments will do well to transfer the essential resources to the local level institutions to formulate their own programmes to eliminate poverty and exclusion. This could bring down the cost of administering such programmes on the one hand, and improve tremendously the targeting on the other. This will also prevent committing the E-mistakes, which have resulted into excessive coverage of people who have benefited at the cost of the poor. It is appropriate to note here that in a country such as Belgium the constitutional provisions governing the federal set up have been changed such that the central and the state governments cannot make an enactment or sign a foreign treaty without the approval of the local level governments. The public distribution system is a case in point. In most of the Indian states more than 50% of the ration cards are bogus and they have been issued to people who are not poor. The involvement of people would improve the quality and supervision of the poverty programmes. Time and cost overruns would come down drastically and the leakages could be checked effectively.

The elimination of poverty and exclusion needs a comprehensive backup of social services comprising education, drinking water supply, sanitation and housing. Everything should be done to ensure the access to primary education facilities to the children in the age group of 4–14 years. Such education should be provided free of cost in the vicinity of the place where the child resides. The lack of primary education is the biggest curse facing India. The resources should not inhibit the access to primary education for all the eligible children. The higher education for the socially weak and poor should be financed by banks. The supply of potable water is a prime requisite for the survival of the poor and the socially excluded. The basic health facilities including first-aid should be provided by the primary health centres and the outpatients departments of the hospitals run by the government and the private agencies. The mid-day meal scheme should be implemented on the national scale. All the States must ensure the supply of the minimum calorific requirements to the people. The Indian agriculture should be given a shot in the arm by increasing investments, providing extension facilities, R&D, making available inputs at competitive costs and ensuring increased incomes to the farmers through better realisation of prices for their produce. The wages for agriculture labour should increase and the non-farm employment opportunities for the farm labour should need to be stepped up on a much higher scale.

The new dispensation from WTO should be managed such that the Indian agriculture becomes competitive. This would require the availability of cheaper credit to the farmers. The micro credit could come in very handy in this regard. The self-help groups could be promoted for obtaining credit from financial institutions. The micro credit could bring down not only the costs of the credit but also minimise the non-performing assets in the case of the lending institutions. There is a need to speed up the agricultural reforms which would include reenergising programmes such as land reforms, land consolidation, increasing the area under crop irrigation, setting up agri-business facilities and promoting the second green revolution. The first green revolution visited India in the middle of 1970s. Its gains have been consummated during the last three decades. A second green revolution must usher in to take care of the needs of the next 20 years.

The problem of social exclusion needs to be analysed afresh and a strategy to combat social exclusion needs to be chalked out anew. As mentioned elsewhere, the tribals, widows, senior citizens (people above 60 years), under-privileged women, children and poorest of the poor among the scheduled castes and backward casts face the problem of exclusion. They are economically too week to secure the basic minimum needs for their survival. It is imperative to design a special strategy to provide them access to education, entrepreneurship and employment. Table.... Shows that the total expenditure incurred on social justice and empowerment to deal with the problem of social exclusion was more or less at 0.6% of the total expenditure incurred by the Government during the period 1991-2001. The per capita expenditure for scheduled castes persons declined from ₹ 55 in 1991 to ₹ 51 in 2000-01 and for the scheduled tribe persons from ₹ 29 to ₹ 24 during the same period. The public distribution system (PDS) is not able to ensure the supply of the minimum foodgrains to these people. Though the government is faced with the problem of storing the foodgrains, the off take of foodgrains under the PDS has been low on account of narrowing differentials between PDS and open market prices. Another problem associated with this scheme is that the poor particularly the poorest generally do not accumulate enough cash to buy 25 Kgs of foodgrain at a time. There is a need to put in place a system that could either allow the purchase of PDS grains in installments or allow to pay in installments. There have been complaints that a large chunk of foodgrains lifted from the PDS is of substandard variety.

All this may require a substantial mobilisastion of resources. Does India have enough resources to combat poverty and exclusion? As a matter fact what India lacks is not the shortage of resources but socio-economic and political will to measure upto the challenge. The reduction in subsidies itself could open the floodgates for funding the poverty alleviation programmes under reference. The subsidies doled out under the various heads by the Central Government constitute 15 per cent of the GDP amounting to ₹ 3,00,000 crore per annum (approximately US $ 60 billion per annum). A reduction of 50 percent of such subsidies could provide approximately ₹ 1,50,000 crore per annum (approximately US $ 30 billion per annum) to the government for pro-poor programmes. This is approximately seven times more than the money provided for poverty alleviation programmes in the Central Government budget for 2001-02.

The New Economic Policy should reenergise the growth momentum. The target of 8 percent growth must be achieved at any cost. The mobilisation of resources for this purpose is to be comprehensively planned. The Government could get credit rated and tap funds from the external capital markets. The internal costs of funds to the government varies between 7 and 9 percent per annum. The recent raising of funds has been done at 2.5 percent to 2.7 percent per annum from the capital markets abroad which have had London Interbank offered rate (LIBOR) and Singapore Interbank offered rate (SIBOR) of approximately 1.75 percent . Incentives could be contemplated to attract the Foreign Direct Investment to the poverty and social justice programmes. The Government needs to innovate such schemes which could lure the global agencies to such programmes. The Global institutions have hammered out such programmes for the third world and India should take advantage of this facility. The Monetary Policy of the Government and the financial sector reforms initiated as a part of the new economic policy must ensure a free flow of credit at reasonable rates for the poverty alleviation programmes and entrepreneurship development. The output elasticity of employment during post-reform period is found very low as compared to the output elasticity of employment during pre-reform period on account of negative differential output elasticity of employment showing that the economic growth during post-reform period is not labour intensive.[11] This trend has to be reversed.

The administration of poverty and exclusion scheme needs to be toned up. The multiplicity of these schemes both at the central and the state levels have led to duplication, and high cost of administration. It is suggested that self-targeting schemes should be given priority. The populist schemes should be discontinued and a continuous review should be undertaken to ensure their meaningful implementation. It is suggested that most of the schemes should be implemented by the local administration and the role of the central government and the state governments should be restricted to policy formulation and review.

8. CONCLUSION

Relating concepts of poverty propounded by Amartya Sen, it could be pointed out without any hesitation that poverty and exclusion constitute the most dangerous threat to the politico-socio and economic fabric of India.[12] From the middle of 1970s, the government started realising the repercussions of these twin problems and launched a number of programmes for their alleviation. Although the proportion of the poor and socially weak has declined a great deal, the problem of rural and urban poverty continue to stare at the face of India. The statistics of poverty are not, as A.K. Sen once remarked, an issue for 'unleashing one's personal morals' yet they seem to become a stone on which many people are happy to grind their axes.[13] There has been a bitter debate on the concepts and measurement of poverty. There is a broad consensus that the minimum should include nutritionally satisfactory diet, a reasonable standard of clothing, housing and other essentials and access to a minimum level of education, health care, clean water supply and sanitary environment. Norms for specific elements with regard to each one of these elements have been specified. The income necessary for people to afford the elements defines the poverty line ensuring the minimum standard for amenities are deemed to be the responsibility of a state. Minimum living standards and poverty are however deceptively simple notions. Complex and contentious issues are involved in deciding the basis on which the minimum bundle is to be determined and valued. Conceptual problems are confounded by problems of empirical measurement. The most important and richest source for assessment of poverty is the national sample survey which is in existence for the last 50 years. The National Council for Applied Economic Research, National Nutrition Monitoring Board, National Family Health Survey and International Crop Research Institute and National Accounts Statistics conduct large scale sample surveys to measure poverty and seclusion. The methodology of poverty estimates have long been the subject of debate. A critical scrutiny of the assumptions and procedures underlying official estimates of poverty points out to the deficiencies in the assessment of poverty. Changes in sampling, reference periods, questionnaire design and interview procedures have made a great difference. Further, the lack of decisive preference between the head count ratio and income estimation method of poverty has only made the problem of measurement more complex. The different sources using different methods, give quite different estimates. The Government is alleged to have shown a decline in the number of poor by adopting methodologies suggested to under-estimate the poor. However, the application of the various methods unhesitatingly reveals that there has been reduction in the proportion of the poor and socially weak people in India. But this has to be seen against the fact that: (i) whereas the rural poverty has reduced substantially, the success in the case of urban poverty has not been encouraging; (ii) the poverty alleviation programmes suffer from political overtones as a large chunk of programmes indulge in political populism ; and (iii) the framework adopted by the Government to combat poverty and exclusion is not strong enough to remove the root cause of their existence.

There is a need to develop a new framework to combat the poverty and exclusion. Poverty alleviation programmes must secure the support of the people. The local administration should be empowered to implement the poverty alleviation programmes and the central and the state Governments should be charged with the responsibility of formulating and monitoring such programmes in consonance with the local administration. The weaker sections of the society should become the focal point of such programmes through self-targeting schemes. The spending on these programmes should be enhanced considerably. The present level of subsidies should be reduced to 50 percent to divert a huge chunk of money for the implementation of poverty alleviation programmes. The agriculture and allied sectors should receive special attention and the non-farm employment need to be considerably stepped up. The New Economic Policy should ensure cheaper and increased flow of credit to poverty alleviation programmes by making micro-credit institutions measuring up to the new challenge and designing built-in-incentives for the financial institutions to disburse the requisite credit at reasonable rates of interest.

REFERENCES

[1] Kala, Shalini, and Mehta, Aasha Kapur, Hunger and Stravation, Alternative Economic Survey 2001-2002 (Economic Reforms: Development Denied), Rainbow Publishers, Noida, 2002, pp 156-158.

[2] Vaidynathan. A, Poverty and Development Policy, *Economic & Political Weekly*, May 26, 2001, Bombay, p. 1808.

[3] Kozel, Valerie, *Poverty Measurement,* Monitoring and Evaluation in India: An Overview- A Summary of Papers and Proceedings of the Seminar on Poverty jointly organised by the World Bank and Planning Commission at New Delhi, Economic & Political Weekly, January 25-31, 2003, Bombay, pp. 296-301. Also see Deaton, Angus and Jean Dreze (2002) 'Poverty and Inequality in India: a Reexamination', Princeton, Research Programme in Development Studies, and Delhi School of Economics, processed (July). Available at http://www. wwws.princeton.edu/-rpds.

[4] Planning Commission (Government of India, New Delhi), Report of the Expert Group on Estimates of Poverty and Number of Poor, New Delhi, 1993.

[5] Ministry of Finance, Government of India, Economic Survey : 2002-2003, New Delhi, February, 2003, pp. 216-217.

[6] Dev, S. Mahendra, Economic Reforms, Poverty, Income Distribution and Employment, *Economic & Political Weekly*, Bombay, March 4, 2000, p. 832. Also see: Dev S. Mahendra, Alleviating Poverty- Maharashtra Employment Guarantee Scheme, *Economic and Political Weekly*, Bombay, October 14-21, 1995 p. 2663.

[7] Radhakrishna, R, Agricultural Growth, Employment and Poverty : A Policy Perspective, *Economic & Political Weekly*, Bombay, January 19, 2002, p. 249.

[8] Filmer, Dean and Lant, Pritchett, Educational Environment and Attainment in India: Household Wealth, Gender, Village and State Effects, *Journal of Educational Planning and Administration*, Vol. 13 : No. 2, 1999, New Delhi.

[9] Usha Devi, MD, Poverty Database in Education : Strategies for Monitoring Poverty Reduction, *Economic & Political Weekly*, Bombay, July 21, 2001, p. 2779.

[10] Bhagwati, Jagdish, Gorwth, Poverty and Reforms, Convocation Address to the Punjab University, Chandigarh, December, 2000 (Mimeo). Also see : (i) World Bank, World Development Report, 1990, Washington, (ii) Asian Development Bank, *Asian Development Review*, Volume 18: Number 2, 2000, Manila.

[11] Upender, M, Differentiating Output Elasticity of Employment during Post Economic Reform Period in the Indian Economy: An Empirical Note, Paper presented at the Seminar on Economic Reforms and Indian Economy: A Development Experience, 15-16, March, 2003, Department of Economic, Osmania University, Hyderabad, p. 9 (Mimeo)

[12] Sen, Amartya, Poverty and Famines: An Essay on entitlement and deprivation, English Language Book Society/Oxford University Press, Oxford, 1986, p. 9.

[13] *Ibid.*

Development Approach Similarity between China and India and their Choices of National Strategies

Zhang Zhanbin

As two large countries in the world, China and India share similarities in their development approaches. Through nearly 30 years' and 20 years' of rapid development, these are two giants among the four BRIC countries. By mid 21st century, Europe, China, US and India shall become world's four largest economies. The oriental booming market as the economic engine of the world shall change the global economic order greatly. China challenged by the vigorously developing India shall study and borrow some experiences from India. However, before they become real strong powers in the world, China and India shall go through a long way of mutual studying and borrowing of excellences from each other to solve the four major strategic issues: urban-rural planning, social justice, conservation culture, and government reform.

Keywords: Comparison between China and India; Development approach; National Strategy.

1. SIMILARITY BETWEEN THE TWO GIANTS: CHINA AND INDIA

With more than five thousand years' history and culture, China and India are two giants that had been invaded by foreign countries in ancient times and suffered from multi-state chaos, wars, civil strifes, natural disasters, and generations of kings. For more than two thousand years, the extra-stable feudal system had reigned over the ancient agricultural societies of China and India. These two countries are in a state of "involution", an expression from economic historians.[1] Not only the social system and people's life style are self-sustained, self-conserved, and self-duplicated, but also the development of economy and society remained static for along time. By statistics and research of economists such as Angus Maddison, findings *The World Economy: A Millennial Perspective* 2001 and Deepak LaI's *The Hindu Equilibrium*, China and India were both found to be trapped by the "high-level development pit", according to Mark Eivin, a western Sinologist. The consequent issues such as "Needham's Puzzle" and "Max Weber's Perplexity" often draw discussions and disputes in the academia. The discussions or debates for China mainly focus on the issues such as Feudal Despotism, Confucian Thought, and emphasising agriculture but restraining commerce etc. For India, the discussions or debates focus on Caste System and Village Economy. What strength had made these two major countries maintain so vigorous a life force? What weaknesses had made them remain trapped by the "high-level development pit"? Currently there is no agreed view about these problems. The academia feels perplexed, but they think it is exciting.

We shall note that in so long a history, China and India have maintained their integrity. With consistent histories and cultures, these two countries had made outstanding contributions to the development of human civilisation, especially agricultural civilisation. In their territories the forces for national consolidation and social harmony have always been reinforced. In modern times China had for nearly one hundred years been a semi-colonial and semi-feudal society; India also had been colonised by England for nearly one hundred years. They both obtained national liberation and state independence by enormous efforts in the middle of 20th century.

The domestic and international conditions that constrain the development of independent China and India moved the decision-makers to choose the development strategy with a priority on the development of heavy industry. In the opinion of Chairman Mao of China the true independence of a country can only be obtained by industrialisation. Premier Nehru of India had always pointed out that industrialisation means development of heavy industry. Their thoughts and strategic choices, determined by the domestic and international political and economic environments, directly showed the economic pursuit and political ambition of leaders of China and India. Meanwhile as developing giants with similar histories, independent China and India have many similarities in the development and strategic choice of industrialisation.

Particularly these similarities are seen: Firstly, China and India both hold industrialisation as a prerequisite for becoming a developed country. During 1950s to 1970s they had essentially given up their comparative advantages and followed the overtaking strategy of Soviet Union (although at different degrees) to set high priority to development of heavy industry, aiming at the status increase of state and nation by industrialisation. Secondly, both China and India neglected the development of agriculture and light industry because of their too high ambition to develop of heavy industry and economy very fast. This had resulted in an unbalanced economic structure featuring emphasising on heavy industry and neglecting agriculture and light industry. Thirdly, at different degrees both countries intensified the role of public enterprises in national industries, increasing the ratio of public sector in domestic economy. China carried out the process of high-level nationalisation at a high speed. India gave nationalisation a leading role in domestic economy. However, the difference between the two countries' social and economic systems resulted in the ratio of China's public economy higher than that of India. Fourthly, their governments conducted the process of industrialisation through five-year plans. China gave up the thought of building new-democratic economy and forged command economic system. India had the market controlled by its government in a tyope of socialism, although its economy was called market-oriented.

By long-term observation and research findings of economists, the prior development of heavy industry became unsuitable to the environment of these two countries resulting in their slow economic growth, unbalanced industrial structure, and insufficient micro-excitation. So these two countries have low-level technology and efficiency, and the actual speed of capital accumulation and technical progress were lower than their potential.[2] By logical deduction and based on development practices we know that the economic reform and development of China and India shall gradually build or amend the market economic system by replacing the "overtaking" strategy with the comparative advantage development strategy in order to make the industries and technological development suitable for their backgrounds and to reduce the cost of reform. Reform began in China from the end of 1970s, and in India from the beginning of 1990s. China's development is labour-intensive mode focusing on manufacturing; India's development is technical-intensive mode focusing on information service industry. In economic growth China mainly relies upon its manufacturing, and India on its service industry. In some experts' opinion China became "world factory" with the assistance from overseas Chinese; India will become "world lab" with the assistance from overseas Indians.[3] In general China and India became leading performers in the global economy, and China's economic development has a level higher than that of India. India's economy lags behind China by 10 years or more.

With their population accounting for 40% of the world, China and India attracted the attention of all countries around the globe during the past nearly 30 years' and the very rapid development and booming growth during the past 20 years. In 2004 Remo, former editor of the American magazine *Time*, senior consultant on political and economic issues for Goldman Sachs, for the first time delivered the conception of "Beijing Consensus", pointing out that China and India, two countries defying the "Washington Consensus", have obtained remarkable economic growth,[4] The international society calls China "Dragon", and India "Elephant",[5] Putting them into the "four BRIC countries" with highest economic potential and being the dynamos of global economy. Some experts stated, "It is impossible to obstruct China from being a world power. This topic will always be hot as before."[6] These remarks are encouragement and affirmation of their confidence in the development of China and India. We are happy to hear western countries' remarks on the progress of China and

India, and we hope western countries understand China and India a great deal more. However, we shall never be proud and lose our sobriety and rationality.

Some critical sectors of India are overtaking or have overtaken China, although the integral strength of economy and society of India trailed China. At present we have no clear opinion whether the success of India in some critical sectors can help it to catch up or overtake China in integral strength. But one thing is true, that India is at its rising period of development, and India has the ability to play its great role as China in the world. It is promising that India becomes the economy with fastest economic growth. Other countries of the world are looking at India, this "tortoise"[7] at the beginning of 1990s and today's "tiger" transformed from "staid elephant".[8] Indian Government has set the prospect of 2020 to be world No.4 or No.5 economic giant; correspondingly plans and measures have been made. China also showed its ambition by delivering the strategic target and approaches to build a well-off society in the first 20 years of 21st century. It shall be exciting to see the race between China and India at the "Olympics" stage of international economy.

2. WHAT CAN CHINA LEARN FROM INDIA? AND WHAT DOES CHINA NEED TO LEARN?

At present China's strengths integrated by its economic aggregate, GDP per capita, foreign exchange reserve, foreign trade aggregate, and imported foreign capital is far higher than that of India. *IMD World Competitiveness Yearbook*, China placed higher than India in economic performance, governmental efficiency, infrastructure, and the general growth of macro-economics. Economist Amartya Sen, Nobel Laureate in economy, in his book *India: Economic Development and Social Opportunity* stressed the advice to learn experiences from China.[9] As we have understood, the special contexts and environments of the two countries call for their mutual learning and borrowing excellences from each other. As a country carrying out reform earlier than India, China has excellences and experiences valuable for India to learn and borrow. However, China shall never underestimate the development speed of India, although India's integral economic strength is weaker. China must study and borrow some experiences from India.[10]

Firstly, India is a pioneer to China in the adjustment of agriculture's underestimated importance in the economic structure during the process of industrialisation. India has basically formed its strategy for long-term sustainable development. In a period following 1950s China and India had been punished for their negligence of agricultural development. In the later period of Nehru Era, the intensified disaster of grain shortage even caused social turbulence and economic crisis. Forced by enormous frustrations, leaders of Indian Government changed their opinion about neglecting agricultural development. After the middle of 1960s, Indian Government called for "green revolution", "white revolution", and "blue revolution"; gradually agricultural production has sufficient development and progress. Today India is a grain net exporter transformed from a net importer. During 2001 to 2002 the grain output reached a record of 202-million tons in India. During 2002 to 2003 India suffered a drought unseen in 30 years, grain output reduced to 28-million tons. However, India kept the price of grains stable. In the national store of India, a grain reserve of 63-million tons is available for coping with natural disasters. We also shall note that, by foreign capital India supports the development of agriculture, especially the construction of a great number of water conservancy and irrigation projects and fertiliser factories, and the procurement of agricultural machinery. India has excellences in agricultural modernisation.

Secondly India has basically kept the industrial development speed stable in its independent economic development. No sharp fluctuation was seen. The annual growth ratio of India's industry is relatively steady, although India's regime has been adjusted and changing in these tens years, and had suffered instability in between. In its First Five-year planning period the annual growth ratio was 5.6%; Second Five-year 7.1%; Third Five-year 10.2%; Fourth Five-year 4.1%; Fifth Five-year 7.7%; Sixth Five-year 7.7%; Seventh Five-year 8.1%; Eighth Five-year 8%; and Ninth Five-year 5.8%. These data showed that the earlier "mixed economy" market system was beneficial for the country's economic growth. China shall pay attention to it. For in China, the economic growth has experienced sharp fluctuations. The highest growth ratio reached 34.3% (1969), lowest going to −15.8% (1967). Chinese Government's anxious instructions violating objective law shall bear the major part of the responsibility in the quick but volatile industrial growth, although we cannot deny the impact and damages from "Great Leap Forward" and "Cultural Revolution". Even today the GDP-oriented instructions from local governments are still an issue to be severely dealt with.

Thirdly, India has an excellent soft investment environment in general with high foreign-capital utilisation and economic independence better than that of China. India's infrastructure, especially public utilities including water, electric power, gas, communication, and transport cannot meet the requirements of the rapid growing economy. It is hard for Indian Government to break this bottleneck of economic development in a short period. China is better than India in infrastructure. But India is attractive in property rights protection and media supervision. The "outsourcing" and "offshore" service centers of western countries such as America have migrated to India for years. India is prosperous in outsourcing industry. As predicted by experts, in the coming future the foreign direct investment (FDI) in India shall be greatly increased. India is an emerging "world office", although it only absorbs 4 to 5-billion dollars of foreign capital annually, far lower than the 50 to 60-billion dollars through FDI in China. As stated by American scholars, India's high economic growth by FDI far lower than that of China means that India has a foreign capital utilisation ratio far higher than that of China. In some other experts' opinion, the economic growth of India relies upon Indian people's intellectual resource and financial resource, not like the traditional manufacturing industry dependent on the import of techniques, devices, and products from foreign countries. With special economic zones, India regulates import of foreign capital more strictly than China. Therefore, India's economic growth has much more FDI dependence than that of China. With lower risks of foreign capital dependence, India's economy may be more sustainable than that of China.

Fourthly, Indian enterprises can carry out financing in domestic capital market quicker than Chinese enterprises, for India has more efficient financial system and commerce. China has deposits of financial assets and household saving ratio higher than those of India.[11] However, in India the industry of finance and banking has been in existence for a long time. Moreover, India has a well-established financial system; the efficiency and transparency of its capital market operations are better than that of China. Many industries of India have been open to private investors, including foreign investors. In the opinion of some American scholars the long-term development of India by its local enterprisers' using domestic high-efficient banks and capital market may drive India's economy to overtake China. Certainly this is only a prediction that needs time to prove it. However, this prediction is a warning to the development of China's capital markets. Chinese Government shall pay attention to this prediction and improve the efficiency of China's capital market. According to *IMD World Competitiveness Yearbook*, while being better than India in economic performance, government efficiency, and infrastructure, China is far behind India in business efficiency. Therefore, increasing business efficiency is a prerequisite to quicken China's economic development and increasing it international competitiveness.

Fifthly India has unique competence in high-tech sectors including information technology, especially software industry. The IT-focused network economy is booming in India. As a well-knows software power in the world, India has great numbers of software engineers and bases, and 1,900 institutes for IT education. Every year India trains 70-thousand English-speaking professionals. Armed with the world's largest software talent reserve, India has more than 200-thousand people working in the Silicon Valley of America. Moreover, India owns the world No.1 number of software companies that have passed various quality standard certifications. Estimated by Mckinsey& Company, in 2008 India's gross value of software output shall reach 85.0-billion dollars, of which 50.0-billion dollars are of export; 2.20-million new jobs shall be created. Bill Gates had even said that in the future the world's largest software development base and super-power must be India, not Europe and Japan.[12] It is hard to calculate correctly the term of comparative advantages maintained in manufacturing, although at present the manufacturing industry is a competent one in China. In the globalisation pioneered by the information-based service industry, the practices of India overthrew the traditional view that the service industry cannot grow without industrial development. In information industry and software technology India is 5 years ahead of China. If India overtakes China in the future, we shall know the significance of local enterprises to the long-term development of economy, and know also limitations of China's economic development relying upon foreign capital.

Sixthly, India is better than China in standard and democratic management of business. India has successfully built some private companies able to compete with the most powerful companies of Europe and America on the international market. For example local Indian enterprises Infosys, Wipro, Ranbaxy and Dr Reddy's for pharmacy and biological technology, and Sundaram of automobile industry are successful in independent innovations, and most of them are industries based on high-tech and information technology. They demonstrated the standardised management and business democracy in India. From certain view China's economy is booming, and Lenovo and Haier are international market players. However, from a stricter view China has no great private enterprises. Especially big enterprises full of independent innovations in the forefront and high-tech sectors are rarely seen. At present China has no world-class private enterprises able to compete with multinational companies on the international market. We can see the facts from the changes in the "going out" strategy.

3. COMMON DIFFICULTIES CHALLENGING CHINA AND INDIA AND THEIR STRATEGIC COUNTERMEASURES

Currently China and India have evident comparative advantages, such as highly developed domestic economic system, industrial facilities, enormous consumption market, low labour cost, human resource potential, and reform etc. By optimistic estimation China and India can keep fast development for another 30 to 50 years or more. These two countries have enormous development potential. In the middle of this century, Europe Union, China, America, and India shall become the world's top four economies. The oriental market shall become the economic engine of the world. The world's economic order shall be changed greatly, for the growth of China and India shall result in the growing up of Asia and the revival of oriental civilisation. Jeffrey Sachs, Professor of Economics in Colombia University, Expert on world development issues, said, "The return of China and India to the global economic growth in the 21st century may re-built the global politics and society. We can see no more the times when the western countries controlled the world for consistently over 50 years. We shall look at their development with respect and hope."[13] From the sub prime lending crisis of America and the depressed economy of Europe, we shall think the opinion of Sachs has not come out of modesty or politeness.

Challenged by the globalisation of economy, China and India shall set right their national strategies, exert the comparative advantages, and eliminate the comparative disadvantages before they can become real powers in the world. At present the difficulties challenging China and India are: the adjustment of industrial structure, the change of development style, and the improvement of infrastructure. The two countries shall attach high importance to four common issues at present and in the coming future. The settlement of these issues promises the growing up of China and India.

Firstly, urban and rural areas shall be under united economic planning. In China and India most people are of agricultural population. Complex historical reasons are behind the urban-rural dual economic structure. The overtaking-type development strategy determined that the only choice for "original accumulating" required industrialisation, which led to the neglect of the traditional agricultural residuals by unequal exchange between industrial and agricultural products. Consequently, the agricultural and industrial relationship and the urban-rural relationship became distorted in both the countries. The dual economic structure is reinforced, and the problems of "agriculture, countryside, and farmer" are prominent and deteriorating. China has sober understanding of the importance of amending market defects and put the urban and rural areas into coordinated planning. During the last five years the key documents of the Central Governments dealt with the important task of "constructing new rural areas" to countermeasure the problems of "agriculture, countryside, and farmer". In 2006 China annulled agricultural taxation, and the government's financial input and public services became more inclined towards rural areas. The adjusted development strategy and policy of China has already resulted in a healthy context featuring "industry feeding back agriculture, and urban areas supporting rural areas". China is building a mechanism to promote the agricultural development by industry, and to push forward rural areas by urban areas. This mechanism is to be effective for a long period of time. On this issue India's urban and rural united planning has defects for they have too enormous an agricultural population, although it has begun correct issue early. China and India shall learn from each other and amend their defects, for many problems are waiting for solutions.

Secondly, social justice shall be a target pursued in the society. Before reforming and opening to the world, China's Gini Coefficient is smaller than 0.2. While being developed rapidly, the big gap between the rich and the poor has caused the Gini Coefficient reach 0.45, which is a number exceeding the threshold acknowledged by the world, a case similar to Russia. China joined the countries having too big a gap between the rich and the poor. In China the gaps between urban and rural areas, different regions, different sectors, and different citizens are enlarging consistently. Unfair distribution became an evident contradiction in China. It is the same case in India. In some respects India's case is worse. In India's large and middle cities houses are old and shabby; rookeries, rubbish, and beggars are seen everywhere. Buses are overcrowded. Moreover, the existence and influence of caste system has accumulated too many social problems. These years China gave special attention to social justice, and delivered the strategy to build harmonious society, quicken the establishment and amending of social security system, and put the promotion of social harmony and justice on a higher plateau. The two governments shall use macro-control in economic development and pay more attention to the life of people in poverty; their public service shall be inclined to people in poverty. Moreover, the two governments shall coordinate various economic stakeholders and avoid the "Pit of Latin America".

Thirdly, eco-friendly civilisation shall be built in the environment and resource sectors. In the new century, China and India with obviously quickened progress of industrialisation entered a new rising period of economic development. Environmental issues had come up in stages over the last one hundred years and more, not because of the industrialisation process of developed countries in China and India are now crowded. The contradiction between the economic development and the resources and environment management more and more intensive. The case is worse in China, though India also faces the troubles from relatively deficient resources, fragile eco-environment, and deficient capacity of environment. To save resources and energy and solve environmental issues is the responsibility of these two developing giants, and the blessing for 1.3-billion Chinese people and 1.2-billion Indian people. These years Chinese Government put forward "ecological civilisation" as a new requirement of the comprehensive construction of a well-off society. This new development thought of Chinese Government plays an important role in promoting the comprehensive development of economy and society by conducting resource and environment protection with scientific development strategy, saving energy, reducing consumption, constraining pollution and emissions. Chinese Government is now making efforts to eliminate the environmental troubles that harm people's health and the sustainable economic development. The two governments shall overcome this issue, for it becomes more and more important due to economic growth.

Fourthly, The governmental administration system shall be reformed in political sector. Both China and India are at the critical stage of economic development and economic transition. The government is challenged by heavy task for the reform of administration system. The new leaders of China's Central Government attach high importance to the reform of administration system. In their opinion the reform of the governmental administration system is an important part of the reform of political system, and it is necessary for the superstructure to be suitable for economic foundation and meet objective laws. These years on the agenda of Chinese Government. Reforming the public administration system is critical for the coordination of various reforms and the planning of economic stakeholders. While adjusting economic system and supervising the market, Chinese Government attaches higher importance to reinforce its social administration and public service function. It aims to build a Chinese-style socialist administrational system of the people and for the people by 2020 when China becomes a well-off society. The newly organised Central Government of China carried out reform of "big department system", aiming at the consistent reform of the governmental administration system to meet the requirements of economic and social development. In contrast Indian Government shall eliminate corruptions of officers and improve governmental efficiency.

REFERENCES

[1] [India] Deepak Lal. The Hindu Equilibrium: India c. 1500 B.C.-A.D. 2000 [M]. Beijing: Peking University Press, 2008. Wei Sen's preface for Chinese edition. "Closed Model" called by some experts. Li Dewei etc. Choice of Policy for China Resurrection [M]. Beijing: China Economy Publishing House, 2008. pp. 8-36.

[2] Huang Yasheng, Tarun Khanna. Will India Overtake China? [J] *America. Diplomacy Magazine*. July 8, 2003.

[3] Lin Yifu etc. China's Miracle: Development Strategy and Economic Reform [M]. Shanghai: Shanghai People's Press, 1994. pp. 53.

[4] [America] Joshua Cooper Ramo, Beijing Consensus[J], edited by Huang Ping, Cui Zhiyuan. China and Globalisation: Washington Consensus of Beijing Consensus [M]. Beijing: Social Sciences Academic Press, 2005. pp. 1-62.

[5] [England] David Smith. The Dragon and the Elephant: China, India, and the New World Order [M], Beijing: Modern China Press, 2007.

[6] [Germany] Karl Pilny, Indien und China prägen die Welt [M]. Beijing: China International Culture Publishing House, 2008. Preface.

[7] [America] Jim Rohwer. Asia Rising [M]. Shanghai: Shanghai People's Press, 1997, Chapter 2.

[8] [England] David Smith. The Dragon and the Elephant: China, India, and the New World Order [M], Beijing: Modern China Press, 2007. Introduction.

[9] [India] Amartya Sen etc. India: Economic Development and Social Opportunity [M]. Beijing: Social Sciences Academic Press, 2006. pp. 99-102.

[10] Zhao Mingqi. India's Way: Probe into the Industrialisation Way of India [M]. Shanghai: Academia Press, 2005. Epilogue.

[11] Cheng Jiming etc. Comparative Research on the Economic and Social Development of five Major Countries [M]. Beijing: Press of Economy and Science, 2006. pp. 200-201.

[12] Hang Kang etc. The 21st century: World Contest of Economic Strategies [M]. Beijing: Press of Economy and Science, 2003. Chapter 1.

[13] [America] Jeffrey Sachs. The End of Poverty: Economic Possibilities for Our Time [M]. Shanghai: Shanghai People's Press. 2007. pp. 163.

Scenario of Public Sector Enterprises in Karnataka

D. Venkateshwara Rao and R.K. Mishra

The arena of fiscal federalism in India, which had been a minefield of political conflicts even in the pre-reform era, has been showing signs of becoming a full-fledged battlefield in the wake of the economic reform programme initiated in 1991. The experience of federal governance in different parts of the world has been one of persisting tensions and conflicts of various types between the central and sub central governments. Independent India, having opted for a federal structure with a strong Union, has been no exception to this. Viewed against this backdrop, Government of India's radical agenda of economic reforms, the Government of India has resulted in industrialisation of the country rather than improving agriculture, which was in vogue since so many decades. Govt of India has also made several sojourns like categorisation of industries into A, B and C, demarcating them for different types of sectors. Category A was mainly for public sectors, whereas category B was for public and private sectors. Category C was the tiny and cottage industries to mobilise enough potential for the weaker sections of the society, to uplift the employment generation. The result, inevitably, was a coordination link between the Centre and the States for establishment of different industries under various sectors catering to the needs of the locational operations.

The State Government has improved upon Govt of India's classification and set up different categories viz., Development Enterprises like Karnataka State Small Industries Development Corporation and Karnataka State Industrial Investment and Development Corporation Ltd; Service Enterprises like Karnataka State Police Housing Corporation Ltd. And Karnataka Land Army Corporation Ltd.; Marketing Enterprises like Mysore Sales International Ltd and Karnataka Food & Civil Supplies Corporation Ltd; Production Enterprises like Hutti Gold Mines Company Ltd. And Karnataka Soaps & Detergents Ltd; Organisations formed under special statutes like Karnataka State Financial Corporation and Karnataka State Road Transport Corporation; Corporations for social welfare like SC/ST Development Corporation, Minority Development Corporation, Backward Classes Corporation etc.

Keeping in view the upliftment of weaker section and generation of employment both Centre and State have established several industries catering to the needs of the country and people in private and public sector. This led to the generation of more employment and also improved standard of living, better than on the day of independence. Unfortunately, the performance results are not that encouraging compared to the capital deployed. In vie of this, both the Centre and State Governments has started reforms independently.

1. INDIA'S ECONOMIC REFORMS 1991-2001

Up to the year 1991the country faced an economic disaster to meet the fiscal deficit because of the heavy imports, low performance of the indigenous industries and also to due untapped and unidentified resources. Since population growth continued to be very high, the country could not cater to even for basic needs of people, let alone luxuries and comforts. Hence, the then Government thought of launching high reforms in the form of liberalisation and also brought in the WTO agreement for spreading the role of the market in the economy.

As far as the State is concerned, i.e., Government of Karnataka, was the number one in the country to deploy huge capital amounting to ₹ 4566 crores in 1991 to ₹ 35,197 crores in the year 2005 for establishing several state level public sector industries to cater to the needs of the population. The figures indicate that the Government of Karnataka had taken more initiatives for employment of more capital in industrial sector. But this resulted in only marginal improvement in performance leading to the diminishing to 6545 by the year 2001-02. These results have alarmed the State Government and provoked it to form a committee to find out the reasons for backlog of industries and also to suggest ways and means improve the performance of the state level public enterprises. The Committee was headed by Mr. P. Padmanabha, a senior most IAS Officer. The committee studied in detail all the state level public sector enterprises and also discussed matters with the senior executives of the respective PSEs. They also obtained views from the workers and suggested the following recommendations:

1. Change of management wherever necessary – privatisation of industry
2. Closure of unviable industries
3. Creation of a Nodal Agency at the Secretariat level.

The CEOs of the PSEs have started implementing the above recommendations. This resulted in a turnaround of several PSEs. Now the State Government can confidently say the performance has improved. Further, the State of Karnataka have identified Information Technology as a growth centre and made the capital of Karnataka – Bangalore as IT-Hub. This hub not only created more direct employment and generated more foreign exchange to the State of Karnataka but also improving the standard of living. It can also be said that the IT-hub has resulted in more opportunities in developing and creating shadow employment for different categories of population including the illiterate. Thereby power of economic parity has come down to a marginal extent in the State of Karnataka.

Furthermore, the IT-hub of Karnataka, i.e., Bangalore has become a national and international i-pod in the service-sector and also in creation of a boom in communication industry. Nowadays, we can boldly say, more foreign multi national companies are visiting Bangalore and also entering into many agreements to improve the commercial business in India and their own countries. As you are all aware, it is this IT sector which has magnified and opened the doors for communication sector and also boom in verbal and oral communications has diminished the mobility of skilled workers in the services sector.

1.1 Motivational Measures Taken

Keeping in view, the globalised economy and survival of public sector enterprises, Government of Karnataka has formulated a new industrial policy and provided incentives for upliftment of not only existing industries, but also to initiate the new generation of various new industries. The following are some of the salient features of the New Industrial Policy 2006-2011:

1. It aims at increasing the percentage in GSDP growth, strengthen manufacturing industry, increase share of exports from Karnataka in the national exports, to generate additional employment to at least 10 lakh persons in the manufacturing and service sectors to promote diversified industrial base to reduce regional imbalance in economic development and employment opportunities and ultimately, to achieve overall socio-economic development of the State;

2. The strategies for further industrialisation of the State during the next five years include zoning of various taluks with special emphasis on most backward taluks for the purpose of industrial growth, develop industrial infrastructure in various key locations of the State in an integrated manner, implement mega industrial water supply schemes for potential locations through SPVs, encourage specialised industrial infrastructure for specific sectors and SEZs, encourage development of industrial clusters/corridors and give priority to up-gradation of infrastructure in existing and new industrial areas. Towards this end, an Infrastructure Up-gradation Fund with an initial corpus of ₹ 500 crores was set up to promote Human Resource Development, Agro Food Processing Industry to take up technology up-gradation for Survival and growth of SSI sector and to create a Technology Up-gradation Initiative Fund with a corpus of ₹ 25 crores to provide marketing assistance to SSI sector and promote local entrepreneurship etc.

3. Extending various incentives and concessions relating to Entry Tax and Special Entry Tax, waiver of conversion fine, exemption of stamp duty and reduction of registration charges have also been considered.

The new industrial policy encourages many multinational companies to promote their industrial sectors/branches in the State of Karnataka. As all of you know very well, industrial development cannot take place without giving due importance to the infrastructure and utilities, like power, providing water, effluent treatment plants and disposal of garbage.

Having understood the importance of the above, the Government of Karnataka has also released new Infrastructure Policy 2007 with efflux of time giving specific incentives and concessions for infrastructure projects. There have been changes in the tax and stamp duty regime, formulation of Government of India's policy on Public Private Partnership in infrastructure projects and the concept of Viability Gap Fund.

The main objective of Government of Karnataka is to provide a fair and transparent policy framework to help, facilitate the process of economic growth and encourage Public Private Partnership in upgrading, expanding and developing infrastructure in the State. The Government is also taking several steps for generation of power and initiated a Power Policy for making the state self-sufficient in power generation and also to meet the heavy demand of power for industry as well as domestic needs. To regulate power generation, consumption and tariffs, the Government has also constituted an Authority called Karnataka Electricity Regulatory Commission which will go into the details of all the needs of power. Under PPP, the Government has initiated steps for construction of new International Airport and also implementation of Metro Rail system to defuse the backlogs of traffic jams etc.

2. IT HUB

As indicated earlier, Karnataka is in the forefront of Information Technology and is called as Silicon Valley of India and its capital Bangalore is called as IT-Capital of India. Karnataka is the pioneering first state to announce an IT Policy way back in 1997, ahead of all the States with the following objectives:

- To utilise Information Technology for eradicating poverty and empowering women;
- To effectively reduce unemployment by absorbing the major share of educated youth into the IT industry;
- To promote the usage of Kannada in Information Technology;
- To use e-governance as a tool and deliver a Government that is more pro-active and responsive to its citizens;

- To unleash the Karnataka Incubation engine;
- To encourage business with non-English speaking countries;
- To maintain the pre-eminent position of both Bangalore and Karnataka in the field of Information Technology.

The new policy facilitated the multinationals to establish many laboratories in the IT Capital, Bangalore. To name a few: Sun Microsystems, IBM, Microsoft, Informix, CISCO etc. The above objectives have been fulfilled by creating more employment and also to develop human resource with required skills in IT Sector. The State Government and the established laboratories have taken initiatives to educate the people at different levels, diploma, degree and post graduate. These resulted in promoting many IT schools. Besides, the main IT Hub, several connected services have been improved to create further employment.

3. CENTRE FOR E-GOVERNANCE

Utilising the IT facilities, the Government established e-governance like e-mailing, internet facility etc to reduce laborious effects of the employees and also to save time for the common man in obtaining several clearances for establishment of the facilities /industry. The results are tremendous, not only in rural areas in catering the day-to-day needs, like land registrations, e-stamping for reducing illegal effects in stamp duties, but also in publication of under graduate, graduate and post graduate level examinations through internet.

Further, software IT Parks and also industrial parks for export promotion have also been created for smooth running and utilisation of resources efficiently and effectively to carry on the exports. At this juncture, I would like to congratulate the then Government of Karnataka for visualising the IT as a main hub for facilitating and also creating employment opportunities on a large scale and also for earning major foreign exchange for the country. I also congratulate the then Prime Minister who has initiated liberalisation and also given importance for globalisation, which has eradicated the licencing raj.

4. MONITORING AGENCY

The process of public sector reforms to turn them around is facing all kinds of hurdles – from trade unions, lack of buyers for prestigious PSUs and also for change of management in restructuring of the Boards etc. Hence, as suggested by Mr. Padmanabha Commission, a central cell with administrative powers cutting across all Government departments, staffed by legal, labour and financial experts known as Department of Public Enterprises (DPE) has been created in the

Government of Karnataka Secretariat. It is headed by a senior Indian Administrative Service officer of the rank of Principal Secretary. This is a nodal agency for monitoring all matters related to the public sector enterprises, either to divest or restructure or diversify and to invest further inflow to the company for making them viable. In order to have transparency with respect to the activities, the Department has released a Government Order providing for the following:

1. Creation of new Corporations or Companies
2. Providing share capital exceeding Rs.50 lakhs by the KSIIDC and the KSFC to a new or an existing Corporation or Company
3. Winding up / amalgamation of major schemes of PSEs
4. Increase in capital cost estimates of PSEs
5. Laying down policies relating to privatisation or restructuring of PSEs
6. Execution of MoUs between PSEs and DPE
7. Performing the role of HPC
8. Undertake in-depth study of PSEs
9. Functioning of data bank in respect of all PSEs
10. Bring out annual survey reports of all PSEs
11. Function as Secretariat for all State PSEs
12. Conduct regular training courses to all the personnel and officers of PSEs.

The Department is monitoring day-to-day affairs of public sectors individually and also thinking of entering into MoUs for better performance. The main aim of entering into MoU with PSEs is to give able leadership with a definite tenure, may be 3–5 years, to give autonomy almost on par with private companies, to give exemptions from important acts like Transparency Act, RTI Act. etc. and to put in place, able personnel to manage optimum utilisation of resources and monitor constantly. In order to cope up with the above activity and also because of the technology upgradation in the industry globally, it is felt that the skills of the human resources are to be upgraded based on the needs of the industry. To cope up with this, training programmes have been organised for enrichment of skills along with the management tools in different fields of production, marketing, finance and IT related etc. To manage the resources effectively, the direction from the top is more important and hence, the Board has been restructured with professionals concerned in different fields of the industries, academicians and administrators.

As it is a liberalised economy, and also India is following and implementing WTO guidelines, it is observed that new market segments have to be created, which requires more strategic planning and decision-making in an effective manner to optimise the resources. This being done effectively by monitoring systems, reviewing and meetings of the top executives occasionally on several platforms to exchange ideas. The Government is also actively participating and also liberalising clearances for better performance which is known as Single Window System monitoring.

5. ENVIRONMENTAL MEASURES

Last, but not least, I would like to emphasise before the August gatherings here that Bangalore is known as Garden City of India. Hence, the Government is also taking measures to reduce pollution to improve the lifespan of the human kind. Towards this end, as a first step, the Government is putting a condition to the new industries that only 33% of the land allotted to them should be used for production purpose and the remaining area should be used for green plantation. Secondly, the industry should take effective measures to dispose off effluents without affecting the surroundings. If necessary, the industry should establish their own effluent treatment plants. Like this, Government of Karnataka has taken several measures to check pollution. To monitor all these activities, Government of Karnataka has established a separate Board called Pollution Control Board.

Due to the above measures, it is observed that the performance of the public sectors have improved for the past 3-4 years and turn around into considerable profits, which is satisfactory. I hope their performance would further improve in the course of time because of definite and conspicuous role played by Department of Public Enterprises. Changes may occur in the investment pattern as well as the mobilisation of industries, by creating first generation entrepreneurs which will further improve the employment potential and self-sustaining capacity.

30 Years of Development after the Reforms and the Opening upto the World: Achievements—A Case of China

Wang Haibo

1. MACROECONOMIC INDICES KEEP INCREASING

Firstly, for the first time in its history China's economic growth has been consistent, rapid, and stable on a long-term basis. From 1979 to 2007 China's GDP increased by 9.8% annually. With a highly increased baseline, this growth ratio was 3.7% higher than the average annual growth ratio 6.1% from 1953 to 1978; the average annual growth ratio was increased by 60%.[1] Calculated by some foreign scholar, 11 countries and regions had average annual economic growth ratio higher than 7% in 25 years from 1950s. China had average annual growth ratio at 9.8% consecutively for 29 years from the inception of economic reforms and opening to the world. Obviously the economic growth at a speed of 9% or so would last for some period of time. China's long-term and continuous economic growth is peerless in history and in the world.

Besides, being long-term, continuous, and quick China's economic growth is also stable. "Stable" means that the growth has moved from the period with ultra-sharp fluctuation (valley year and peak year have economic growth ratio gap above 20%), period with sharp fluctuation (gap above 10%), period with medium fluctuation (gap above 5%) to period with slight fluctuation (gap below 5%). For example, the economic growth ratio in peak year 1953 and valley year 1954 was 15.6% and 4.2% separately. The later is 11.4% lower than the former ratio. So we call it a period of sharp fluctuation. The economic growth ratio in year 1958 and year 1961 was 21.3% and 27.3% separately, showing a gap of 48.6% and a period with ultra-sharp fluctuation. In 1978 and 1981 the economic growth ratio was 11.7% and 5.2% separately, showing a gap of 6.5% and a period with medium fluctuation. Then by comparing valley year 1999 (economic growth ratio 7.6%) and peak year 2007 (economic

---

[1] *China Statistical Yearbook 2007*, China Statistics Press, Page 60; www.stats.gov.cn, Apr. 10 2008.

growth ratio 11.9%), the gap turns out to 4.3%, showing a period of slight fluctuation.[2]

Secondly, for prices[3], China keeps low inflation while economy is growing fast. To explain this point we shall give two preconditions: 1. The conception of hot and cool economies and the general indices for measuring hot and cool economies. Firstly we should know that economy hot or cool is a general conception for economy, not a partial one. Hot or cool economy means that the total social supply is lower than or higher than the total social demand. The hot or cool indicates the degree that the former is lower than or higher than the later. So the general indices measuring hot or cool economy shall reflect the gross context of the economy, not partial context of the economy. The potential of social production cannot be maximised if the gross social demand is less than the gross social supply, showing actual economic growth ratio lower than the potential economic growth ratio. Otherwise, if the total social demand is higher than total social supply, it means that the actual economic growth ratio is higher than the potential economic growth ratio. From their mutual relationship we know that hot or cool economy can be understood as the actual economic growth ratio is lower or higher than the potential economic growth ratio.

A simple method for the estimation of potential economic growth ratio is to use the average annual economic growth ratio over a long term. The high or low potential economic growth ratio mainly is determined by the degree of the development social productivity. It is a dynamic concept, not static. Therefore, the potential economic growth ratio increases not only in the long period after China's reform and opening to the world, but also increases in times featuring rapidly developing social productivity and different stages of reform. From 1953 to 1978 the average social labour productivity increased by 3.4% annually. From 1979 to 1990 the average increase was 4.8% annually. From 1991 to 2007 the average increase was 9.2% annually. So we see three periods to estimate the potential economic growth ratio of every period. The average annual economic growth ratios were 6.1%, 9.0%, and 10.3% during periods from 1953 to 1978, from 1979 to 1999, and from 1991 to 2007.[4]

---

[2] *China Statistical Yearbook 2007*, China Statistics Press, Page 60; www.stats.gov.cn, Apr. 10 2008.

[3] The broad sense price (including prices of goods and services) index includes GDP price deflator, producer price index, and consumer price index. For discussion convenience this paper neglects the former two indexes.

[4] Note: Currently the economic development has imposed upon China's resources and environment pressures reaching their limit, or even exceeding their limit. So we shall include the indexes of resource and environment into the factor category for determining the too hot economy. This significant issue deserves research. However, this issue is complex, and we need data. We have neglected this point in the above discussion. The potential economic growth ratio designed by this paper shall decrease at proper degree if resource and environment are taken into the category of observation.

If the above estimates are correct, the peak year of the rising stage of the present period can only be somewhat hot in economy. China's history of economic growth after its reform and opening to the world showed that the actual average annual growth ratio exceeding the potential average annual growth ratio by two percent would result in hot economy. The four peak years, 1978, 1984, 1987, and 1992, have economic growth ratios 11.7%, 15.2%, 11.6%, and 14.2%, separately. They are 5.6%, 6.2%, 2.6%, and 3.9% higher than the potential growth ratios, separately. From 2003 to 2007 the economic growth ratios are 10%, 10.1%, 10.4%, 11.6%, and 11.9%.[5] These ratios are at the top of the potential growth ratios, or within 1 percent above the potential economic growth ratio. The economy of these years can only be somewhat hot. However, inappropriate macro-control may result in hot economy.

Based on the historical experiences and current situation after the foundation of PRC, we may set four grades corresponding to different economic growth ratios and consumer price index increase or decrease ratios. Four grades for economic growth are: 1. Too hot: The economy grows at a ratio of two percent or so above the potential economic growth ratio. 2. High growth: The economy grows under the upper limit above the potential economic growth ratio. To simplify problems and facilitate the correspondence to grades of consumer price index, generally we may put warm economy (i.e., the economy grows at a rate of 1 percent or so above the potential economic growth ratio). 3. Medium growth: The economy grows within the medium section of the potential economic growth ratio. 4. Low growth: The economy grows within the lower section of the potential economic growth ratio or at a speed below the potential economic growth ratio. Corresponding to these grades, the four grades for consumer price index are: 1. High inflation: The consumer price index increased by 10% or more; 2. Moderate inflation: The consumer price index increased below 10%; 3. Low inflation: The consumer price index increased below 5%; 4. Deflation: The consumer price index is negative.

By these preconditions we may begin to explain the characteristics of prices in peak years of the new economic period based on the facts of economic development after the foundation of PRC. Therefore, we should make a simple comparison among the prices of peak years of every economic period after the foundation of PRC. There are 8 peak years after the foundation of PRC if 1956 is counted as the first peak year. The economic growth ratios and corresponding price indices of these peak years are: 115.0 and 99.9, 1956; 121.3 and 98.9, 1958; 119.4 and 100.0, 1970; 111.7 and 100.7, 1978; 115.2 and 102.7, 1984, and 113.5 and 109.3, 1985; 111.6 and 107.3, 1987, and 111.3 and 118.8, 1988; 114.2 and 106.4, 1992, and 114.0 and 114.7, 1993, and 113.1 and 124.1, 1994. The five years from 2003 to 2007 have economic growth ratios and

---

[5] *China Statistical Yearbook 2007*, China Statistics Press; www.stats.gov.cn, Apr. 10 2008.

corresponding price indexes as following in sequence: 110.0 and 101.2, 110.1 and 103.9, 110.4 and 101.8, 111.6 and 101.0, 111.9 and 104.8.[6] These data show: 1. The price indices of the early four peak years are characterised by: Deflation (1956 and 1958) or approximate deflation (1970 and 1978). Obviously the administrative instructions from the Government to meet requirements of overtaking strategy and prior development of heavy industry strategy had caused deflation by its planned price system. Indeed from 1978 China had begun the reform of economic system, but only by a long period prices completed the change from being specified by administrative instructions of the government to being adjusted by the market. For example in the change of price system for goods, for the total amounts of consumable retail sales, agricultural by-products procurement, and production means sales, the administrative pricing by the government had occupied a share of 97.0%, 92.2% and 100% in 1978 (the remainder share is occupied by the prices conducted by the government or adjusted by the market, same as below), 47.0%, 37% and 60% in 1985, 5.9%, 12.5% and 18.7% in 1992, and 2.8%, 1.2% and 5.6% in 2006.[7] The change of price system of services in general more lagged. As we had seen, the pricing specified by government instructions restrained the rising of prices even after 1978. 2. The 5th, 6th, and 7th peak years had change of prices characterized by: Low inflation (1984), moderate inflation (1985, 1987, and 1992) or high inflation (1988, 1993, and 1994) in hot economy, for prices were gradually adjusted and freed (a significant progress of economic reform), economy was becoming hotter and hotter year after year, and for the predicted creeping inflation. 3. The 8th peak years (2003–2007) had change of prices characterised by: Low inflation in somewhat hot economy, i.e., low inflation in high growing economy.

Thirdly, employment made historical breakthrough. There had never been hundreds of millions of people on the peril of unemployment in the planned economic system and urban and rural dual social structure before China's reform and opening to the world. Moreover, millions of new workers appeared in China every year. State-owned enterprises and collective enterprises could not create new employment opportunities but would free millions of unemployed people due to the progress of reform. So employment would be an urgent social issue after reforming.

However, China had made historical breakthrough for this issue after reforms 1. The total employment was almost doubled. During 26 years from 1953 to 1978, China's employment was increased to 401.52-million from 213.64-million, an increase ratio of 87.9% with average annual increase ratio 2.4%. During 29 years from 1979 to 2007, China's employment was increased to 769.90-million from 410.24-million, an

---

[6] *China Statistical Yearbook 2007*, China Statistics Press; *Price Yearbook of China* (years mentioned), China Price Press.

[7] *Price Yearbook of China* (years mentioned), China Price Press.

increase ratio of 91.7% with average annual increase ratio 2.3%. But we should see that employment in 1979, the first year of the later 29 years was 1.9 times that of 1953, the first year of the former 26 years. The social labor productivity of the later 29 years had an average annual growth ratio of 7.3%, 2.1 times 3.4% the average annual growth ratio of the former 26 years. This means that during 29 years after the beginning of reforms, China's organic composition of capital had been greatly improved, resulting in greatly reduced employment elasticity. We see that the maintenance of the approximate average annual growth ratio of employment of 26 years before reforms begin with the employment of 29 years after the reforms began is a great achievement, if we take into account the greatly increased employment, highly progressed technology, and greatly reduced employment elasticity. 2. Preconditioned by disadvantages such as, in rural areas a great number of potentially unemployed people came to employment, public-owned enterprises released a mass of unemployed people, new urban and rural labours appeared in abundance, and employment elasticity decreased greatly. It is a wonder to have the urban unemployment ratio restrained, and in consecutively 5 years from 2003 to 2007 the government reduced the unemployment ratio. In 1978 the registered urban unemployment ratio was 5.3%, which decreased to 4.3% 2003, and to 4.0% 2007.[8] A more important thing is that, for a long time, people have been mostly worrying about an important issue, i.e., how to transform idle rural labours, at quantity of hundreds of millions, into labours for non-agricultural industry during the modernisation of China. Originally it was designed that this transformation needed a long period to complete. However, reform practices built a solid foundation for this transformation and it took less than what people predicted. We have now seen clearly the prospect of complete transformation. This means that the labour supply of China's non-agricultural industry would have turned into basically balanced supply and demand in a short period. This is a milestone. As estimated by some scholars, rural areas had 300-million idle labours or so to be transferred to non-agricultural industry after the beginning of reforms. So far 120-million people had been transferred to township enterprises; 110-million people are working in urban areas; and 70 million or so idle labours are left to be transferred. The basic completion of this transfer needs 10 years or so because of the joining of new urban and rural labours, reduced employment elasticity caused by increased urban and rural labour productivity. The completion time would be year 2015 or so. The above data showed that China has already realised a historical breakthrough in dealing with the significant but difficult issue – employment. Certainly we have much more to do.

---

[8] Data Source: *China Statistical Yearbook* (years mentioned), China Statistics Press; www.stats.gov.cn, Feb. 28, Apr. 10 2008.

Fourthly, the balance of payments has jumped. China's balance of payments were on a had small scale and grew at a low rate before economic reforms, partially for the closed or semi-closed policy applied in planned economic system, partially for the limitation of the international situation of that time. At the end of 1952, China only had 294-million dollars of balance of payments, and 868-million dollars in 1978. Calculated by current dollar price, by 26 years the balance of payments only saw an increase of 1.95 times, average annual increase ratio 4.2%. The balance of payments jumped after China's economic reform and in the background of rapidly growing economy and the development of open economy. It grew to 247.025-billion dollars 2006 from 6.291-billion dollars 1982. Calculated by the exchange rate of that time, by 24 years China saw an increase of 38.3 times in balance of payments, average annual increase ratio 16.5%.[9]

2. PEOPLE'S MATERIAL AND CULTURAL LIVING LEVEL HAS BEEN COMPREHENSIVELY IMPROVED

Firstly, people saw the rapid increase of their income, which is the source for the improvement of their consumption level. From 1978 to 2007, the urban resident disposable income per capita increased to 13,786-Yuan from 343.4-Yuan; the rural resident net income per capita increased to 4,140-Yuan from 133.6-Yuan; an increase of 6.4 times and 6.2 times respectively.[10] And we must add that these incomes do not mean the total income of residents. They are just the salaries. Business net income, property income, and transfer income, not including the allowances given by the government to residents and other legal incomes are not included; nor does it include a great number of gray incomes and black incomes. So, people's income level was underestimated to some extent. We also should note that the increase of the taxable income level also has increased resident income. In 1999 China began taxing individual income at a level of 800-Yuan, which was adjusted to 1,600-Yuan in 2006, and to 2,000-Yuan in 2008.[11]

Secondly, there was saw rapid increase in their consumption level. In 1978 the resident consumption level increased to 184-Yuan from 91-Yuan of 1952. Rural residents' consumption level increased to 138-Yuan from 65-Yuan, and urban residents from 154-Yuan to 405-Yuan. Calculated by comparable prices, the annual growth ratios of these three indexes are 2.3%, 1.8%, and 3.0% respectively. In 2006 the resident consumption level increased to 6,111-Yuan from 184-Yuan of 1978. Rural residents' consumption level increased to 2848-Yuan from 138-Yuan, and

[9] *China Statistical Yearbook* (years mentioned), China Statistics Press.
[10] *China Statistical Yearbook 2007*, China Statistics Press, Page 345; www.stats.gov.cn, Feb. 28 2008.
[11] *Economic Daily News*, eighth space, Dec. 24, 2007.

urban residents from 405-Yuan to 10359-Yuan. The annual growth ratios of these three indexes are 7.5%, 5.9%, and 6.3% respectively. Comparing to the former period, the later indexes increased 2.26 times, 2.28 times, and 1.1 times.[12] We also should emphasise that from 1978 to 2007, China's rural population in poverty decreased to 14.79-million from 250-milion.

Thirdly, the increase of Engel's Coefficient (proportion of income that goes into food) is a significant index for the improvement of residents' material life. From 1978 to 2007 the rural residents' Engel's Coefficient decreased to 43.1% from 67.7%, and urban residents' Engel's Coefficient to 36.3% from 57.5%. The decrease ratios are 24.6% and 21.2%, respectively. Fourthly, the improvement of housing level is a significant index for the improvement of people's material life. From 1978 to 2006, the urban housing area per capita increased to 27.0-m^2 from 6.7-m^2, rural housing area per capita to 30.7-m^2 from 8.1-m^2; the increase ratios are 3.0 times and 2.8 times respectively.

Fifthly, the extensive use of modern transport and communication tools and the increase of the proportion of expenditures of transport and communication in consumption pattern indicate modernisation of residents' life. For example, by 2006 in average a hundred of resident families in China owned 152.88 mobile phones. This number is 62.05 in rural areas. By 2007 China had had 122-million broadband users, No. 1 in the world.[13] A corresponding fact is that, in 2006 the urban residents' transport and communication expenditures had a proportion in consumption per capita increased to 13.19% from 1.20% of 1990; rural residents to 11.95% from 2.24%.

Sixthly, the increase of the number of college and university graduates is one of the most significant indexes of improvement in people's cultural life. From 1978 to 2007 the graduates of ordinary colleges and universities had a number increased from 165-thousand to 4.48-million; the number of masters and doctors increased from 9 to 310-thousand. The increase ratios were 26.1 times and 34443.4 times, respectively. In the consumption expenditure structure of urban and rural residents we can also see a clear improvement in people's cultural life. From 1990 to 2006, the proportion of the educational, cultural, and amusement expenditures in per capita consumption of the urban and rural residents increased from 11.12% to 13.83%; rural areas from 8.36% to 12.63%.[14]

---

[12] *China Statistical Yearbook* (years mentioned), China Statistics Press.
[13] *Science and Technology Daily*, Dec. 24, 2007.
[14] *China Statistical Yearbook 2007*, China Statistics Press, Pages 347, 371, 390; www.stats.gov.cn, Feb. 28, 2008.

The above first to fifth points are significant signs of the improved material and cultural life of people. Tourism is a composite carrier for material and cultural life and healthcare, and time of leisure is an important condition for the material and cultural life and for the comprehensive development of people. These are the new things that appeared because of the significant improvement in the material and cultural life of people since the beginning of reforms.

Seventhly, domestic tourism has bee booming. From 1994 to 2006, the domestic tourism saw traveler person-times increased from 5.24-million to 13.94-million, of which urban resident travelers increased from 2.05-million person-times to 5.76-million person times, and rural resident travelers from 3.19-million person-times to 8.18-million person-times. The three increase ratios are 1.66 times, 1.81 times, and 1.56 times respectively. During this period the per capita travel expenditure increased from 195.3-Yuan to 446.9-Yuan, of which urban residents from 414.7-Yuan to 766.4-Yuan, and rural resident from 54.9-Yuan to 221.9-Yuan; the three increase ratios are 1.29 times, 0.85 times, and 3.04 times respectively.[15]

Eighthly, greatly increased time of leisure. China changed the single day weekend before reform into double-day weekend after beginning reform. Later national holidays Labor Day, National Day, and Spring Festival were given to working people. These holidays were adjusted and total rest days increased from January 1 2008 Tomb-sweeping Day, Dragon Boat Festival, and Mid-autumn Festival were set. Thus the average holiday time in a year is more than one third if we combine legal holidays, weekends, and employees' paid annual leave.[16]

Ninthly, life expectancy is a comprehensive index for the improved material and cultural life of people. From 1978 to 2006, life expectancy in China increased from 68 years to 72.4 years.[17] In general, Chinese people's material and cultural life improved in an unprecedented, quick, and comprehensive way after the reforms. Certainly China will still remain in the initial stage of socialism for a long time. As a developing country, Chinese standard of living is lower in general when compared with that of developed countries.

3. CHINA AS AN ECONOMIC GIANT

Firstly, with a 2,645.2-billion dollar GDP, China ranked No.4 in the world in 2005, 2006, and 2007, following America, Japan, and Germany. China was ranked No.10 in 1978, it may be added. Correspondingly, the increase of China's economic aggregate

---

[15] Data Source: *China Statistical Yearbook 2007*, China Statistics Press, Page 765.
[16] For details see Economic Daily News, Second space, Dec. 17, 2007.
[17] *Guangming Daily*, Fifth part, Jan. 8 2008.

also contributed more to the growth of the world's economy. From 2003 to 2005 China's economic growth contributed to 13.8% of the world's economic growth, ranking at world No.2. It is anticipated that in 2007 this percentage shall go up to 16%, world No.1.

Secondly, the outputs of the major agricultural products grains, meat, and seed cotton were ranked at world No.2, No.3, and No.4 respectively in 1978. After 1990 these outputs are world No.1. For steel and cement the major raw material for industry, China was world No.5 and No.4 in 1978, and world No.1 after 2000. The major energy sources, coal, crude oil, and electric power, were world No.3, No.8, and No.7 in 1978. Of these, China became world No.1 in coal after 1990; crude oil increased to world No.5 or No.6 after 1990; and electric power turned into world No.2 after 2000.[18] Currently China's manufacturing is world No.4; of it the high-tech manufacturing is world No.2.

Thirdly, in 2007 there were 18.55-million of students in ordinary colleges and universities. China has 70-million people who have had higher education experience.[19] China has become a higher education giant and human resource giant. According to the report of "China Technology Cases Research" issued by the Ministry of Science and Technology in September 2007. Today China has 35-million people working in scientific and technological fields, a world No.1. In 2006 China had 1.42-million researchers and developers, a world No.2. This is the first point. For the second point, in 2006 the total amount of scientific and technological expenditures of China was 450-billion-Yuan, and the total value of research and development was 300.31-billion Yuan, a world No.5. The input into research and development was 1.42%. The third point we should note is that, currently the total amount of patent applications reached above 4-million, and consecutively for three years domestic patent applications are higher than that of foreign patent applications; in 2006 the domestic percentage was 53.4%. China has world No.4 invention patent applications.[20]

Fourthly, in 2007 China's import& export trade volume increased to 2,173.80-billion dollars from 20.64-billion dollars in 1978. Calculated by current dollar price, the increase ratio was 105.3 times. China's import & export trade volume was ranked at world No.27 in 1978, and became world No. 3 after 2004.[21] As reported by the International Trade Institute of Korea International Trade Association in August

---

[18] *China Statistical Yearbook (2007),* China Statistics Press, P1024; www.xinhuanet.com, Jan. 5, 2008.

[19] *Economic Daily News,* Third space, Dec. 24, 2007; www.stats.gov.cn, Feb. 28 2008.

[20] *People's Daily – Overseas Edition,* Sep. 26, 2007; *Economic Daily News,* Fourth space, Jan. 9 2008.

[21] *China Statistical Yearbook 2007,* China Statistics Press, P. 1024.

2007, China has 958 types of products with world No.1 share in the global market. China is the country owning most varied commodities with world No.1 market share.[22] China's actual foreign-capital utilisation increased from 18.187-billion dollars of 1979 – 1980 to 74.8-billion dollars in 2007. For many years this utilisation has been world No.1. In 2007 China's international direct investment reached 18.7-billion dollars, the No.1 among developing countries. China's foreign exchange reserve increased to 1,528.2-billion dollars in 2007 from 167-million dollars in 1978. Calculated by current dollar price, the increase ratio was 9149.9 times[23], world No.1.

Fifthly, as estimated by some foreign organisations, in 2006 China's consumption volume contributed to 5.4% of the world's consumption volume, world No. 5.[24]

Firstly China is from an aggregate view an economic giant. This means that on the one hand, in some fields China is not an economic giant yet. On the other hand, China is not only an economic giant in some fields, but a technological power as manifested by the third milestone of development of China's aviation and space flight, the first lunar prospector mission of 2007 in addition to the first launch of man-made satellite, and the first launch of space ship. China has been great power in the aviation and space flight sector a. Secondly, more comprehensive comparison on economic indices shall find that China's economy is not ranked so high in the world. For example, by GDP China was world No.4 in 2005. But by GNI (GDP + Net factor income from abroad), China's gross economic volume was 2,286.7-billion dollars in 2005, in which year America, Japan, Germany, England, and France have economic volumes 14,503.9-billion dollars, 4,941.8-billion dollars, 3,630.9-billion dollars, 3,579.6-billion dollars, and 2,791.0-billion dollars. China is ranked at world No.6 not No.4 in economic volume. Another example is that in 2005 China's foreign trade volume was world No.3 1,422.1-billion dollars. But the actual foreign trade volume was 874.1-billion dollars in 2005, if we take into account the foreign capital's contribution to foreign trade. In that year Germany, Japan, France, and England had foreign trade volumes at 1,744.8-billion dollars, 1,111.9-billion dollars, 955.0-billion dollars, and 878.1-billion dollars, higher than that of China.[25] However, China is in general an economic giant, even after we take the above factors into account.

In summary China has obtained splendid achievements in economic development during 30 years after reform and opening to the world, demonstrated by the improving macro-economy indices, comprehensively improved people's life, and the general position as an economic giant.

---

[22] *Legal Mirror*, Aug. 21, 2007.
[23] *China Statistical Yearbook 2007*, China Statistics Press, P774; www.stats.gov.cn, Feb. 28 2008.
[24] *The Report to the 17th National Congress of the CPC (Tutorial Reading)*, People's Publishing House, 2007, P93.
[25] *China Economic Times*, June 15, 2007.

Certainly China's economic development is challenged by many difficulties and problems, because all things have the nature of duality. As summarised by the 17th National Congress of CPC, these difficulties and problems are: Economy grows at too high a cost of resources and environment; economic and social development of urban and rural areas and different regions remains unbalanced; stable agricultural development and sustainable income increase of rural residents face many difficulties; labour and employment, social security, income distribution, education and health, resident housing, safe production, judicature and public security etc are facing many issues; some people are suffering in poverty; the administrative ability of CPC is slightly unsuitable for the new situation and tasks; no thorough investigation and research has been made into some major issues for stabilizing reform and development; some root CPC units are fragile and loose; some CPC members and officers enjoy their Pharisaism and bureaucratic privileges, and have behaviours of waste, extravagance, and corruption. We should attach high importance to these problems and solve them by prudent ways.[26]

3.1 Reforms and Opening up are the Driving Forces of China's 30-year's Economic Development

We should first mention two historical factors. Firstly in history China had never been an economic giant. However, in contemporary times China has rosy prospect for development. By the data calculated out by Professor Madisan based on the international dollar 1990, in 1820 the GDPs of China, America, and Japan were 228.6-billion dollars, 12.6-billion dollars, and 20.9-billion dollars respectively, accounting for a share of 32.4%, 1.8%, and 3% in the world's total GDP amount; they are world No.1, No.6, and No.5 respectively. Certainly the contemporary China contains many factors different from the old China. However, as the development process of any country, the actual development of China's economy has some relation with history, general nature of people (for example high population and excellent scientific and cultural tradition etc.) Therefore, the contemporary China by using various past advantages and long-term hard work to attain the achievements. Secondly we should know that China owned huge potential for economic development, for it was constrained by the planned economic system before reform and opening to the world. An evident expression of this potential was that in rural and urban areas there were hundreds of millions of idle workers. Certainly we need a series of conditions to make most out of the potential of economic growth mentioned above or to turn the huge development prospect into reality. Reform and opening give us the essential strength. Through 30 years of reform and opening to the world, China

---

[26] *Collection of Documents of the 17th National Congress of the CPC*, People's Publishing House, 2007, P5-6.

has initially established the framework of socialist market economic system, forming a general economic structure that open is to the world in a comprehensive, widespread, and multi-layer way. Reform and opening, became the driving forces behind the sustainable and quick development of economy.

Here we face the first theoretical problem: Why the reform of economic system has so powerful a force in developing social productivity? According to the theory of historical materialism, the basic contradictions of human society are the contradiction between productivity and production relations, and the contradiction between economic foundation and superstructure. These contradictions are the fundamental forces driving forward social development. History has given us full evidence: This theory is completely right. However, the history also proved that as the particular expression of the production relations (economic foundation), the economic system has significant function in developing social productivity, which cannot be denied.

The birth, development, and eclipse of the economic system are determined by and, at the same time, counteractive to the development of social productivity. Economic system can be the driving force of productivity, or the constraints of productivity. Economic system is the expression of basic economic regime (production relations or economic foundation), and in turn it is counteractive to the basic economic regime. Economic system is able to maintain or destroy economic structure. The government of the superstructure may protect the economic system, and in turn the economic system may be counteractive to the government. The reform of economic system to meet the requirements of developing productivity needs the government as a driver, and it reinforces the government in turn. The government shall collapse if reform is not carried out in tune with the requirements of productivity. Here we shall point out some important differences between basic economic regime and economic system. First difference is that the former has the capacity to contain social productivity higher than the later. Second difference is that the former has a lasting period longer than that of the later. Third difference is that the essential reform of the former needs revolution in a class society, that generally a class shall overthrow the sovereign of another class. The later reform is of self-improving of a government preconditioned by the maintenance of the basic class structure.

We must emphasize that the use of economic system concept is helpful to further discover the development law of ancient society, capitalism society, and socialist society. By the development of China's feudal society we began. The change from feudal suzerain system to feudal lord system can be explained in two historical scenes: Firstly China's suzerain economy existed for less than 600 years, as recorded in history. The feudal lord economy existed for nearly 2,400 years. The later had a life of about four times the former. Also we should note that the feudal lord economy's productivity was faster than that of the suzerain economy. Secondly the feudalist-suzerain system in Europe lasted for one thousand years, where as China's feudalist-suzerain economic system lived for 3,000 years. Many factors have determined this difference. The current situation makes us believe that Marx's or Lenin's prediction on capitalism and imperialism is correct, except that they lasted longer. Many factors caused this situation. Theoretically an important factor they neglected was that they did not see (and could not see) that of the productivity a modern market economic system is very much higher than that of the classical market economic system. Essentially this limitation came from the times when Marx or Lenin lived. This explanation meets Marxist Epistemology and historical materialism. In 1859 Marx issued a clear and classic statement: "No social system will be ruined before its productivity capacity is maximized."[27] Therefore, we shall not doubt the correctness of Marxism and Leninism or their prediction on capitalism. At last, by development of socialist society we see that Soviet Union was disintegrated in 1991, and China's economy got rapid development after year 1978 and reinforced more socialism. This difference was caused by many factors. Soviet Union stayed in planned economic system for a long period, resulting in very slow social productivity. China after 1978 is gradually taking the way of market-oriented economy, pushing forward the development of social productivity.

We have discussed the important function of economic system in developing social productivity in general. The economic system has more important and unique role in developing social productivity under the environment of China's socialist market economy. The basic characteristic of socialist market economy is that it is combined with the basic economic regime of socialism, although it is also a market economy with governmental interference. Viewed from a long term normal development perspective, the socialist market economic system shall have greater capacity for social productivity than the modern market system of developed countries. It also has much greater power in promoting the development of social productivity.

At the present China's socialist economic system has many unique functions in promoting the development of social productivity. Here we mention the development of competition relating to the development of socialist market economy. Competition is the basic nature of market economy. However, in China, unique competition is occurring when China began to transit from planned economy to socialist market economy. Some major determinants are: 1. The contemporary developed countries stepped out of the original capital's accumulation stage in a period of three hundred years. Their people are living in rich style, and their economy developed. Certainly competition exists at this time, and in some fields it is very intense. But in general the competition today is more moderate than that of the original capital's accumulation

---

[27] *Selected Works of Karl Marx and Frederick Engels*, Volume 2, P83, People's Publishing House, 1972.

stage. At the beginning of its reform, China's non-public economy occupied a share less than 1% in GDP, and 250-million people living in poverty. Therefore, the non-public economy shall strive for the accumulation of their original capital; people living in poverty shall strive for their life. Facts showed that the competition of this stage is more intensive than the competition of the developed economy stage. This is the difference between competitions in different stages. 2. Competitors in the market of developed countries are mainly private enterprises, for they have few state-owned enterprises. But in China, the competition exists between state-owned enterprises and collective enterprises, between public-owned enterprises and private-owned enterprises, between the enterprises under the urban and rural dual-structure, and between foreign-invested enterprises with many advantages and local enterprises, especially the competition exists among local governments owning a mass of production resources. These market players of high quantity and different advantages and disadvantages have complicated the competition scenario. 3. For the purpose of competition, the developed countries have well-established market system, social credit system, and legal system, and corresponding orderly and optimised fair competition. Certainly in these developed countries there will be competition for excess profits, and for monopolised profits. However, in contemporary China, the market trade is in chaos, social credit missing, legal system is incomplete, and fair competition is non-existent. Many industries that promise high profits are waiting for development. The long-term co-existence of planned system and market economic system builds a huge lease-hunting space. Under these conditions many enterprises are striving for sudden huge profits, for they are not satisfied with profits of medium level, or even excessive or monopolized profits. Their behaviours worsened the status of competition, and caused social fortune to be collected by a few people in a short period. A great number of '*arrivistes*' appeared in China. The demonstrative effects of this fortune grabbing in return promoted the intensification of competition. 4. Viewed from the market of production factors, China has excess labour, and hundreds of millions of these workers suffer unemployment (especially rural labour). The progress of reform shall throw out millions more workers from public-owned enterprises. The employment elasticity is undergoing evident decrease due to technological progress and optimisation of industrial structure. All these shall intensify the competition at the labour market. China has low land area per capita. The contradiction between supply and demand of land is becoming more and more prominent due to urbanisation and the growth of the GDP supporting industry, real estate. Although the difference between deposit and loan of state-owned or state-controlled banks is increasing, the mid and small enterprises, rural areas, and remote areas do not have sufficient money supply, leading to rapid growth of non-governmental loan with excessively high interest rates. All these factors have intensified the competition at the factory market of labour, land, and capital. 5. Repeated construction and repeated production are a severe problem in planned economic system in China. This problem does not cease after China's began reforms, but even worsens, for in China a united and open market has not been built yet. This is also an important factor in intensifying competition. 6. In general China is at the low end of the industrial chain. In China's industry the high-tech plays a small part, and the quantity of products with independent intellectual property rights is low. China's most exported products are labour-intensive. This low-tech and simple exported product structure puts related enterprises into a context of intensive competition. From a positive view, the intensive competition inspired by market-oriented reform has energised the economy at the present stage. So for a long period this competition shall promote the rapid development of China's economy. However, from a negative view this intensive competition shall impact or harm economic development. However, the negative view is secondary.

Now we shall discuss the important function of reform and opening up of the economy in promoting growth. Firstly reform and opening has optimised the distribution of social and productive resources. One optimized distribution is among different ownerships. Before reforms, public ownership (especially state ownership) almost covered every sector. After reform and opening to the world, China has basically formed a context featuring the leading role of state-owned economy, the backbone role of public-owned economy, and the general development of multiple ownerships. We take the industry that plays a leading role in domestic economy as an example. From 1978 to 2006, the gross value of industrial output increased to 31,658.89-billion Yuan from 423.7-billion Yuan, of which the output of public-owned industry (including state-owned and collective industries) increased to 13,422.097-billion Yuan from 423.7-billion Yuan, and the non-public industry increased from 0 to 18236.8-billion Yuan. Their ratios in the gross value of industrial output were decreased from 100% to 42.4% and increased from 0% to 57.6%, respectively.[28] However, during this period, not only the non-public economy achieved rapid growth by its special energy, but the state-owned industry that plays a leading role in the public-owned industry has greatly energised economic activity and evidently increased benefits due to the progress of reform, especially due to the adjustment of state-owned economy strategy, the progress of state-owned enterprise stock alteration, and the reinforcement of state-owned assets supervision from the later period of 1990s. From 1998 to 2006 the overall labour productivity of the state-owned and state-controlled industrial enterprises increased from 98,70 Yuan to 548,284 Yuan. Even we take inflation into consideration; the labour productivity has increased greatly.[29] Another optimisation is of the resources among different

[28]Data Source: *China Statistical Yearbook 2007* (years mentioned), China Statistics Press.
[29]*China Statistical Yearbook 2007*, China Statistics Press, P518-520.

industrial sectors. From 1978 to 2006, the employees of the first, second, and third industries had ratios in the total number of domestic employment decreasing from 70.5% to 42.6%, increasing from 17.3% to 25.2%, and increasing from 12.2% to 32.2%. During this period the average annual growth ratios of labour productivities of the first, second, and third industries are 4.1%, 7.4%, and 4.5% separately. The purpose to use these data for demonstration is to explain the optimized distribution of labour resource, the most important factor of social resources after China's reforms and opening to the world. This demonstration does not deny the severely unbalanced industrial structure in China. Secondly, the operational benefits of production factors are increased. For example, the average annual growth ratio of the social labour productivity from 1979 to 2007 after China began reforms is 2.1 times that of 1953 to 1978. Thirdly, opening to the world means, China's external spread of domestic economy reform. Opening to the world is the necessary channel for China to use two kinds of resources (domestic and foreign) and two kinds of markets (domestic and foreign markets). From a certain view the opening to the world is the approach to optimize the distribution of social and production resources worldwide. So opening to the world became an important factor in promoting China's economic development. In fact after reforming, China's opening to the world has advanced the economic development in employment enlargement, tax increase, moderating of contradiction between market supply and demand, moderating of resource and environment pressure, adjustment of industrial structure, and improvement of international competence and promotion of economic reforms. For example, from 1978 to 2007, China GDP had average annual growth ratio at 9.8%, while the average annual growth ratio of foreign trade and imported foreign investment reached 17.4% and 17.1% high. Certainly at present China is challenged with the issues to adjust the scale and to improve the quality of foreign trade and import of foreign investment.

As emphasised before that reform and opening are the driving forces behind China's economic development, but we did not deny other problems in reform and opening, nor did we deny admitting other factors' important functions in promoting economic development. Important factors are: First, factor the effects of technological progress in the times of intellectual economy; second, factor the stage effects for China's being at the mid and later period of industrialisation; third, factor the positive effects of high population and economic giant; fourth, the comprehensive and multi-layer macro-control experiences suitable to the development of modern market economy; fifth, the long-term stable political context; sixth, the long-term international peace. However, maximisation of the effects of these factors at high degree necessitates reform and opening. So from this view we can say that reform and opening to the world are the driving forces behind China's rapid growth.

Technological Reforms: A Case Study of E-Governance in India

S.S. Subrahmanyam

Technology reforms are key to the growth and development of any economy. The history of growth and development of the last 250 year points out that the countries with an advantage in technology had also economic predominance and social advantage. Technology is an omnibus term including in its ambit the technologies ranging from most traditional to the most modern technologies pervading defence, rocket science, bio-technology, nanotechnology, computer and information technology, etc. The e-Governance, an off-shoot of the computer and information technology, provides a connect between science and people and enhances the welfare of the later through rapidity in transactions and savings in time and space.

The successful governance in the country requires a direct dialogue between people and government. The governance has to be simple, moral, accountable, responsive and transparent (SMART). The e-Government sought primarily with a view in cutting the cost of governance in the developed world. Though this has been stated as one of the reasons for developing nations too, it would appear to be lower down the order of priority with savings in cost accruing primarily form process optimization and labour costs in India. E-Governance is emerging as a new tool to establish SMART governance paving the way for the socio-economic transformation of the country, its modernization and integration with the rest of the world. The paper highlights centralization vs. decentralization dimensions in relation to e-Governance and incorporates case studies on e-Governance in Andhra Pradesh which is recognized as the change leader in the country.

1. CONTEXT AND SITUATION

The 21st century is characterized by high level of public awareness, high people's expectations, and technical skills of high order, flexible and adaptable structures and simplified and goal oriented procedures. The institutions of public administration and persons with it cannot endure for longer period without adapting themselves to the changing times. According to Gerald Caiden, 'Unless the administrative system is geared to keep pace with cultural transformation, social discontent, alimentation and violence may ultimately lead to the breakdown of the social fabric'. To be effective and efficient, the public institutions need to shoulder more responsibilities to the changes in the social structures, political need and economic challenges and the key to responsiveness is organizational adaptability to the change. e-Governance promises a plethora of benefits to its citizens by accelerating and automating government-citizen interface and bringing about transparency in government functioning. It is said that 'after e-commerce and e-business, the next in line are internet revolution and e-Governance'.

The successful governance in the country requires a direct dialogue between people and government. The governance has to be simple, moral, accountable, responsive and transparent (SMART). The e-Government sought primarily with a view in cutting the cost of governance in the developed world. Though this has been stated as one of the reasons for developing nations too, it would appear to be lower down the order of priority with savings in cost accruing primarily form process *optimization* and labour costs in India. e-Governance is emerging as a new tool to establish SMART governance paving the way for the socio-economic transformation of the country, its modernization and integration with the rest of the world. The paper highlights centralisation vs. decentralisation dimensions in relation to e-Governance and incorporates case studies on e-Governance in Andhra Pradesh which is recognized as *the change leader in the country*.

Principally, e-Government has the power to improve government processes, connect citizens and build interaction with and within civil societies, all of which are in turn the objectives of good governance itself[1] (Heeks, 2001). The Administrative Staff College of India – Computer Society of India research project offered the recommendations for the culmination of e-Governance in India from information to transformation phase[2] (Bagga, R.K) by ensuring comprehensive implementation of G2G (Government to Government), G2C (Government to Citizens), G2B (Government and Business) and G2E (Government to Employee)

Although India has a leadership position in IT, e-Governance in India has a long way to go. Sadagopan, S, (2006) noted that the UN e-Government Readiness Index 2005, ranks US, Denmark, Sweden, UK, Korea, Australia, Singapore, Canada, Finland and Norway as top 10 nations. India is placed at 87th position among 179 countries.[3] The companion e-Participation Index 2005 of the same UN Survey puts India at 59th position among the 191 nations; UK Singapore, US, Canada, Korea, New Zealand, Denmark, Mexico, Australia and Netherlands being the Top 10 countries. Brazil (18) and China (50) are ahead of India while Russia (62) is behind.

Michiel Backus (2001) investigated the challenges faced by the developing countries. He focused on political, social, economic and technological aspects and analysed them through SWOT. He suggested the implementation of e-Governance through a mix of short-term steps (projects) and long-term goals (vision).[4]

Pre and post computerization effects – Worldwide

Country	Type of government application	No. of days to process before application	Number of days to process after application
Service Center, Bahia, Brazil	Registration of 29 documents	Several days	20-30 minutes per document, one day for business licenses
Chilean Tax system on-line	Filing taxes onlines	25 days	12 hours
Interstate Check Posts, Gujarat	Collect fines for over loading	30 minutes	2 minutes
Mandal computers, AP India	Issues of Caste Certificate	20-30 days	15 minutes
Customs Online Philippines	Release of cargo	8 days	4 hours – 2 days to release cargo
Online-Tax, Singapore	Issue of Tax Assessments	12-18 month	3-5 months
Beijing's Business E-Park, China	Online application for 32 business services	2-3 months for business license. Many visits to multiple offices for filings	10-15 days for business license Several seconds for routine filing for companies

Source: Presented during Annual Bank Conference on Development Economies, 2003.

2. POLICY AND PROGRAMMES

The policy and programme relating to e-Governance of the Government of India and the various state governments have made a great headway during the last ten years. Both the central and state governments are in unison about deepening and widening the applications of e-Governance. The Government of India with the help of the India Informatics Centre under its aegis has taken initiatives for building: e-Governance awareness and commitment, e-Governance strategic capacity, e-Governance implementation capacity, infrastructure for e-Governance implementation, e-Governance pilot projects and evaluation of e-projects. The Ministry of Communications & Information Technology, Department of Information Technology, Government of India, has set up a Centre for e-Governance (CEG) which showcases several e-Governance applications and solutions that have been successfully deployed in various states.

Programmes and Services in Major States

State / Website	Projects names	Services
Delhi http://delhigovt.nic.in	Bhagidari	• Application Forms for certificates Licenses • Apply online Certificates • Environment Health Education • Property tax Birth Certificates • Important Tel. Numbers • DDA Housing Procedures Land • For Weaker sections, women and child and labour welfare • Mandi Rates • Stock Exchange information • Service matters
Gujarat http://gswan.gov.in	Gujarat State Wide Area Network (GSWAN)	• Provides integrated voice, data and video services to the state government departments
Haryana http://haryanait.nic.in	Haryana State Wide Area Network (HARNET)	• Integrated Finance Management • Municipal Corporation • Education Department • Excise and Taxation Department • Government House Allotment • Court cases monitoring system • File Tracking System • Scheme monitoring system • Chandigarh Transport Computerization • E-granthalaya
Kerala http://www.kerala.gov.in	PEARL (Packages for effective Administration of Registration Laws)	• Administration of Registration Laws
	Project GRAMEEN	• Provides education to local citizens about IT
	Sulekha, Sevana and Sanchita	• Computerization of Local Bodies
Rajasthan www.rajasthan.gov.in	Janmitra, Lokmitra and Aarakshi	• Rajasthan State Roadways Transport Corporation, Transport, MIS for secondary Education and Land and Building Tax Departments • Hospital Management Information System • Electoral Rolls, Management Software, Rajasthan Housing Board

e-Democracy, the latest development in the realm e-Governance, is the move very effectively promoted by the central government as a part of which India has used electronic polls in the election for its billion strong population. The election commission used about 8,00,000 electronic voting machines (EVM). The Election Commission has introduced a new method of polling by EVM. This is a simple, safe and secure method that takes minimum time. These machines are easy to handle even by an unlettered villager. This is one of the example of governing by electronic way. The programmes and services of e-Governance in some of the states are given in the table.

The Government of India has started ranking different states of India e-Governance. Sadagopan S, (2006) in his article pointed out that during the year 2004, Karnataka, Tamil Nadu, Andhra Pradesh, Maharasthra, and Chandigarh are in the Leadership position. Kerala, Gujarat, Goa, Delhi, Punjab and Haryana are in the aspiring leaders positions. West Bengal, Pondicherry and MP are in the expectant category and other states are lagging behind.

3. ROLE OF PRIVATE AND RURAL SECTOR PARTICIPATION IN e-GOVERNANCE

A very large number of e-Governance pilot projects are under various stages of development, deployment and improvement. These include Bhoomi, Akshaya, Khajane, e-seva, SARI and Honey-bee Network. Information and Communication Technology (ICT) helps rural households in decision-making relating to production, consumption, operations, marketing and savings. The important initiatives namely Gyandoot, NaiDisha and Drishtee. Warana Project in Maharashtra, though heavily funded initially by the state of Maharashtra and Delhi, is currently funded by the sugar cane cooperatives in the area, and offers tangible benefits to sugar producers and to sugar cane growers in the area. In Nellikuppam, Tamil Nadu - EID Parry funded a project, which expects advantages in terms of improved information to their producers about best agricultural practices. ITC-IBD has set up a series of IT "chaupals" for soya, shrimp and coffee farmers with the goal of reducing the costs of production that currently go to middlemen. The commercial interests may justify the expense of establishing rural info-kiosks, which can also provide much general information in addition to specific product information.

3.1 e-Panchayat

e-Panchayat is introduced in Andhra Pradesh by National Informatics Center of Department of Information Technology. The function of this electronic knowledge based panchayat are birth and death registrations, house tax assessment and collections, trade licenses, old age pensions, works monitoring, financial accounting and all other activities of panchayat administrations are all being executed through this system. This system is being adopted by the states of Haryana, Orissa and Maharasthra. The key challenges faced by the system were to: equip rural areas with technology infrastructure so citizens could conduct web based transactions; facilitate easy access to information and enable e-learning; introduce business to consumer e-government services; improve revenue collection process; encourage self employment; help bridge the digital divide between urban and the rural areas.

3.2 Gyandoot

Gyandoot stands heads and shoulders above the peer projects and most other such projects have their origin in this application. Gyandoot has won several awards. Gyandoot has been implemented in Dhar—a tribal district of Madhya Pradesh by installing computers at 30 panchayats connected through intranet. Local rural youth act as entrepreneurs for running cybercafés called Soochnalayas. Gyandoot project is different from e-Governance initiatives taken elsewhere in that it provides a G2C interface whereas most other projects were oriented towards a G2G interface. The project demonstrated a new model for a more effective, accessible, prompt and transparent model of governance, which benefited not only the citizens but also the government by making the citizen a partner in the process of the governance. The entire cost of setting up Gyanboot network has been borne by panchayats. In Gyandoot complaints and applications reach directly in panchayats in a computerized form and get sorted in organized databases.

3.3 NaiDisha

NaiDisha is a web portal dedicated to citizen services, is an ICT based interface between Haryana Government and its subjects. It stands for new agent of information – district level integrated services of Haryana for all. It is a step towards making government services available to citizens anytime, anywhere via internet. NaiDisha brings state/local government and district administration closer to citizens, as if they are only a mouse-click away from their government and its services. NaiDisha has been developed with 23 types of citizen services. It has been implemented in Panchkula and is being replicated to five more districts in first phase. The application packages include public grievances, public information and facilitation system, payroll, periodic returns transmission systems, postal monitoring system etc.

3.4 Drishtee

A 12 person ICT organization, Drishtee Private Ltd, is one of the very few companies in the world that has become profitable by offering information and communication related services in rural India. Drishtee has successfully launched about a hundred kiosks throughout rural India. Drishtee provides technical expertise and management consultancy to build the information technology infrastructure and the human capacity to link service providers to rural citizens. Previously, villagers were forced to make extended and multiple trips to district authorities to obtain such documents as a marriage license; a copy of a land title or an income, caster and domicile certificate. This process could take months. Now, villagers can file their applications online and often receive the documents within a week, saving considerable time and money.

3.5 e-Governance in Andhra Pradesh

Andhra Pradesh has become a trendsetter and a front– ranking State in e-Governance crusade in India. The www.aponline.in links the various government departments. The state is known for the assimilation of *hi-tech* in its activities. To help its citizens gain one-stop access to government information and services in a secure way and to provide better more efficient transparent and responsive services, the Government of Andhra Pradesh has embarked upon a scheme of e-Government to leverage the tools of ICT for serving its citizens efficiently. The e-Governance projects intended to convert the state secretariat to a paperless, electronic office.

The Government of Andhra Pradesh was quick to recognize the potential for employing Internet communications and web technologies to improve government services in the overall context of speeding up citizen empowerment and economic development. The technologies used included: government portal – common gateway for all state services; secure intranet – communication infrastructure connecting all government office locations; data centre – focal point for hosting all major applications and data of government departments; kiosks (rural areas) – access points for rural locations with implementation under public-private-partnership mode; public key infrastructure – secure transaction over internet and digital signatures implementation under public – private – partnership mode; citizen identity cards – unique identification number for citizens using smart cards and data warehousing – projects implemented jointly with government of India.

The Government of Andhra Pradesh has successfully implemented e-Government projects that have yielded extremely encouraging results. The following are some worth mentioning initiatives:

CARD (Computer-aided Administration of Registration Department): The Department of Registration and stamps is one of the oldest wings of the AP state government in India. It was initially established to administer the Indian Registration Act, affecting citizens property rights and liabilities, and the Indian Stamps Act, which manages the supply, distribution and sale of official registration stamps through sub-registrar offices and licensed stamp vendors. CARD is a simplified procedure for registration of legal documents like sale deeds, mortgage deeds, gift deeds, etc. The involved automation of processes at 239 sub – registrar offices. 2.8 million deeds were registered digitally and 1.4 million title searches and 2.1 million property valuations were done in three years after the launch of CARD.

Features

- Enables employees with minimal technical and IT skills to manage and share documents at 387 sub-registrar offices across the state of Andhra Pradesh
- Ensure fair and speedy provision of all services, including registration, valuation and stamp duty assessment
- Consolidate all citizen profiles into a central database, including data about age family religion land holdings, dwellings, occupation, income and business type
- Track all historical changes made to registered documents such as changes of ownership, transfer of property titles, re-classification, subdivisions, and title mergers
- Expedited registration and the issuing of certificates by developing electronic templates for forms and deeds
- Lessened the time and effort required to search and manage documents by deploying an intuitive graphical user interface
- Reduced fraud and malpractice by providing a transparent method of property valuation and stamp duty calculation.

The following table depicts the pre and post computerization effects of CARD.

Pre and post computerization effects

Aspect	Pre-Computerisation	Post-Computerisation	Effects
Valuation of property	Few days	5 minutes	Less time consuming
Provision Certificate of registered documents	Few days	10 minutes	Less time consuming
Encumbrance certificate	2 – 3 Weeks	5 minutes	Faster delivery of services
Land registration	7-15 days	2-3 hours	Faster delivery of services

(Net revenue increased by 20% due to this system).
Source: IPE research.

3.6 e-Seva

This project operates through 75 outlets in Andhra Pradesh delivering 19 services at one point. These services include among others payments of telephone bills, electricity bills, municipal taxes, drinking water bills, passport fees, driving license fees, purchase of train tickets and bus tickets etc. The e-Seva outlets remain open from 8.00 am to 8.00 pm on working days and 11.00 am to 5.00 pm on Sundays. The bills could be paid in less than five minutes. The e-Seva centers have become a tremendous success because of their convenient location, personal touch and speed of delivering services. The e-Seva counters are managed by Government functionaries run by public/private agencies.

e-Seva Services

	Gender		Services					Bills belong to			Location		Mode of payment			Preferred day	
	Male	Female	Elec. Bill	Water bill	Tele. Bill	Property tax	Others	Own	Acquaintance	Employer's	Office	Residence	Cash	Bank	Credit card	Sunday / holiday	Working day
Sitafalmandi	10		9	9	8	6	1	10				10	10			7	4
Mushirabad	9		7	4	5	2	1	8		2	3	7	7	2		2	7
Greenlands	7	1	7	3	5	1		7	1	1	1	7	6	2		3	5
SR Nagar	14		13	6	4	2		13		1	2	12	15	2	1	11	3
Tirumalgiri	8	5	9	5	9	1		11		2	4	9	10	2	1	6	8
Vijayanagar Colony	7	5	6	5	7	1	1	9	3	1	1	10	6	6	2	5	8
Vamastalipuram	6	2	7	4	4	2	1	7		1		8	6	3		3	4
Habsiguda	20	1	17	7	11	3	1	19	4	3	9	14	17	5		13	11
Total	**81**	**14**	**75**	**43**	**53**	**18**	**5**	**84**	**8**	**11**	**20**	**77**	**77**	**22**	**4**	**50**	**50**

Source: Mishra. R.K. and J. Kiranmai, e-Governance: Challenges ahead, Institute of Public Enterprise, Hyderabad, 2005, Mimeo.

The important facts revealed from the study of e-Seva centers located at eight different locations in the twin cities of Hyderabad are discussed below:

- Male populations paid the majority bills while rushing to office as the center is open since 8.00 am
- Working people preferred to pay bills in the evening rather than morning

- The staff were found to be very courteous with the customers
- The centers were located at a convenient places – near to residences
- All the services are available under one roof.

The following some of the setbacks found:

- Staff are not aware of the technical concepts
- Staff should be further trained
- The gift scheme declared were not implemented.

4. COST ISSUES

NASSCOM in its projection of domestic revenue in software development in 1999 indicated that the highest share in the government sector at 28.40 percent of the total revenue, compared with banking and finance at 15.60 percent. In Maharashtra, e-Governance reduced the costs and saved time spent by employees doing manual work thus by increasing the efficiency of the government significantly (www. worldbank.com). The government has spent more approximately ₹ 100 crore on e-Governance. This expenditure should be viewed in terms of economic benefits that it could bring the common man rather than financial benefits. The joint venture by private organizations with an Indian PSU to provide e-governance and IT services in the state is planned. Nearly 7,000 electronic kiosks would be set up all over the state and the JV would have to maintain Web application servers, system delivery operations throughout the network, develop data warehouses and facilitate government revenue collection.

The Government of Delhi invested about ₹ 1,000 crore on e-Governance initiatives. The planning commission had allocated 2-3 percent of every organization on IT. If the total budget outlay for all industries is ₹ 45,000 crore, 2 percent would be about ₹ 1,000 crore, which is for IT or e-governance.

The Government of Gujarat's Sales tax collection is a new system which has produced three-fold increase in tax collection over 2 years. Revenue increased from US$ 12mn to US$ 35mn, paying back the total project cost of US$ 4mn in just 6 months. On an average, vehicles are cleared in 2 minutes instead of 30 in the manual system. Harassment of truckers continues, abetted by the problems with the video monitoring system. The large and medium transport owners are happy with the system because they can come to know the exact date and time their driver passed the check-post. The pre-paid card means that the driver does not have to carry much money.

5. RESULTS AND EFFECTS

e-Governance has brought about a great transformation in the government – citizen relationship. The scope of e-Governance is widening from this relationship to the Parliament – citizen interface wherein the Parliamentarians could be in direct touch with their electorate and through interactive relationship the electorate could also communicate with the parliamentarians without any obstruction. Some of the results and effects of e-Governance are mentioned below:

- Integration of the departmental activities and synergy in action: the government departments through inter-connection have integrated their activities and have increased the intensity of their action through intra and inter-departmental synergy. The district administration is an important component of public administration in India. The National Informatics Centre (NIC) took up a programme for implementing the All India Satellite - based Government Informatics Network connecting various district collectorates, the state government , secretaries and the central government offices in Delhi. Collectorate – 2000 software was developed for this purpose incorporating subjects such as land, revenue, magisterial functions, directorates, welfare schemes, petitions, government orders and geographic information systems. Whereas Collectorate-2000 has simplified and economized on the government activities, it has resulted in the saving of time and cost on the part of the citizen.

- Improvement in Law and Order: The maintenance of law and order is a crucial problem in India. The police administration has been facing this as an ardent challenge. As a part of e-Governance, Cyber–Cops were configured around a specific set of objectives to meet existing challenges before the police in the country. Through Cyber-Cops, the police administration established connectivity among the different police stations in the districts, introduced videoconferencing, piloted networking among court – jail – district police headquarters and established networking among police stations – central reserve police force - special police battalion. Cyber-Cops has resulted in grievance redressal as through e-mail, fax, etc the police could receive complains and respond to them. Further, it has led to considerable operational convenience.

- Change management: e-Governance entails a paradigm shift in governance. It has led to grass root participation, overcoming misconceptions, inculcating information technology culture, shift of focus from reactive to proactive administration, increased efficiency, enhanced transparency, increased savings and higher morale of the work force.

- Cost optimization, improved service delivery and merger of the identity of the business with the client: e-Governance has brought down substantially the costs of operations, improved the service delivery through reducing the time by process improvements and promoted a better user-provider interface. e-Governance has introduced the flexibility in changing the paradigm of the service delivery and product innovations. It has improved the project management practices.

6. LEARNING FROM INDIA

The Indian model of e-Governance has a lot to tell to the rest of the World. Some of the key findings on e-Governance in India are discussed here below:

- *Direct Ownership vs. use of Information and Communication Technology*: e-Governance in the developed world has succeeded due to direct digital connections to the individual citizens. India citizen direct ownership of information and communication technology is applicable to only a small fraction of small population. A greater number of people have gained access through non-ownership but direct use of information technology. All the government projects at the Central and the state levels are being implemented through non-ownership of digital equipments.

- *Certainty Trough*: The Mackenzie's theory of Certainty Trough talks as to why certain sections of people are more confident about technologies through they are not directly involved with them. The second part of Certainty Trough deals with people who are committed to the popularization of technology. The third part of the Trough concerns people who generate the technology. It is the second part of Trough which has popularized e-Governance in India. These are people involved in civil services which carryout the day-to-day administration of the country. They are large in numbers and wield very great influence.

- *Bottom up Approach*: The Indian approach to e-Governance is based on the bottom up requirements wherein all the related programs have been formulated keeping the needs of common man as the central consideration. That is why citizen services have been brought under the umbrella of e-Governance. The activities of the government having a direct bearing on the masses have also been computerized and networked.

- *PPP Dimension*: e-Governance in India covers a wide gamut of activities and sectors. To intensify e-Governance, it is necessary that PPP makes deep inroads into it. The participation in e-Governance has to go beyond a few non-government organizations and corporate houses. This will result in the mobilization of adequate resources to meet the hardware and software needs of the e-Governance projects.

7. RECOMMENDATIONS

If e-Governance has to take firm roots, it is imperative to resolve certain issues as discussed below:

- *Technology Issues*: e-Governance initiatives would have to address the technology issues by identifying functional areas in every government organization which need to be taken up for e-Governance by identifying the appropriate hardware platforms and software application packages for cost effective delivery of public services, making this knowledge repository widely available through appropriate Demo- mechanisms, offering a basket of these models to the central and states, which could be suitably customized as per location and work specific requirements. This may require amendment in state laws through study and consultation.

- *Management of Change Related Issues*: The issue of management of change, which would have to be quite rapid at times, is the other most fundamental challenge to be addressed by the practice of e-Governance. This would involve delivery of public services like utilities, rural and urban development schemes through Internet and other IT based technologies and would necessitate procedural and legal changes in the decision and delivery making processes as well as institutions; fundamental changes in government decision management; changes in the decision making procedures in terms of decision making levels and delegation of authority; and mandatory changes in legal provisions to give effect to the technology objectives.

- *Funding Issues*: While e-Governance could have very laudable objectives and ambitious work plans, these have to be weighed in terms of available resources both in the plan sector and outside it. It is here that leveraging of ongoing projects can be made more cost and value effective with the use of IT in a modulated fashion without any critical incremental costs. The kiosks by themselves can bring in little in terms of better delivery of services, unless the same are made economically viable and of demonstrated use to the stakeholders, viz the public and the citizenry.

- *Digital Divide Concern*: India is experiencing an interesting phenomenon known as digital divide which separates north from south. The South India has become a hub of information technology. Many global companies are situated in South. A major part of the information technology exports takes place from South. The tele-density, PC and TV penetration is higher in South as compared to North. The IT spending by the state governments and the private sector organizations is also higher in South India. The IT courses have made a great mark both in terms of numbers and enrollment. The use of IT by executive – political and civil – is on ascendancy in South. The condition of the eastern parts of India is even worse than North India. India would do well to remove this digital divide by initiating appropriate policy measures.

8. SUMMARY AND FINAL REMARKS

e-Governance is considered as SMART governance in India. It is being used as a conduit between government and people, non-government organizations and their beneficiaries, enterprise and customers, bank and clients, and rural institutions as providers of service and rural citizenry as user of the service. Whereas it has instilled credibility in the 'government and government like organizations' as an institution, it has also empowered people to ascertain their will relating to several socio-economic and political issues. It has contributed significantly to the reduction of social exclusion and improving social equity. However, several crucial issues are impeding the progress of e-Governance in India including technological, change management, PPP and funding related issues. The experience of states such as Andhra Pradesh and Karnataka very prominently indicates that e-Governance holds a very bright future in India. The corporate sector in India has demonstrated very strongly as to how e-Governance helps it in improving its profits through better cost and effective customer service management. e-Democracy has taken off well in India with the limitations of human bias afflicting the polling teams stationed at the polling booths.

REFERENCES

[1] Heeks, R (2001). Understanding e-Governance for development I-Government Working Paper Series, *Working Paper No.1*, ISBN: 1 902518934. Manchester: University of Manchester.

[2] Bagga, R.K. IT Policies and their implementation in India: The ASCI–CSI Research Project, *ASCI Journal of Management*, Vol. 30 (1&2) March 2001, Hyderabad, p. 20.

[3] Sadagopan, S (2006). e-Governance: A long way to go, *The Economic Times*, February 11, Hyderabad, p. 8.

[4] World Bank: e-Government. Available at: http://web.worldbank.org/ Wbsite/ External/Topics/Extinformationandcommunicationandtechnologies/Extegovern ment/0,,menuPK:702592~pagePK:149018~piPK:149093~theSitePK:702586,00. html. Accessed on August, 10 2006.

SMEs Clusters in India

R.K. Mishra and J. Kiranmai

1. INTRODUCTION

Nowadays, economic activities are moving toward knowledge-intensive business, accompanied by rapid development of technology in globalized economy era. This condition has impact on the tight competition, and rapid change in business environment. Domestic manufacturing products are directly competing with foreign products and business world must accept reality that technology advancement has become a reason on the obsolent production facilities, short product life-cycle, and lower profit margin. To attain the momentum Clusters development initiated. Clusters are geographic concentrations of interconnected companies, specialized suppliers, service providers, and associated institutions in a particular field that are present in a nation or region. Clusters arise because they increase the productivity with which companies can compete. The development and upgrading of clusters is an important agenda for governments, companies, and other institutions. Cluster development initiatives are an important new direction in economic policy, building on earlier efforts in macroeconomic stabilization, privatization, market opening, and reducing the costs of doing business.

Small and medium enterprise clusters has always been the engine of growth and job creation for every country, be it in developed, developing or transition economies. The cluster building creates a sound industrial base amongst developing countries. They, along with micro enterprises, have been identified as high potential sector for employment generation and source of livelihood to millions of people in Asia, Africa and Latin America. The SME cluster dominated the economies of the most developed countries. SMEs are spring boards for technological innovation and entrepreneurship. They also play vital role for engagement of poor skilled manpower. Many developed countries are on their way of industrialization through SME cluster. Japan's SME cluster contributes 55 Million jobs and 52% exports.

A thriving SME cluster is vital to economic growth of India as well. The importance of small and medium enterprises (SMEs) cluster as a pillar of Indian economy cannot be over looked. We cannot depend only on a few large industrial houses for driving our industrialization process. The employment intensive nature and the greater regional spread of SMEs make them attractive option for industrial growth India has nearly three million small and medium enterprises. SMEs account for nearly 50 per cent of India's industrial output and contribute over 30 per cent of exports. They constitute 80 per cent of the total number of industrial enterprises and over 50 per cent of private sector employment. It is the micro-enterprises and SMEs that discover the dynamic comparative advantages of a country. Since the SMEs are an important constituent of the supply chain, it is indeed quite intriguing to know what holds them back from realizing their potential in the international markets. Indeed, they have the potential to become leading business conglomerates of tomorrow. Gaining access to global markets is the key to realizing this potential for high growth. In order to access the international markets they must learn to manufacture quality products and at the same time be cost competitive. China has become the workshop of the world precisely because of its cost competitiveness.

SMEs and Industrial Policies in India: In any country, the domestic policy environment consists of three parts:

- The macro economic environment. Any macro economic instability in a country leads to balance of payments crisis, high inflation and current account deficits and appreciation in exchange rates. Given their small size and limited resources SMEs have fewer options to defend against such instability compared to large firms. Therefore, ensuring macro economic stability is an important way to help Small Enterprises emerge, grow and prosper. This might be the best support a government could give to SMEs.

- Incentive policies: The most important task the policy makers have to perform is creating a level playing environment for SMEs through various incentive policies, to compete and succeed internationally, and

- Institutions: Building institutions and a responsive support structure for SMEs is no less important. The existence of a good legal system and faster dispute settlement mechanism is also of equal importance.

'The strategic objective of Indian Policy Makers, immediately after achieving independence was creation of a self reliant economy and reduction of the high levels of poverty that existed, all within a democratic political framework. In order to achieve these objectives the authorities steadfastly followed a socialist strategy of state-directed, heavy industry-oriented and capital-intensive industrialization complemented by an across-the-board import substitution policy and complex industrial and statutory requirements. Notwithstanding some notable successes, the highly state-centric and interventionist development-policies adhered to during the period of insulation, led to a severely distorted production structure.

The six industrial policy resolutions adopted by the successive Governments at the Centre aimed at promoting industrial growth and determined a pattern of State intervention and assistance. They have setout the guide lines for the country's industrial development. The basic framework for industrialization is provided in the Industries Development and Regulation Act of 1951. Small Scale Industries were given due importance under the provisions of the Act. The Act determined the licensing policies for the sector and the reservation of products for exclusive manufacture by the sector. Promotion of Small Scale Sector has always been an important thrust of India's industrial policy since independence though the priorities changed with each five year plan.

2. CLUSTER DEVELOPMENT IN INDIA

The concept of clusters is not new to India. Clusters have been in existence in India for decades, perhaps centuries, in some cases. According to a Survey conducted by UNIDO in 1996, there were about 350 SSI Clusters in India and approximately 2000 rural artisan- based Clusters in India. Some of these clusters are so big that they contribute about 70 – 80% of Indian output in that particular product. It is estimated that these clusters contribute about 60% of the finished goods exports from India. Notable among these clusters are:

- Panipat in Haryana accounting for 75% of the total blankets produced in India.
- Thirupur, a small township in Coimbatore district of Tamilnadu accounting for 80% of the cotton hosiery exports.
- Agra in U.P. virtually a Footwear City with 800 registered and 6,000 unregistered small and cottage footwear production units, making 1.5 lakh pairs of shoes per day with a production value of 1.3 million dollars per day and exporting shoes worth US 57.14 million per year. (Pl. see' Special feature on Leather and leather goods', The Economic Times, New Delhi, October 21, 1996.
- Ludhiana, well known as Manchester of India, contributes 95% of the country's woolen knit wear, 85% of the country's sewing machines and 60% of the nation's bicycle and bicycle parts,
- The city of Bangalore deserves an explicit reference in its contribution to software sector.

3. INDIAN INITIATIVES

In India, the Small Sector Industries (SSI) has been given a distinct place and plays a crucial role in the process of economic development by value addition, employment generation, equitable distribution of national income, removal of regional disparities, wide dispersion of industries, mobilization of capital, up-gradation of entrepreneurial skills and substantial contribution by way of export earnings. The small scale industries in India present a wide spectrum consisting of tiny, cottage and village industries and modern sunrise industries, i.e., from traditional sector to sophisticated state of the art technology. The enactment of the Small and Medium Enterprises (Development) Act, 2006 and the policy on credit announced in 2005 have, triggered a change in the mindset of small and medium entrepreneurs in India. The new thrust is towards up-scaling the size, finances and technological upgradation. After due consultation with the stakeholders and on the recommendation of the Advisory Committee, the Ministry of Small Scale Industries of Government of India has identified 180 items for de reservation. In order to give a fresh impetus to lending following new initiatives have been envisaged by the Small Industries Development Bank of India (SIDBI). (i) Recognize SMEs in the services sector, and treat the small scale enterprises in the services sector at par with the small scale enterprises in the manufacturing sector; (ii) Raise the corpus of the Credit Guarantee Fund from ₹ 1,132 crore at end-March 2006 to ₹ 2,500 crore in five years. In 2006-07, a sum of ₹ 118 crore was proposed; (iii) Advise Credit Guarantee Trust for Small Industries (CGTSI) to reduce the one time guarantee fee from 2.5 per cent to 1.5 per cent for all loans; and (iv) Extend insurance cover to approximately 30,000 borrowers, identified as chief promoters, under the CGTSI. The sum insured would be ₹ 200, 000 per beneficiary and the premium will be paid by CGTSI.

The National Common Minimum Programme (NCMP) of the present Government draws attention to the fact that in the past few years, the most employment-intensive segment of small-scale industry has suffered extensive neglect. This also states that the SSI sector will be freed from "Inspector Raj" and will be given improved access to credit, technological and marketing support. It also assures small businesses that infrastructure upgradation in major industrial clusters will receive adequate attention. Government of India is proposing to increase the financial assistance to existing clusters of micro, small and medium enterprises up to 80 per cent of their financial requirements during the Eleventh Plan (2007-2012). Financing SMEs linked to large corporates, covering suppliers, ancillary units, dealers etc. would enhance competitive-ness of the corporates as well as the SME participants. There are 25-30 very active and successful NGOs in South India and some other states, which have outstanding record of successful micro credit management. They provide ideal role models for training and development of groups and individuals in other parts of the country. Besides NGOs, there are other successful micro-credit institutions who service small, tiny and individual entrepreneurs in Tamil Nadu, Andhra Pradesh and Karnataka.

Growth of SMEs would be the key to significant growth in GDP as well as in creating employment over time. Small and Medium Enterprises (SMEs) are integral part of the national economy. While globalization is creating new opportunities for them, they are also faced with many difficult challenges. Recognizing the challenges that technology, globalization and market changes will create for SMEs the following need to be focused:

  (i) entire Business Development

 (ii) problem-solving Techniques for SMEs

(iii) Outsourcing Strategies for Small and Medium Enterprises

(iv) Incubators for SMEs

 (v) Supply Chain Management for SMEs

(vi) Cluster Approach for Industrial Development

(vii) Quality Management for SMEs

(viii) Strategic Alliances among SMEs through Technology Fusion.

Government and quasi-government agencies need to do much more to act as facilitators, so as to make SMEs more competitive. While eleven years of liberalization in India have given big businesses much more freedom to operate, still there exist problems for small businesses. While the big can still afford to deal with a myriad of rules and regulations, those whose whole business often comprises only a dozen people (or less) cannot afford to have even one of them tied down in filling forms and "managing" the governmental system.

Micro, Small and Medium Enterprises :-At present, a small scale industrial unit is an undertaking in which investment in plant and machinery, does not exceed Rs.1crore, except in respect of certain specified items under hosiery, hand tools, drugs and pharmaceuticals, stationery items and sports goods, where this investment limit has been enhanced to ₹ 5 crore. Units with investment in plant and machinery in excess of SSI limit and up to ₹ 10 crore are treated as Medium Enterprises (ME). The Government of India has since enacted the Micro, Small and Medium Enterprises Development (MSMED) Act, 2006 which was notified on October 2, 2006. So much so, the Government of India has changed the name of Department of Small Scale Industries to Department of Small and Medium Enterprises. Consistent with the said notification the definition of micro, small and medium enterprises engaged in manufacturing or production and in providing or rendering of services is being modified and is required to be implemented by the banks along with other policy measures.

(a) Enterprises engaged in the manufacture or production, processing or preservation of goods as specified below:

  (i) A micro enterprise is an enterprise where investment in plant and machinery [original cost excluding land and building and the items specified by the Ministry of Small Scale Industries vide its notification No.S.O.1722(E) dated October 5, 2006] does not exceed ₹ 25 lakh;

(ii) A small enterprise is an enterprise where the investment in plant and machinery [original cost excluding land and building and the items specified by the Ministry of Small Scale Industries vide its notification No. S.O. 1722(E) dated October 5, 2006] is more than ₹ 25 lakh but does not exceed Rs.5crore; and

(iii) A medium enterprise is an enterprise where the investment in plant and machinery [original cost excluding land and building and the items specified by the Ministry of Small Scale Industries vide its notification No. S.O. 1722(E) dated October 5, 2006] is more than ₹ 5 crore but does not exceed ₹ 10 crore.

(b) Enterprises engaged in providing or rendering of services and whose investment in equipment [original cost excluding land and building and furniture, fittings, and other items not directly related to the service rendered or as may be notified under the MSMED Act 2006) are specified below. These will include small road and water transport operators (owning a fleet of vehicles not exceeding ten vehicles), retail trade (with credit limits not exceeding ₹ 10 lakh), small business (whose original cost price of the equipment used for the purpose of business does not exceed ₹ 20 lakh) and professional and self employed persons (whose borrowing limits do not exceed ₹ 10 lakh of which not more than ₹ 2 lakh should be for working capital requirements except in case of professionally qualified medical practitioners setting up of practice in semi-urban and rural areas, the borrowing limits should not exceed ₹ 15 lakh with a sub-ceiling of ₹ 3 lakh for working capital requirements).

(i) A **micro enterprise** is an enterprise where the investment in equipment does not exceed ₹ 10 lakh

(ii) A **small enterprise** is an enterprise where the investment in equipment is more than ₹ 10 lakh but does not exceed ₹ 2 crore; and

(iii) A **medium enterprise** is an enterprise where the investment in equipment is more than ₹ 2 crore but does not exceed ₹ 5 crore.

4. SME CLUSTERS IN INDIA

The SME clusters for the following analysis have been chosen and categorized mostly based upon the secondary data available such as write-ups and studies by researchers, judgment of informed persons, each one cross checked and reconfirmed from several possible sources to improve the reliability of information. There may be some limitations or differences in view point. Due to the scarcity of research studies available for most of these clusters, this improvised method of data collection is entirely the responsibility of the researcher with a few possible limitations or differences in view point.

Size and heterogeneity in the cluster network: It has been estimated that there exist about 350 SME clusters in India. These clusters are overwhelmingly predominant with small industries and the share of medium and large industries in the sales turnover, production and employment is nominal. The size in terms of the number of units and the quantum of output of clusters may vary significantly. Some of them are so big that they produce up to 70 to 80% of the total volume of that particular product produced in India. For example, the township of Panipat produces 75% of the total blankets produced in the country. Similarly, Tirupur, a small township in the Coimbatore district of Tamilnadu contributes 80% of the country's cotton hosiery exports. Yet another example would be of the city of Agra, virtually a Footwear City with 800 registered and 6,000 unregistered small and cottage footwear production units, making 1.5 lakh pairs of shoes per day with a production value of 1.3 million dollars per day and exporting shoes worth US $ 57.14 million per year.

State-wise Distribution of SME Clusters: It would be interesting to note that the industrially developed States of Maharashtra, Gujarat, Punjab, Rajasthan, Tamilnadu and Haryana have the maximum number of clusters. The top six industrially developed states account for about 54% of the SSI units and 71% of the clusters are located in them. The common States among them are Gujarat, Punjab, Uttar Pradesh and West Bengal. Surprisingly, the State of Madhya Pradesh which has the maximum number of small scale enterprises (12.7%) as per the Second All India Survey of SSI, seems to have very few clusters (1.4%).

State-wise Distribution of Clusters

Sl. No.	State	No. of clusters
1.	Maharashtra	25
2.	Gujarat	20
3.	Punjab	15
4.	Rajasthan	14
5.	Uttar Pradesh	13
6.	Haryana	12
7.	West Bengal	9
8.	Tamil Nadu	8
9.	Himachal Pradesh	5

Region wise distribution of clusters: Out of 138 clusters, the largest concentration of clusters is in Western India which has 58 clusters and which is closely followed by Northern India wherein 52 clusters exists. The concentration in these two parts of the country can be attributed to the fact that these areas are rich in entrepreneurial talent and are industrially well developed. Also since these parts are agriculturally better developed, they provide a rich base for consumption of goods produced in SSI.

Distribution of Clusters

Sl. No.	Industry group	NIC code	No. of clusters
1.	Machinery & Parts except electrical	35	20
2.	Cotton Textiles	23	15
3.	Chemical & Chemical Products	31	14
4.	Metal Products	34	13
5.	Hosiery & Garments	26	10
6.	Food Products	21, 20	9
7.	Non- metallic Mineral Products	32	9
8.	Electrical Machinery & Parts	36	8
9.	Wool, Silk & Synthetic Fibre Textiles	24	8
10.	Transport Equipment & Parts	37	7
11.	Others 8 Categories	Several	25
	Total		**138**

Rural clusters: Cluster formation in rural areas has taken place for the products where there is less need for infrastructure and supply of raw material. According to the Second All India Census, the number of modern SME clusters that exist in rural areas or small towns are much lesser. One possible reason for this variation can be that the units that have come up in rural areas are small firms which cater to limited local markets that are not significant enough to induce formation of a cluster. The clusters in metropolitan cities are either demand based arising from large population or they cater to export markets or to the large mother units as ancillaries to them. The detailed break up of the locations of these clusters is given as under;

Location-wise Distribution of Clusters

Sl. No.	Location	No. of clusters
1.	City	50
2.	Metro	14
3.	Town	61
4.	Small Town / Rural	13
	Total	**138**

The induced clusters are those where government takes a decision and makes a conscious effort that results in the concentration of similar units in that area. On a close examination, we could classify 125 clusters out of 138 as natural. This means 90.5 7°/s of the clusters that exist in the country have come up on their own. This seems to be in line with the pattern of cluster development at the international level.

Cluster Formation: Induced and Natural

Sl. No	Type of cluster	No. of clusters
1.	Natural	125
2.	Induced	13
	Total	138

5. SME CLUSTER : CHALLENGES AND OPPORTUNITIES

- **Globalization of the financial services industry:** Globalisation and technology are fundamentally changing the financial services industry worldwide. Competition has accelerated and is fierce for "Best Credits"/Corporates in most countries as new competitors entered the market. Margins and fees are narrowing significantly. Development of securities markets is disinter mediating banks. Impact on the domestic Financial Intermediaries (FIs) has been great due to deregulations, mergers, acquisitions, consolidations, global networks/alliances. FIs have the interest to tap new markets but the enabling environment is not friendly for SME finance and FIs lack strategies and skills to tackle impediments associated with SMEs and micro enterprises.

- **SMEs and Economic Development:** SMEs are expected to boost efficiency and growth and lead to economic development because of being engine of job creation, seedbed for innovation and entrepreneurship. SMEs play an important role in promoting growth and development, including for the poor. SMEs are more likely to be able to play important role in economic development in countries with better financial development and low financing constraints, good policies and good institutions like control of corruption, rule of law, property rights, etc.

- **Financial Institutions facing the choice**: In many transition and developing countries, deposit-taking FIs are awash with deposits. For many Governments, the development of SMEs is crucial for economic and social development, but SMEs are perceived as high risk and high cost.

5.1 Constraints Faced by Indian SME Clusters

The Financial constraints faced by Indian SMEs is attributable to a combination of factors that are rooted in :

(a) legal/regulatory framework that makes recovery of bad loans to SMEs, bankruptcy and contract enforcement difficult for creditors;

(b) institutional weaknesses such as the absence of good credit appraisal and risk management/monitoring tools, that increase banks' transaction costs in dealing with SMEs;

(c) Absence of reliable credit information on SMEs, and the lack of sufficient market credibility of the SME sector. This has made a difficult for lenders to assess risk premiums properly, creating differences in the perceived versus real risk profiles of SMEs and resulting in untapped lending opportunities to SMEs.

6. SUPPORT OF GOVERNMENT OF INDIA

In recent years, the Indian Government has taken several steps to support SME financing and development to overcome this situation.

- There has been a welcome shift in focus from "SSI" to "SME" as Government of India announced Rs.100 billion [US $ 2.3 billion] SME Fund operated by the Small Industries Development Bank of India (SIDBI), which is the apex bank for SMEs in India.

- To strengthen the framework for tackling loan defaults and contract enforcement, Government of India has enacted the Securitisation and Reconstruction of Financial Assets and Enforcement of Security Interest (SARFAESI) Act. The Act empowers secured creditors to foreclose and enforce securities in case of default, without intervention of a Court or Tribunal, and has also created an enabling framework for asset reconstruction companies and securitisation in general. A new bankruptcy legislation was enacted in 2003 and Sick Industrial Companies Act (SICA) has been repealed. The challenge is now to ensure the efficient implementation/enforcement of these laws as they apply to SMEs.

- RBI has issued a directive requiring all banks to introduce standardized credit appraisal systems and guidelines. Most public sector banks require upgradation of credit scoring tools for SME loans. The latest scoring tools would help banks better understand, appreciate, and mitigate SME credit risk, making them more confident in lending to the sector.

- Efforts have also been made in recent years by SIDBI and others to improve business development services for SMEs and enhance market linkages, which are critical to ensuring the longer term commercial viability, bank ability of SMEs.

7. CONCLUSIONS

SME sector is expanding. Micro enterprises which have been growing at rapid pace and providing institutional support to the disadvantaged people, are joining the SME sector. This new development will change the SME cluster horizon and call for new approaches and strategies for both financial institutions and the Governments. The facilitating and supporting environment by the Financial institutions and Government authorities through better financing pattern; minimum financing constraints; good governance policies; low inflation; minimum entry level regulation and processing time; good skilled manpower; coupled with transparent processing procedures; least supervisory hurdles; can make SMEs prosper the developing economies. Since from the Government point of view, the development and growth of SMEs are important for economic growth, social development, poverty alleviation, employment generation and technological innovation, there is need for paradigm shift in financial services for SMEs. The shift includes change of mind set of bankers, shift from product focus to customer focus; and shift from just lending to package of financial services.

Policy Restructuring for Industrial Cluster Upgrade in China

Li Jiangtao

Ever since the reform and opening up to the outside world, the industrial clusters, as a modern organisational mode of industrial economy, have played an essential role in the continued growth of the Chinese economy. Having experienced the embryonic, growing and partially mature stages, the industrial clusters are now entering an important turning point on the path to further development. Recently the large-scale retreat of Hong Kong and Taiwan enterprises from Pearl River Delta has exemplified the challenge facing the existing industrial clusters. The question is whether China is able to further upgrade industrial clusters. If the answer is yes, the industrial clusters will enter a new stage of qualitative change by technological and institutional innovation. If the answer is no, the industrial clusters will gradually weaken and finally disappear from the economy. As a matter of fact, as an important organisational form for promoting industrial upgrade and economic growth, the effectiveness of industrial clusters has been proved by economic practices of developed countries. The immature development of industrial clusters in China was caused by multiple factors. Among them, the lagging government policy was a major constraining force. Whether government policy will be restructured directly determines the long-term economic growth when Chinese economy enters a new development stage.

1. GENERAL CHARACTERISTICS OF THE CURRENT DEVELOPMENT OF INDUSTRIAL CLUSTERS

Encouraged by the policy of reforming and opening to the world of 1980s, industrial clusters appeared in East China coastal areas such as Guangdong, Zhejiang, and Jiangsu. China's largest electronic and information industry cluster lies in the famous electronic and information industry corridor of Shenzhen, Dongguan, Huizhou, and Guangzhou at the bank east of the Pearl River. One fourth of 404 towns in the Pearl River Delta have formed typical industrial clusters. Textile of Shaoxing, metal and hardware of Yongkang, leather shoe of Wenzhou, leather of Haining, ties of Shengzhou, low-voltage electric apparatuses of Yueqing, and pen of Tonglu industrial clusters are widespread in Zhejiang, and they are the important production bases for Zhejiang's developing international and domestic markets. Large numbers of industrial clusters have been the major motive force of economic development. The nine major supporting industries formed by industrial clusters in Guangdong contributed over 70% to the gross value of the provincial industrial output. In 2003, Zhejiang had 149 manufacturing industrial clusters with gross value of industrial output of over 1-billion Yuan. Of these 149 clusters, 35 have gross value over 5-billion Yuan, 26 over 10-billion Yuan, and 6 over 20-billion Yuan. The gross value of the output of these 149 manufacturing industrial clusters reaches 1-trillion Yuan, about 52% of the total provincial amount.

As an organisational mode, industrial clusters began to be popular in the whole country because of their increasingly huge contribution to economic growth. Currently the development of industrial clusters in China is generally characterised by the following:

1.1 Regional Distribution from East China Coastal Areas to Middle and West China Areas

As an effective organisational form, firstly industrial cluster has gradually obtained people's acknowledgment and understanding. Industrial cluster became an important approach for economic development in working reports and regional plans of China's central and local governments. Areas of middle and west China began to incubate industrial clusters to become the foundation of sustainable economic growth. High achievements have been obtained. For example, Sichuan Province has incubated 40 or so industrial clusters by 2007. In these industrial clusters 3,236 companies are located. The total sales of these industrial clusters reached 67.14-billion Yuan, harvesting profits of 5.49-billion Yuan, 11.2% of the total sales income of and 16.8% of the gross gains of companies with sales of 5-million-Yuan or above.

1.2 Industrial Up-gradation from Light Industry to Heavy Chemical Industry, High-Tech Industry, and Third Industry

The booming industrial clusters in China are highly linked to the development and changes in people's demand. The desire for "eating and dressing" was the fundamental force for the high-speed economic growth of China during 1980s to 1990s. So China's industrial clusters first appeared in the light industry. More than one half of top-100 industrial clusters are in the light industry category, according to the Industrial Economy Institute of the Chinese Academy of Social Sciences, October 2007.

The development of information technology during 1990s has resulted in the rise of a series of new industries, and a great number of new industrial clusters appeared, for example IT industrial cluster of Haidian District, Beijing, Digital Household Appliance industrial cluster of Mianyang, Sichuan, etc. As the leading industry for

China's economic development at the beginning of this century, the heavy chemical and manufacturing industries formed large numbers of industrial clusters, for example major technological equipment industrial cluster of Deyang, steel industrial cluster of Baoshan, Shanghai, optoelectronic industrial cluster etc. Meanwhile some service industrial clusters emerged, for example finance industrial cluster of Pudong.

1.3 Technical Extension from Labor-Intensive to Capital-Intensive and Technical-Intensive Industries

Most of the early industrial clusters in East China coastal areas are labour-intensive industries or in the labour-intensive phase of high-tech industries, for example socks of Zhuji, Zhejiang; electronic information industry of Dongguan, Guangdong etc. It is urgent for China to upgrade industrial clusters because low-cost clusters have gradually lost advantages in domestic and international markets. The emergence of industrial clusters of heavy chemicals, high-tech, and service industries showed a trend of upgrading of industrial structures. The quality improvement, increased variety, amended process and up-gradation of value chain occurring in the process of further innovation of the existing industrial clusters was reflected in the trend of industries upgrading themselves.

1.4 Leading Role Transferred from the Market to the Government, or to the Combination of the Government and the Market

Most industrial clusters of light industry coexist along with a great number of mid- and small enterprises. The leading role of this type of industrial clusters shall be governed by the market. Recently the government or the combination of the government and the market have increasingly become the leading force of the industrial clusters. Reasons for this situation are: Firstly local governments have the strong impulse to realise rapid GDP growth by industrial clusters for they have become aware of the huge contribution of industrial clusters to long-term economic growth and have a desire to develop economy. Secondly local governments have strong ability for capital domination and resource collection, and high failure risk endurance beneficial for the rapid growth of heavy chemical industry and high-tech industry.

1.5 Reduction of Foreign-Invested Industrial Clusters

The formation of many industrial clusters in Guangdong and Jiangsu during the process of global industrial transfer depended on the incoming foreign investors. The foreign-invested industrial clusters have promoted the rapid growth of regional economy. We should say that recently local strengths are playing a leading role by eclipsing greatly the role of foreign investors in the formation of industrial clusters due to local governments' rich knowledge, reinforced capital domination and ability to raise resources.

2. APPROACHES FOR INDUSTRIAL CLUSTER UP-GRADATION

China has undergone great changes in the 21st century. Firstly China entered the phase of heavy chemical industry. Capital played a role of increased influence in economic growth. The traditional, labour-intensive industrial clusters contribution to economic growth declined. For example, although these years Wenzhou has an economic amount ranking at top prefectures of Zhejiang, by certain view its economic growth ratio ranking at the last one of Zhejiang Province has constrained the provincial economic growth. Secondly many new factors are forcing China to quicken the steps of industrial up-gradation and changes in economic growth style, for example implementation of the new Employment Contract Law, RMB appreciation, and hike of raw material prices have further reduced the originally low gains of enterprises. Moreover, these factors have just begun affect China's economy.

2.1 New Issues in the Development of Industrial Clusters

This new background in China may remain for a long period. Under such a new background, China's industrial clusters show many new issues:

a. The abundance of "gathered but not grouped" clusters

Professor Michael E. Porter has a classic definition of industrial cluster: Clusters are geographic concentrations of interconnected companies, specialized suppliers, service providers, and associated institutes in a particular field (generally with a leading industry) that are present in a nation or region; clusters shall form strong and lasting competence. However, the industrial clusters existing in China are more like an "industrial gathering".[1] Moreover, these industrial clusters lack associated supporting institutes. That is to say, often China's industrial clusters are the gathering of the similar enterprises at a geographic location. These enterprises have no horizontal or vertical industrial relations, and they have no cooperation or competition relationship.

b. Emphasis on the new construction of heavy chemical and high-tech industrial clusters

Local governments attach greater importance to the construction of heavy chemical and high-tech industrial clusters to upgrade industrial structures because it is the main driving force behind regional economic growth; especially the development of heavy

---

[1] A particular case is that local governments saw the large-scale construction of industrial production bases as the incubation of industrial clusters.

chemical industry has brought local governments rapid growth of GDP and huge profits in a short period. The industrial cluster upgrade driven by industrial strengthening shall have a strong and lasting impact. Moreover, local governments shall undergo the high risk of failures. Therefore, local governments have almost no desire for the industrial cluster upgrade though industrial strengthening approach.

c. "Importing Investment" mode

Obviously it is not appropriate for independent market-oriented development of industrial clusters in different areas, for these areas are competing intensively. Therefore, most local governments used the traditional "importing investment" mode to quicken the formation of industrial clusters. The "importing investment" mode may incur some negative effects. The idea of "importing investment" is to realise rapid GDP growth in a short period. Therefore, local governments may import investment for they see it as an excellent tool for GDP growth. Meanwhile often "importing investment" is the political task of government officers. A negative result is that the imported enterprises have no interconnections to form real industrial clusters. The "importing investment" mode depends upon favours from government policy, not specialized division, cooperation and competition, market discovery, or geographic and brand advantages of true industrial clusters etc. The industrial clusters favoured by government policies shall have eclipsed market competence. Moreover, it is impossible to form clusters if local governments attach importance to the import and cultivation of big enterprises and projects while neglecting the development of mid- and small enterprises and projects that are ancillary to the big enterprises and projects.

d. The unbalanced development of public utilities

Associated institutes of finance, scientific research, information, consultation, labour market, laws, accounting, and auditing are the prerequisites for the existence of industrial clusters. However, local public utilities of education, medical treatment, social security, and infrastructure are significant considerations for the aggregation of associated institutes in addition to the development potential of the major industries. An area with undeveloped public utilities shall be hard to attract talented people into associated institutes, resulting in the low service quality of associated institutes, or even their absence. Particularly in China multiple factors of history have made sharply unbalanced availabilities of public utilities in urban and rural areas. China's high-level colleges, universities, research institutes, and medical treatment providers are crowded in a few big cities such as Beijing, Shanghai, Guangzhou, Xi'an, and Chengdu etc. This unbalanced state of China's public utilities cannot be changed in a short period. This shall constrain the formation of sustainable local industrial clusters to a great extent.

2.2 Industrial Cluster Up-gradation

a. Industrial upgrade and industrial cluster upgrade

Recently China has realised the urgent need to quicken industrial upgrade and industrial cluster upgrade because for investors from Hong Kong, Taiwan, and South Korea have withdrawn from East China coastal areas on a large scale. It is necessary to probe into new approaches for industrial upgrade and industrial cluster upgrade at once. Here we shall distinguish the two conceptions.

In the author's opinion industrial upgrade includes two aspects: Firstly, the evolution of industrial structure. Industrial structure means the interconnections and numerous relationships among different industries. Industrial upgrade by the evolvement of industrial structure means that different industries are rational and highly dynamic in domestic economic structure. This view of industrial upgrade is based on the time and geographic context of industries of different kinds. Secondly, the strengthened development of industry, means that in the context of international divisions, a country carries out the finish-processing and technology-intensive development through gradual development of all industries in general or through strengthening of a particular industry. Such industrial upgrade is expressed forms of increased product variety, quality improvement, increased process level, and amended value chain phases. This view of industrial upgrade is based on the existence of the same industry at different times and geographic locations.

Industrial upgrade, the industrial cluster upgrade mainly means lengthening of the lifecycle of industrial clusters by strengthening industry and innovation. So the future industrial upgrade of East China coastal areas may include: a) Eliminate some industrial clusters that have severely blocked the way of industrial strengthening and innovation; b) Stimulate and encourage the upgrade of those industrial clusters that can lengthen their lifecycle by industrial strengthening and innovation; c) Build completely new industrial clusters, for example modern service industrial cluster, and high-tech industrial cluster at high-end phase etc. Most industrial upgrades of Middle and West China areas are of the later two varieties.

b. Approaches for Industrial Cluster Upgrade

In the future the industrial upgrade of Southeast China coastal areas[2] may face the following difficulties: The upgrade of industrial clusters and the construction of new industrial clusters must be successful while eliminating some industrial clusters; else this area shall suffer the high risk of economic depression from industry hollowing out. However, history shows that it is very probable that the upgrade of industrial clusters and the construction of new industrial clusters shall fail.

---

[2] Middle and west China areas have much lower risks of industrial upgrade for they are focusing on the new construction of industrial clusters.

The core of industrial strengthening and innovation is technical innovation. Theoretic analysis shows that clusters have the ability to create networked technical innovations by specialised divisions, cooperation and competition, and the disclosure and sharing of information and knowledge. However, the development of China's industrial clusters gave us a contrary answer. Why? In the author's opinion at least the following facts caused the weakened innovating ability of China's industrial clusters. a) China's industrial clusters are still at the primary development stage; most clusters are focusing on obtaining external scale benefits; their products are focusing on processing or assembly, or simulation without differentiation, and their competencies lie in low cost and low prices. b) There is no healthy interactive relationship among enterprises in industrial cluster, or between enterprises and associated institutes, especially scientific research institutes; no official or non-official public mechanism beneficial for industrial strengthening or innovation is available. c) The intellectual property system and trade credit system are incomplete, and enterprises shall bear too high trade costs. d) Government has no sufficient investment to conduct innovation encouragement, and healthy public service and technical platform are not available.

We must say that it may be long and quite difficult for China's existing industrial clusters to realise cluster upgrade based on the market-oriented networked technical innovation system. A more realistic approach is to use the dual-driver mode wherein to adapt to the changes of market demand in a long period, the government plays an active role in establishing innovation- encouraging policies, adding R&D investment, constructing public service and technical platform, amending mechanism and rules, and cultivating innovative spirit and culture. In the dual-driver mode "market directs innovations and government conducts the innovation platform".

2.3 Restructuring Policy System for Industrial Cluster Upgrade

a. Defects

We shall admit that the policy may be the first tool for the primary development of industrial clusters, because on the one hand a favourable policy for industrial cluster means government's approval, full understanding, and firm support to the development of industrial clusters, and on the other hand government provides or will provide particular and feasible behaviour warranty and security for the multiple-aspect development of industrial clusters. However, the current policy of China's industrial cluster has many defects.

b. General insufficiency at state level

Currently the state level policies encouraging the development of industrial clusters are only shown in the demand of the "Eleventh Five-year" Plan to develop industrial cluster and Some Opinions on Promoting the Development of Industrial Clusters issued by the National Development and Reform Commission in 2007. Defects of these policies are: cursory description, no detailed measures dealing with finance, money, and regional planning, and focusing on mid- and small enterprises' industrial cluster.

c. Most policies of local governments are still on taxation and land aiming at "importing investment"

Most areas are still insisting on favourable policies for taxation and land, except for the issue of opinions or planning by few regions such as Guangdong, Jiangsu, Zhejiang, Fujian, and Hebei specially for the promotion of industrial cluster development

d. No policy for encouraging industrial strengthening and innovation

China has no policy for industrial upgrade by industrial strengthening and innovation in industrial clusters, nor it has a systematic policy for promoting industrial strengthening and innovation in the domestic economy as a whole, for there is no systematic research for industrial development theory distinguished from industrial strengthening and innovation available in China.

e. Replace "industrial cluster policy" by "industrial policy"

The purpose of industrial mainly policy is to develop major industries in certain period by some intended favourable policies, protecting industries unequipped with competence at market by prior allocation of resources.[3] This means that industrial policies are a kind of supply policy that they may constrain competition – industries enjoying favourable policies may lose their competence because of the excessive protection. As the combination and extension of industrial policies, technological policies, and regional development policies, industrial cluster policies are to promote and realise the healthy development of industrial clusters capable of containing all industries in domestic economy. Therefore, it is necessary to make industrial cluster policy independent of industrial policies. However, Chinese government is using "industrial policies" as "industrial cluster policies" for the unclear theoretical research and theoretical knowledge, resulting in frequent occurrences of a great number of cases such as "gathered but not grouped" and "replacing industrial clusters by regional leading industry".

2.4 Industrial Cluster Policies in Developed Countries

Most developed countries have made effective cluster policies to solve the market malfunction and system malfunction of industrial clusters, optimised the drive

---

[3] These industries may be major industries to be developed, or industries suffering depression.

mechanism of clusters, improves clustering environment, and made most out of the industrial clusters. Moreover, their policies became systematic and institutionalised because of long years of practice that caused qualitative jump.

American government defines itself as servant to the clusters of computer, communications, and biological technology in Silicon Valley. The active policies featuring long-term interaction and cooperation with educational institutes and industrial society, including policy for military goods public procurement, policy for civil application of national defense high-tech, migration policy, employment policy, policy for free international trade, and environment policy, have been the classic cluster policy mode to be simulated by countries around the globe.

Japan set its industrial cluster policy in year 2001, aiming at building networked environment of enterprises to promote the development of an environment favouring enterprise innovation. Japan issued two action plans: One is the "industrial cluster plan" prepared and implemented by the Ministry of Economy, Trade, and Industry; another is the "intellectual cluster plan" prepared and implemented by the Ministry of Education, Culture, Sports, Science and Technology. The former plan launched 19 projects of industrial cluster; the later plan launched 10 projects of industrial cluster. During the process of project implementation, the government furnishes overall financial support from technological development, cross-industry cooperation, managerial innovation, R&D, market cultivation, enterprise and incubator establishment etc. Moreover, the Ministry of Economy, Trade, and Industry changed its internal organisational structure and working style, making efforts to build a new networked innovation environment by nine "regional economic and industrial teams" serving enterprises throughout Japan.

OECD made cluster policy with an R&D focus based on national innovating system. For example, in Denmark enterprises, associated organisations, and the government by relative reference groups interactively communicate with each other and through prerequisites of significant cluster policies established co-research centre in information technology, biological technology, and medical and pharmaceutical technology sectors, implement new educational plan in transport sector, and start "industrial networked cooperation project" to furnish financial services to more than 300 enterprises. From 1990s, the industrial cluster policies of Finland are expressed by: Allocate research fund to end users based on competition; implement research plan in strategy sector and enlarge research centre in universities; launch cluster plans of communications, food, transport, environment, and forestry to promote the innovation cooperation among technological organisations, industry, and government. Sweden by its innovating system VINNOVA issued national projects and plans to favour the scientific and technological incubating centre for industrial clusters. The governmental industrial system and plan aim at stimulating talks between industries and other stakeholders. The launched projects are for the development of new industrial clusters and the establishment of framework suitable for single cluster. Meanwhile government conducts prospective seminars on the active development of technology for potential innovating clusters.

2.5 Restructuring of policy system for industrial cluster upgrade in China

As stated above, industrial cluster is not only an important organisational form of industrial development, but also a major approach for the development of regional economy. The functional region planning under preparation shall have profound influence on the regional economic development of China in the long run. Industrial clusters have a more evident function on economic development in the context of major functional regions. So the policy system for industrial cluster upgrade in China shall be restructured under the new regional economic development planning to lengthen the lifecycle of the existing industries and to avoid industrial hollowing out to realise long-term economic growth in China.

1. Strengthen system of reform to innovate China's traditional decentralised and separate technical innovation systems.
2. Build industrial cluster policy system at national level to form networked technical innovation system, including national strategy and planning for industrial clusters, technological innovations, policy for taxation, finance, human resource and capital, and public procurement etc.
3. Prepare policies encouraging infrastructure construction, and rebuild public service platform and public technology platform.
4. Design and incubate agencies.
5. Prepare plans for cultivating innovating cultures, build open and innovative social capital, and reinforce fair competition.
6. Establish cross-regional coordinating mechanism for industrial cluster upgrade.
7. Endow local governments with rights to probe into new mode for industrial cluster upgrade.
8. Establish industrial cluster statistics and analysis information systems.

Financial Sector Reforms

J. Kiranmai

In the Indian financial system, the banking system occupies a predominant position and it has come a long way to grow into a mature and stable banking system at present. The nationalization and subsequent massive expansion of bank branches provided the much needed fillip to banking habits of the population; extension of bank credit formed an important element of the massive programme of poverty eradication. The Government used bank resources for funding its large public expenditure. The large pre-emption of bank resources which at one point exceeded 63%, led to automatic monetisation of fiscal deficit. Total regulation of interest rates which were more often pegged at artificially low levels, prescription of credit ceilings and directed credit programmes led to "financial repression" and distortions in allocation of resources.

As a result, banks came to work under a protective environment. In the absence of transparency in their operations, banks booked incomes which were not realized; profitability was relegated to the background and banks were saddled with assets of poor quality. Eventually, as the costs became unsustainable, some of the banks started incurring losses and accumulated them even to the extent, of wiping away their entire net worth.

In 1990-91, the Indian economy faced unprecedented external crisis arising out of macro-economic imbalances. The resolution of the imbalances was attempted through the twin process of stabilization in the short-term and structural reform over the medium and long-term.

Although attempts were made earlier to bring about changes in the financial sector, a cohesive strategy for reforms came about with the report of the Narasimham Committee (1991). The broad aim of the reform process was clear. With the gradual opening of the economy, financial sector cannot be kept in isolation. Accordingly, a movement from financial repression to liberalisation had to be achieved through a shift from an inventiononist approach to market-based mechanisms. This was to lead to improvement in operational efficiency, i.e. reduction in costs of financial inter-mediation and allocational efficiency, i.e. allocation of resources to the best possible uses.

This paper proposes to look into the banking sector reforms concerning prudential norms, asset liability match, bank supervision, technologisation, productivity of the banking system, competition, internationalization, regulation and portfolio transfor-mation during the period of economic reforms.

1. INTRODUCTION

Since the initiation of reforms in the early 1990s, the Indian economy has achieved high growth in an environment of macro economic and financial stability. The period has been marked by broad based economic reform that has touched every segment of the economy. These reforms were designed essentially to promote greater efficiency in the economy through promotion of greater competition.

The main objective of the financial sector reforms in India initiated in the early 1990s was to create an efficient, competitive and stable financial sector that could then contribute in greater measure to stimulate growth. Concomitantly, the monetary policy framework made a phased shift from direct instruments of monetary management to an increasing reliance on indirect instruments. However, as appropriate monetary transmission cannot take place without efficient price discovery of interest rates and exchange rates in the overall functioning of financial markets, the corresponding development of the money market, Government securities market and the foreign exchange market became necessary. Reforms in the various segments, therefore, had to be coordinated. In this process, growing integration of the Indian economy with the rest of the world also had to be recognised and provided for.

The financial sector reforms since the early 1990s could be analytically classified into two phases. The first phase was aimed at creating an efficient, productive and profitable financial sector which would function in an environment of operational flexibility and functional autonomy. In the second phase, which started in the mid-1990s, the emphasis of reforms has been on strengthening the financial system and introducing structural improvements.

The main objective of banking sector reforms was to promote a diversified, efficient and competitive financial system with the ultimate goal of improving the allocative efficiency of resources through operational flexibility, improved financial viability and institutional strengthening. The reforms have focused on removing financial repression through reductions in statutory pre-emptions, while stepping up prudential regulations at the same time. Furthermore, interest rates on both deposits and lending of banks have been progressively deregulated.

As the Indian banking system had become predominantly government owned by the early 1990s banking sector reforms essentially took a two pronged approach. First, the level of competition was gradually increased within the banking system while simultaneously introducing international best practices in prudential regulation and supervision tailored to Indian requirements. In particular, special emphasis was placed on building up the risk management capabilities of Indian banks while measures were initiated to ensure flexibility, operational autonomy and competition in the banking sector. Second, active steps were taken to improve the institutional arrangements including the legal framework and technological system. The supervisory system was revamped in view of the crucial role of supervision in the creation of an efficient banking system.

The banking system's wide reach, judged in terms of expansion of branches and the growth of credit and deposits indicates continued financial deepening as shown in Table 1. The population per bank branch has not changed since the 1980s and has remained at around 16,000.

Table 1: Progress of Commercial Banking in India

S. No	Items	1969	1980	1991	1995	2000	2005
1.	No. of Commercial Banks	73	154	272	284	298	288
2.	No. of Bank Offices Rural and semi-urban bank offices	8262 5172	34594 23227	60570 46550	64234 46602	67868 47693	68339 47491
3.	Population Per Office ('000s)	64	16	14	15	15	16
4.	Per Capita Deposit (₹)	88	738	2368	4242	8542	16699
5.	Per Capita Credit (₹)	68	457	1434	2320	4555	10135
6.	Priority Sector Advances @ (Per cent)	15	37	39	34	35	40
7.	Deposits (Per cent of National Income)	16	36	48	48	54	65

Source: Reserve Bank of India.

The major reforms that have taken place in the banking sector includes:

1. Prudential Measures
2. Capital Adequacy
3. Structure Regulation
4. Reduction in Statutory Pre-Emptions
5. Deregulation Of Interest Rates

6. Financial Supervision
7. Risk Management.

2. PRUDENTIAL MEASURES

Before the reform process, the banks were booking incomes on accrual basis and to the extent banks were booking incomes which were unrealised, their balance sheet was overstated. Therefore, the initial reform measures centered on cleansing the balance sheet of banks.

This was achieved by implementation of internationally followed prudential accounting norms according to which assets have to be classified into 4 categories viz., Standard, Sub-standard, Doubtful and Loss. Further, income recognition from loan assets should be on realised rather than accrual basis. Other than standard assets, the rest are treated as non-performing (NPA) and no interest should be charged to or taken into account from these assets.

Depending upon the classification, provisioning is made ranging between 10 to 100%. While initially, the prudential norms were liberal, gradually the rigours of asset classification have been made more stringent. RBI has also proposed to gradually more towards to internationally adopted norm of 90 days compared to the existing 180 days for NPA recognition.

Gross NPA of public sector banks at the end of March 2001 is estimated at over ₹ 54,700 crore or 13% of gross advances. However, the level of NPAs in the Indian banking industry should be seen in the light of a larger overhang arising out of historical reasons and non-availability of means for quick recovery of dues from non-performing loans

To facilitate quick recovery of non-performing advances, the government has established Debt Recovery Tribunals (DRTs). So far, 22 DRTs and 5 Appellate Tribunals have been constituted and 7 more have been proposed. At the end of March 2001, out of over 47,000 cases pending before the DRTs, over 62% of the cases relate to public sector banks. However, of the total claims of public sector banks, the Tribunals have settled only about 4% at the end of March 2001. Thus, the effectiveness of the DRTs has been far from adequate.

Another important step for resolving' the NPAs, has been, the implementation of Settlement Advisory Committees (SACs) for negotiated settlement with defaulting borrowers of up to ₹ 5 crore. The, scheme generated good response and reports indicate that the banks have been able to recover more than ₹ 2000 crore of their dues. However, it should be noted that these forms of debt forgiveness, if extended for longer time could result, in"moral hazard", thereby 'exacerbating 'rather than 'containing the level of NPAs. Recognising this, the scheme was closed in June *2001*. The suggestion of the Narasimham Committee for setting up Assets Reconstructions Company (ARC) is still in its infancy stage.

Table 2 shows that the overall capital position of commercial banks has witnessed a marked improvement during the reform period.

Table 2: Distribution of Commercial Banks according to Risk-Weight Capacity Adequcy

(Number of Banks)

Year	Below 4 per cent	Between 4-9 per cent *	Between 9-10 per cent@	Above 10 per cent	Total
1995-96	8	9	33	42	92
2000-01	3	2	11	84	100
2004-05	1	1	8	78	88

*: Relates to 4-8 per cent before 1999-2000
@: Relates to 8-10 per cent before 1999-2000
Source: Reserve Bank of India.

3. CAPITAL ADEQUACY

The ownership of public sector banks by the government has acted as a pillar of confidence even though some banks reported losses after the implementation of prudential accounting norms. In a deregulated environment, there is a vital need to link risk-exposure with capital funds. Following the Narasimham Committee recommen-dations, banks were required to attain a capital-to-risk assets ratio of 8%, which was later raised to 9% to be achieved by March 2000. Moreover, banks have also been required to assign risk weight of 2.5% on government securities and open positions in forex, beginning March 2001 to arrive at the level of regulatory capital to be maintained.

An amendment to the State Bank of India Act, 1955 and the introduction of the Banking Companies (Acquisition and Transfer of Undertaking) Amendment Bill, 1994 were made. As per these changes, the paid-up capital of banks can be raised through public issue of shares. The ultimate objective is to disinvest government holding upto the prescribed level. Towards this, the government has already announced that it would reduce its shareholding to 33% while keeping the public sector character unchanged.

4. STRUCTURE REGULATION

Structural regulation broadly refers to norms relating to entry of new banks, licensing of branches, etc. nine such private banks were established (with a merger between

HDFC Bank and Times Bank, the number now stands at eight) including those by some of the public sector financial institutions. In consonance with the objective of enhancing efficiency and productivity of banks through greater competition from new private sector banks and entry and expansion of several foreign banks there has been a consistent decline in the share of public sector banks in total assets of commercial banks. nothwithstanding such transformation, the public sector banks still account for nearly three-fourths of assets and income. Public sector banks have also responded to the new challenges of competition, as reflected in their increased share in the overall profit of the banking sector. This suggests that, with operational flexibility, public sector banks are competing relatively effectively with private sector and foreign banks. public sector bank managements are now probably more attuned to the market consequences of their activities. Shares of India private sector banks, especially new private sector banks established in the 1990s, in the total income and assets of the banking system have improved considerably since the mid-1990s as shown in Table 3.

Table 3: Bank Group-wise shares: Select Indicators

(Percent)

Banks	1995-96	2000-01	2004-05
Public Sector Banks			
Income	82.5	78.4	75.6
Expenditure	84.2	78.9	75.8
Total Assets	84.4	79.5	74.4
Net Profit	−39.1	67.4	73.3
Gross Profit	74.3	69.9	75.9
New Private Sector Banks			
Income	1.5	5.7	11.8
Expenditure	1.3	5.5	11.4
Total Assets	1.5	6.1	12.9
Net Profit	17.8	10.0	15.0
Gross Profit	2.5	6.9	10.7
Foreign Banks			
Income	9.4	9.1	7.0
Expenditure	8.3	8.8	6.6
Total Assets	7.9	7.9	6.8
Net Profit	79.8	14.8	9.7
Gross Profit	15.6	15.7	9.0

Source: Reserve Bank of India.

Table 4 shows the efficiency gains which reflects in the operating expenditure as a proportion of total assets. This has been achieved in spite of large expenditures incurred by Indian banks in installation and upgradation of information technology and, in the case of public sector banks, large expenditures under voluntary pre-mature retirement of nearly 12 per cent of their total staff strength. Intermediation costs of banks in India still tend to be higher than those in developed countries. Similarly, the cost income-ratio (defined as the ratio of operating expenses to total income less interest expense) of Indian banks has shown a declining trend during the post reform period. Indian banks paid nearly 45 per cent of their net income towards managing labour and physical capital in 2004 as against nearly 72 per cent in 1993. Indian banks thus recorded a net cost saving of nearly 27 per cent of their net income during the post reform period.

Table 4: Earnings and Expenses of Scheduled Commercial Banks

(Rs. Billion)

Year	Total assets	Total earnings	Interest earnings	Total expenses	Interest expenses	Establishment expenses	Net interest earnings
1969	68	4 (6.2)	4 (5.3)	4 (5.5)	2 (2.8)	1 (2.1)	2 (2.5)
1980	582	42 (7.3)	38 (6.4)	42 (7.2)	27 (4.7)	10 (1.7)	10 (1.8)
1991	3275	304 (9.3)	275 (8.4)	297 (9.1)	190 (5.8)	76 (2.3)	86 (2.6)
2000	11055	1149 (10.4)	992 (9.0)	1077 (9.7)	690 (6.2)	276 (2.5)	301 (2.7)
2005	22746	1867 (8.2)	1531 (6.7)	1660 (7.3)	866 (3.8)	491 (2.2)	665 (2.9)

Source: Reserve Bank of India.
Note: Figures in brackets are ratios to total assets.

5. REDUCTION IN STATUTORY PRE-EMPTIONS

Cash Reserve Ratio (CRR) and the Statutory Liquidity Ratio (SLR) are the reserve requirements and are part of the instruments of monetary control by the RBI. With the government's fiscal deficit remaining at high levels over the years, these pre-emptions were used to fund government's public expenditure, while at the same time the rate of return for the banks was low. These pre-emptions were progressively increased over a period of time and by 1991 these two ratios put together reached as high as 63.5%. Such high levels of pre-emptions of bank's resources had the deleterious effect of automatic monetistion of fiscal deficit, high inflation, crowding-out private sector demand for credit and seriously eroding the profit position of public sector banks.

As part of the reform process, the RBI has targeted to reduce SLR and is moving towards this end in phases. At present, the SLR stands reduced to 25% of DTL which is their minimum level as per the Banking Regulation Act. Similarly, CRR will be reduced to 5.5% in 2 years. The objective of reduction in these reserve requirements is to release additional resources for the banks which could be profitably deployed in lending. At the same time, government has moved towards raising its resources at market-related interest rates, with the result the yield on government paper has shown improvement. To facilitate the development of a government paper market and money market, RBI has introduced various structural measures.

6. DEREGULATION OF INTEREST RATES

Banks have been given freedom to fix the interest rates, depending upon the risk-perception of the loan. For this, banks are to evolve a Prime Lending Rate (PLR) which will be the rate offered to the first-class clients of the banks and peg the interest rates to be charged for other borrowers to this base rate. Banks have been required to declare the maximum spread they earn over the PLR. Loans in the ₹ 25,000–₹ 2 lac category are to be charged at PLR.

More recently, keeping with international practice, RBI has provided freedom to banks to provide loans at sub-PLR rates to exporters and other credit worthy borrowers. Thus, lending rates have been deregulated for all loans and advances excepting those under Differential Rate of Interest (DRI) scheme, export credit and advances up to ₹ 2 lac. Banks have also been permitted to announce their Prime Term Lending Rate (PTLR) for term loans over ₹ 2 lac.

In "respect of deposit rates also, "interest rates have been mostly deregulated with banks given freedom to determine interest rates on term" deposits of all tenors. Interest rates on saving deposits, however, continue to be regulated and this is also expected to be deregulated eventually.

Thus, the process of deregulation of interest rates has been more or less achieved. The deregulation process during the last decade has provided valuable lessons to banks, particularly in regard to the cost consciousness in resource mobilisation.

7. FINANCIAL SUPERVISION

With deregulation, the supervisory role of the Reserve Bank of India has been enhanced. A Department of Supervision (DoS) headed by a Deputy Governor has been established. The DoS has been entrusted with the task of supervising the banks and other non-banking financial companies. A process of rating banks on the CAMELS (Capital Adequacy, Management, Earnings, Liquidity and Systems) format has been put in place.

Keeping with the shift towards prudential regulation, emphasis is being laid on off-site supervision which will supplement on-site supervision. The off-site supervision system comprises 12 returns focusing on the different supervisory concerns.

8. RISK MANAGEMENT

With the progressive deregulation, risk management has assumed paramount importance. The Reserve Bank of India has issued guidelines to banks to introduce system of Asset-Liability Management (ALM) to address market risks like interest rate risks, exchange rate risk, etc. Although, this is in its infancy, the ALM system is expected to stabilise quickly and the introduction of risk hedging instruments like interest rate swaps, etc. are facilitating the process.

From March, 2001, banks are also annexing the balance sheet of their subsidiaries so that a gradual move towards consolidation of balance sheet could be made.

The first phase of India's financial reforms highlighted above may be termed as "Curative" inasmuch as they were addressed to the issue of cleansing the balance sheet of banks and putting them on a recovery path. The second generation reforms will be "Preventive", aimed at building a strong and robust banking system which can withstand the pressures of globalisation.

The broad tenor of the recommendations of the second Narasimham Committee (1998) is to move towards universal banking. This view has also been echoed by the RBI also. The opening of the Indian insurance sector will usher in bank assurance.

As part of rationalisation of manpower in public sector banks, the Narasimham Committee has suggested scheme for voluntary separation. Following the government's encouragement, public sector banks have implemented the Voluntary Retirement Scheme (VRS). This has been a major step as this was one of the most. contentious issues facing the banking industry. Nearly 1 lac employees of banks, constituting about 11 % of the total staff strength have accepted VRS, the severance package has been estimated to cost over ₹ 10,000 crore.

With interest rates moving southwards, banks will have to learn to work with leaner staff and thinner margins. Banks should also ensure that due to shortage of manpower, the quality of customer service does not suffer. In balance, it appears that VRS could at best provide a partial solution to the issue of reduction in intermediation costs as banks which are burdened with a backlog of NPAs will not be in a position to cut interest rates to the desired extent.

But by far, the most challenging task before banks in the post-VRS situation will be changing the mind-set of employees to face the competitive pressures. This will call for thorough reorientation of the HR initiatives in the banks. The HR strategy, inter alia, will have to deal with career path, provision of incentives for better performance, training in areas like risk management, technology, marketing, relationship management, etc. In other words, employees should be able to adopt a commercial orientation to business so that they can service existing clients well and recruit new customers.

The reduction of manpower could also give a push to the use of technology. Public sector banks have been relatively late entrants in respect of technology, with the result, their level of technology absorption has been low. However, recognising the need for using IT, the banks have gone for large scale computerisation of branches in a rapid pace. Almost all the public sector banks have been able to capture 70% of their business through computerisation.

In fact, technology is credited with 'ending geography', as funds today flow in a seamless world. In fact, unbundling of risks has become possible by use of technology-based solutions, a task which derivatives perform. As the process of deregulation is pursued and structural barriers are lowered, new opportunities will emerge. But in every opportunity, there is an inherent risk as well. Banks cannot perform in a competitive environment unless there are means of mitigating the inherent risks. Derivative instruments like swaps, options, futures, etc. enable such risk mitigation. As the Indian financial market moves towards more sophistication, some of these instruments have emerged as in the case of interest rate swaps, futures, etc. Securitization is in its infancy. But there is a need for more such instruments considering globalisation of the corporate sector and as the Indian economy integrates with the world economy. Acquiring the skills to offer such products will pose a major challenge to the public sector banks. Development of full-fledged GTC markets will take some time till the structural rigidities in the financial markets are addressed.

At the retail level, public sector banks will have to make further inroads into electronic banking. It could be through card-based mechanisms like stored-value products (Smart Cards), interest-based banking, telebanking, remote banking, etc. This will lead to innovative technology-based products and services.

As the Indian banks move gradually towards universal banking and as they position themselves as financial service providers; banking business is getting redefined. Technology is unsetting the earlier business processes and customer behaviour is undergoing change. To survive under these conditions, the public sector banks will have to undertake business process reengineering, redefine their strategy and align their organisation structure. They have to understand their core competencies and dovetail their strategies to exploit such strengths. Besides, banks will have to develop IT and HR strategies which are aligned to the overall business strategy. Banks which are successful in restructuring their operations will be better placed to face the onslaught on competition.

9. FUTURE CHALLENGES FOR INDIAN BANKS

A few broad challenges facing the Indian banks are: threats of risks from globalisation; implementation of Basel II; improvement of risk management systems;

implementation of new accounting standards; enhancement of transparency and disclosures; enhancement of customer service; and application of technology.

9.1 Globalisation – A Challenge as Well as an Opportunity

The waves of globalisation are sweeping across the world, and have thrown up several opportunities accompanied by concomitant risks. Integration of domestic market with international financial markets has been facilitated by tremendous advancement in information and communications technology. There is a growing realisation that the ability of countries to conduct business across national borders and the ability to cope with the possible downside risks would depend, inter alia, on the soundness of the financial system. This has necessitated convergence of prudential norms with international best practices as well consistent refinement of the technological and institutional framework in the financial sector through a non-disruptive and consultative process.

9.2 Opening up of the Capital Account

The Committee on Fuller Capital Account Convertibility (Chairman: Shri S.S. Tarapore) observed that under a full capital account convertibility regime, the banking system would be exposed to greater market volatility, and this necessitated enhancing the risk management capabilities in the banking system in view of liquidity risk, interest rate risk, currency risk, counter-party risk and country risk that arise from international capital flows. The potential dangers associated with the proliferation of derivative instruments – credit derivatives and interest rate derivatives also need to be recognised in the regulatory and supervisory system. The issues relating to cross-border supervision of financial intermediaries in the context of greater capital flows are just emerging and need to be addressed.

9.3 Basel II Implementation

The Reserve Bank and the commercial banks have been preparing to implement Basel II, and it has been decided to allow banks some more time in adhering to new norms. As against the deadline of March 31, 2007 for compliance with Basel II, it was decided in October 2006 that foreign banks operating in India and Indian banks having presence outside India would migrate to the standardised approach for credit risk and the basic indicator approach for operational risk under Basel II with effect from March 31, 2008, while all other scheduled commercial banks are required to migrate to Basel II by March 31, 2009.

It is widely acknowledged that implementation of Basel II poses significant challenge to both banks and the regulators. Basel II implementation may also be seen as a compliance challenge. But at the same time, it offers two major opportunities to banks, *viz.*, refinement of risk management systems; and improvement in capital efficiency. The transition from Basel I to Basel II essentially involves a move from capital adequacy to capital efficiency. This transition in how capital is used and how much capital is needed will become a significant factor in return-onequity strategy for years to come.

The reliance on the market to assess the riskiness of banks would lead to increased focus on transparency and market disclosure, critical information describing the risk profile, capital structure and capital adequacy. Besides making banks more accountable and responsive to better-informed investors, these processes enable banks to strike the right balance between risks and rewards and to improve the access to markets. Improvements in market discipline also call for greater coordination between banks and regulators.

9.4 Improving Risk Management Systems

Basel II has brought into focus the need for a more comprehensive risk management framework to deal with various risks, including credit and market risk and their inter-linkages. Banks in India are also moving from the individual silo system to an enterprise-wide risk management system. While the first milestone would be risk integration across the entity, the next step would entail risk aggregation across the group both in the specific risk areas as also across the risks. Banks would, therefore, be required to allocate significant resources towards this endeavour. In India, the risk-based approach to supervision is also serving as a catalyst to banks' migration to the integrated risk management systems. However, taking into account the diversity in the Indian banking system, stabilizing the RBS as an effective supervisory mechanism is another challenge.

9.5 Corporate Governance

To a large extent, many risk management failures reflect a breakdown in corporate governance which arise due to poor management of conflict of interest, inadequate understanding of key banking risks, and poor Board oversight of the mechanisms for risk management and internal audit. Corporate governance is, therefore, the foundation for effective risk managements in banks and, thus, the foundation for a sound financial system. Therefore, the choices which banks make when they establish their risk management and corporate governance systems have important ramifications for financial stability. Banks may have to cultivate a good governance culture building in appropriate checks and balances in their operations. There are four important forms of oversight that should be included in the organisational structure of any bank in order to ensure appropriate checks and balances: (i) oversight by the board of directors or supervisory board; (ii) oversight by individuals not involved in the day-to-day running of the various business areas; (iii) direct line supervision of different business areas; and (iv) independent risk management, compliance and audit functions. In addition, it is important that key personnel are fit and proper for their jobs. Furthermore, the general principles of sound corporate governance should also be applied to all banks, irrespective of their unique ownership structures.

9.6 Implementation of New Accounting Standards

Derivative activity in banks has been increasing at a brisk pace. While the risk management framework for derivative trading, which is a relatively new area for Indian banks (particularly in the more structured products) is an essential pre-requisite, the absence of clear accounting guidelines in this area is a matter of significant concern. The World Bank's ROSC on Accounting and Auditing in India has commented on the absence of an accounting standard which deals with recognition, measurement and disclosures pertaining to financial instruments. The Accounting Standards Board of the Institute of Chartered Accountants of India (ICAI) is considering issue of Accounting Standards in respect of financial instruments. These will be the Indian parallel to International Accounting Standards 32 and 39. The proposed Accounting Standards will be of considerable significance for financial entities and could, therefore, have implications for the financial sector. The formal introduction of these Accounting Standards by the ICAI is likely to take some time in view of the processes involved. In the meanwhile, the Reserve Bank is considering the need for banks and financial entities adopting the broad underlying principles of IAS 39. Since this is likely to give rise to some regulatory/prudential issues, all relevant aspects are being comprehensively examined. The proposals in this regard would, as is normal, be discussed with the market participants before introduction. Adoption and implementation of these principles are likely to pose a great challenge to both the banks and the Reserve Bank.

9.7 Supervision of Financial Conglomerates

The financial landscape is increasingly witnessing entry of some of the bigger banks into other financial segments like merchant banking, insurance etc. Emergence of several new players with diversified presence across major segments make it imperative for supervision to be spread across various segments of the financial sector. In this direction, an inter-regulatory Working Group was constituted with members from RBI, SEBI and IRDA. The framework proposed by the Group is complementary to the existing regulatory structure wherein the individual entities are regulated by the respective regulators and the identified financial conglomerates are subjected to focussed regulatory oversight through a mechanism of interregulatory exchange of information. As a first step in this direction, an inter-agency Working

Group on Financial Conglomerates (FC) comprising the above three supervisory bodies identified 23 FCs and a pilot process for obtaining information from these conglomerates has been initiated. The complexities involved in the supervision of financial conglomerates are a challenge not only to the Reserve Bank of India but also to the other regulatory agencies, which need to have a close and continued coordination on an on-going basis.

In view of increased focus on empowering supervisors to undertake consolidated supervision of bank groups and since the Core Principles for Effective Banking Supervision issued by the Basel Committee on Banking Supervision have underscored consolidated supervision as an independent principle, the Reserve Bank had introduced, as an initial step, consolidated accounting and other quantitative methods to facilitate consolidated supervision. The components of consolidated supervision include, consolidated financial statements intended for public disclosure, consolidated prudential reports intended for supervisory assessment of risks and application of certain prudential regulations on group basis. In due course, consolidated supervision as introduced above would evolve to cover banks in mixed conglomerates, where the parent may be non-financial entities or parents may be financial entities coming under the jurisdiction of other regulators.

9.8 Application of Advanced Technology

The role of technology in banking in creating new business models and processes, in maintaining competitive advantage, in enhancing quality of risk management systems in banks, and in revolutionizing distribution channels, cannot be overemphasized. Recognizing the benefits of modernising their technology infrastructure, banks are taking the right initiatives. While doing so, banks have four options to choose from: they can build a new system themselves, or buy best of the modules, or buy a comprehensive solution, or outsource. A further challenge which banks face in this regard is to ensure that they derive maximum advantage from their investments in technology and avoid wasteful expenditure which might arise on account of uncoordinated and piecemeal adoption of technology; adoption of inappropriate/ inconsistent technology and adoption of obsolete technology. A case in point is the implementation of core banking solution by some banks without assessing its scalability or adaptability to meet Basel II requirements.

9.9 Financial Inclusion

While banks are focusing on the methodologies of meeting the increasing demands placed on them, there are legitimate concerns with regard to the banking practices that tend to exclude rather than attract vast sections of population, in particular pensioners, self-employed and those employed in unorganised sector. While commercial considerations are no doubt important, banks have been bestowed with several privileges, especially of seeking public deposits on a highly leveraged basis, and consequently they should be obliged to provide banking services to all segments of the population, on equitable basis. Further, experience has shown that consumers' interests are at times not accorded full protection and their grievances are not properly attended to. Feedback received reveals recent trends of levying unreasonably high service/user charges and enhancement of user charges without proper and prior intimation.

It is in this context that the Governor, Reserve Bank of India had mentioned in the Annual Policy Statement 2005-06 that RBI will take initiatives to encourage greater degree of financial inclusion in the country; setting up of a mechanism for ensuring fair treatment of consumers; and effective redressal of customer grievances.

10. CONCLUSION

With the increasing levels of globalisation of the Indian banking industry, evolution of universal banks and bundling of financial services, competition in the banking industry will intensify further. The banking industry has the potential and the ability to rise to the occasion as demonstrated by the rapid pace of automation which has already had a profound impact on raising the standard of banking services. The financial strength of individual banks, which are major participants in the financial system, is the first line of defence against financial risks. Strong capital positions and balance sheets place banks in a better position to deal with and absorb the economic shocks.

REFERENCES

[1] Ahluwalia, M.S. (2002). "Economic Reforms in India since 1991: Has Gradualism Worked?" *Journal of Economic Perspectives*, 16, (3), 67-88.

[2] Borio, Claudio and William White (2003), "Whither Monetary and Financial Stability? The Implications of Evolving Policy Regimes", *BIS Working Paper* No. 147.

[3] Crockett, A (2001), "Monetary Policy and Financial Stability, Lecture Delivered at the HKMA Distinguished Lecture, February.

[4] Mohan, Rakesh (2004a), "Challenges to Monetary Policy in a Globalising Context", *Reserve Bank of India Bulletin*, January.

[5] Mohan, Rakesh (2004b), "Financial Sector Reforms in India: Policies and Performance Analysis", *Reserve Bank of India Bulletin,* October.

[6] www.rbi.org.in.

Economic Reforms in China with Reference to Privatisation of Public Enterprises

R.K. Mishra

Chinese Economy is being intensively studied by scholars and institutions around the world. Chinese economic reforms and privatisation of its public enterprises are of great significance to India, which launched its economic reforms programme in 1991. The sequencing, putting in place appropriate institutional structure, and an optimal trade off between the equity and growth and the pace of privatisation have surfaced as major issues confronting policy makers in India engaged in formulating and implementing the economic reforms, have entered a crucial stage and wherein they are required to traverse from the centre to the states.

1. STAGES OF ECONOMIC REFORMS IN CHINA

Chinese reforms commencing[1] in 1978 have passed through three stages. In the first stage, extending from 1978 to 1984, Chinese Government liberalised agriculture, withdrew controls, modernised industry and its fundamental structure in the national economy. In the second stage, beginning from 1984 and stretching up to 1991, the leadership reforms occupied the centre stage, which concerned themselves with the emergence and continuation of leadership committed to the development of Chinese economy with the specific objective of achieving 10% the rate of growth per annum for the next 20 years. During this stage, Chinese economic reforms also transformed the political structure. During this stage Chinese overhauled their agricultural, industrial, fiscal, financial infrastructure and trade policies. The current stage of reforms began in 1991, and continues to hold its sway way in the present decade of 21st century. It deals with marketising the political structure and the economy. This is the most crucial stage of reform which has helped Chinese in preserving their socio-political and economic systems, on the one hand, and superimposing market economy on this tripod on the other. During this stage of reforms, Chinese have mounted an ambitious programme of privatising public enterprises. The privatisation drive, which has taken off during this stage, has led to privatisation of 1,00,000

---

[1] http://en.wikipeida.org/wiki/chinese_economic_reform

public enterprises out of a total of 2,66,000. The enterprise reforms transformed public enterprises into self-reliant entities.

The economic reforms have transcended the expected benefits. The allocations to the central government of the total resources have increased from 40%-50%. The preponderance of government agencies is being questioned. The roles and responsibilities of the remaining government organs have been classified. The strong hold of the bureaucracy has been substantially weakened. The number of Departments Government has been reduced form 40 to 28. The over-sized Chinese bureaucracy has been trimmed from a massive number of 30,000 to 10,000. The number of bureaucrats belonging to the provincial governments has been reduced from 55,000 to 28,000. A new system of evaluation of civil servants has been introduced which favours action and discourages bias in favour of accumulating files. The bureaucracy at the level of local administration is also getting leaner or weaker?

2. FOCUS OF THE PAPER

The present paper looks at public enterprise reforms in China within the broad ambit of economic reforms in the country. An attempt has been made to study privatisation and non-privatisation reforms, techniques and modalities of privatisation, marketisation process of public enterprise in respect of mobilisation of funds, operational and commercial autonomy and the post-privatisation efficiency. The issue of equity and growth in relation to privatisation and the labour related issues pertaining to privatisation have also been studied besides discussing the comparative aspects of public enterprise reforms in India and China.

3. PUBLIC ENTERPRISE REFORMS IN CHINA–A CRITICAL REVIEW

Public Enterprise Reforms are central to the agenda of economic reforms in China.[2] The various dimensions of public enterprises have experienced a decline after the onset of economic reforms in China. According to the State-owned Assets Supervision and Administration Commission (SASAC), the number of state-owned and state-held businesses fell from 238,000 in 1998 to 150,000 in 2003. Some idea of the rate of decline[3] in the numbers of public enterprises since 1998 can be gathered from Table 1.

About the size of public enterprises in China, it is worth noting that about 60,000 enterprises are considered to be large ones, whereas 1,60,000 enterprises are considered to be small ones. The decline in the number of public enterprises is

---

[2] http://www.chinadaily.com.cn/english/doc/2006-01/24/content_514993.htm
[3] htpp://www.forbes.com/business/2004/11/04/cx_1104mckinseychina6.html

Table 1: Trends in Number of Public Enterprises in China, 1998 to 2002

Year	1998	1999	2000	2001	2002
No. of Public Enterprises	64737	61301	53489	46767	41125
No. of all Public Enterprises and Private Enterprises above designated size*	165080	162033	162885	171256	181557

Note: *All Public Enterprises and Private Enterprises industrial enterprises above designated size refer to all Public Enterprises and the Private Enterprises industrial enterprises with an annual sales income of over 5 million Yuan

Source: China State Statistical Bureau (2003).

associated with falling output and from 77.6% in 1978 to 28.5% in 1999. The retail sale of these enterprises during the same period nose-dived from 54.6% to 24.3%. However, in some sectors public enterprises continue to dominate the position of commanding heights. In the steel industry, these enterprises possess 80% of aggregate market share and in the insurance sector, they account for 70% of the market share. The four major state-owned banks hold more than 60% of Chinese banking assets. The state monopoly continues to dominate the fields of Civil Aviation, Energy, Telecommunications, Metallurgy and some other strategic industries. Public enterprise reform programme has made a great mark on their performance improvement.[4] However, there is another view stating that profitability improvement has taken place only in the case of monopoly PEs and that it has registered a shortfall from 7 per cent to 3 per cent return on assets in the case of deregulated public enterprises. It is argued that the lack of level playing field has contributed to profitability of monopoly public enterprises as they have priority in obtaining bank loans and government subsidies and first claim on natural resources. Table 2 shows the efficiency comparison between public enterprises and foreign funded enterprises in China.

Public enterprise reforms in China commenced in 1978 at the initiative of the Communist Party of China. In the first phase starting 1978 and ending 1984, the reform programme allocated quotas for output and mopped up profits. The appointments of the senior executives were made by the Government who acted as extended arm of the State. The relationship of public enterprises with the Government was like that of the departmental enterprises. In 1979, a departure was made and the Government started delegating power and sharing profits with public enterprises resulting in greater autonomy for these enterprises and their de-bureaucratisation. In 1984, the Government, as a part of its approach of delegating

---

[4] Li Wei (1997) 'The impact of economic reform on the performance of Chinese state enterprises, 1980-1989', *Journal of Political Economy* 105: 1080-1106

Table 2: Efficiency Comparison between Public Enterprises and
Foreign Funded Enterprises in 2002

Enterprises	Ratio of value-added to gross industrial output value (%)	Ratio of total assets to industrial output value (%)	Asset liability ratio (%)	Ratio of profits to industrial cost (%)	Overall labour productivity (Yuan-person-year)	Proportion of products sold
Public Enterprises and State Holding Enterprises	35.27	8.71	59.30	5.93	65749	98.98
Foreign Funded Enterprises	26.41	10.46	54.38	6.40	81313	98.28

Source: China Statistical Bureau (2003).

powers and sharing profits empowered these enterprises to take autonomous decisions in the area of production, operations management, marketing, inventory management, disposal of assets, management of personnel as concerned with wages and bonus.

The second phase of economic reforms starting in 1984 and ending in 1991, introduced the concept of the Memorandum of Understanding (MoU)[5] in the form of a management contract incorporating details on profits, taxes, asset appreciation, debt payment, product and technology innovation and allocation of retained profits. The year 1988 saw the enactment of a full-fledged public enterprise law making executives in public enterprises responsible for their management and accountable to public agencies as also prohibiting the latter from interfering in the working of these enterprises.

The third and the present phase of public enterprise reform began in 1992. The current phase of reform directs public enterprises to cultivate market orientation and compete. During this phase, the Government has drawn a demarcating line between itself and public enterprises leading to separation of enterprises from administration and encouraging them to follow the principles of scientific management. During the current phase, public enterprises are expected to institute modern business systems, spread their shareholdings and corporatarise themselves. Public enterprises no longer

---

[5] Groves, Theodore, Hong Yongmiao, McMillan John and Naughton, Barry (1994) 'Autonomy and incentives in Chinese State Enterprises', *Quarterly Journal of Economics* 109(1): 181-209.

enjoy parity with the Government officials in terms of ranks and privileges, and organize their rank and file as is done by a modern corporate entity.

The reform programme, on the one hand, has led to rollback of the State from the undesirable areas and increased the efficiency of the left over public enterprises, on the other. Table 3 presents efficiency indices of public enterprises in China.

Table 3: Efficiency Indices of Public Enterprises and State-holding Enterprises

Year	Ratio of value-added to gross industrial output value (%)	Ratio of total assets to industrial output value (%)	Asset liability ratio (%)	Ratio of profits to industrial cost (%)	Overall labour productivity (Yuan-person-year)	Proportion of products sold
1998	32.95	6.51	64.26	1.61	29054	97.41
1999	34.11	6.77	61.98	2.89	35741	98.15
2000	33.97	8.43	60.99	6.15	45998	98.88
2001	34.55	8.17	59.19	5.75	54772	98.65
2002	35.27	8.71	59.30	5.93	65749	98.98

Source: China State Statistical Bureau (2003).

The table reveals a steady increase in both the asset–output ratio and labour productivity. The profits to industrial cost ratio also increased substantially. The overall labour productivity rose more than twofold and the production-turnover ratio registered improvement. However, the comparison of public enterprise performance were non-public enterprise stream shows that the former lagged behind substantially. Table 4 compares the total factor productivity and labour productivity trends as related to public enterprises, urban and township enterprises and township-village enterprises. The table shows that public enterprises in China scored lower than the urban and township – village enterprises on both the counts.

Table 4: Estimated Percentage Rates in Annual Productivity Growth in Chinese Industry

	1980-84	1984-88	1988-92
Total factor productivity			
Public Enterprise	1.8	3.0	2.5
Urban and Township Enterprise	3.4	5.9	4.9*
Township-Village Enterprise	7.3*	6.6*	6.9*
Labour productivity			
Public Enterprise	3.8	6.2	4.7
Urban and Township Enterprise	8.6	7.0	13.8

Note: *Preliminary results

Source: Jefferson and Rawski (1994).

Table 5 showing profitability of public enterprises and non-public enterprises entities points out clearly that profitability of public enterprise was lower as compared to the non-public enterprise streams.

Table 5: Profitability of Public Enterprise and Private Enterprises

	Wage share %		Profit-tax ratio (%)	
	1985	1995	1985	1995
Public Enterprises	22.02	37.08	32.94	13.45
Collective-owned enterprises	34.84	33.15	46.96	22.26
Private industry		16.83		50.71
Joint industry	21.08	32.79	64.44	18.45
Share-holding industry		26.22		25.63
Foreign funded industry	23.16	17.80	31.90	20.29
Total	25.14	33.10	35.06	15.64

Source: Chinese State Statistical Bureau (1985, 1995).

It is worth mentioning that one third of Chinese public enterprise make explicit losses, another one third make implicit losses and the rest one third are somewhat profitable. This is at variance with the previous conclusion. But the contradiction could be explained in terms of the distinction between public enterprises and the state holding enterprises. The state holding enterprises are mixed organisations where majority shareholding is in the hands of the Government. The output value and performance of these enterprises outweigh the performance of public enterprises formidably as shown in Table 6.

Table 6: Public Enterprises and State Holding Enterprises

	No. of enterprises (Unit)		Gross industrial output value (100 million Yuan)	
	2001	2002	2001	2002
Public Enterprises	34530	29449	17229.19	17271.09
State-holding Enterprises	46767	41125	42408.49	45178.96

Source: China State Statistical Bureau (2003).

The criticism that non-public enterprise sector is performing better than the public enterprise sector is rebutted by the argument that obtrusive behaviour of the Government in interfering with public enterprises has been the key reason for their non-performance. The problem of non-performance will continue to exist as long as the Government does not separate itself fully from public enterprises. The corporatisation of public enterprises is suggested as an effective remedy to the problem. Consequent to this thinking the Government set up Shenzhen and Shanghai stock markets in 1990. Further, the Government allowed public enterprises to diversify their shareholdings and go in for listing in the capital markets abroad. The Government has set up asset management companies to facilitate the listing and off-loading of shareholdings. This also pepped up the status of corporate governance in Chinese public enterprises. The lack of marketisation of public enterprises has also been construed as a hurdle in these enterprises performing well.[6] The price distortions, soft budget constraints and ineffective cost management have all affected the performance of these enterprises. It is suggested that to make public enterprises intensively competitive, the Government should remove the social burden, hardened budget constraints and make public enterprise managers risk-friendly. The telecom sector public enterprises in China have taken some of these steps. In essence, to turn the corner, Chinese public enterprises have to marketise their functioning and relieve themselves of the ownership syndrome. This will require Chinese Government to institute an effective price system leading to superior resource allocation[7] and establish a robust legal system leading to the abridgment of Government control of business including the removal of barrier to entry from private sector within China and corporate enterprises from public and private sectors abroad. The Government should ensure enhanced study in shares of public enterprises by giving up its share of equity and becoming a minority shareholder.

The Government holds about two thirds of the equity in public enterprises, which has led to partial privatisation depriving the country of the advantage of a market economy. Chinese stock market behaviour has clearly indicated a positive relationship between the announcements about the off-loading of shareholdings of public enterprises and market price of their script. The announcement by the China Securities Regulatory Commission (CSRC) in June 2001 that the state would sell shares equal to 10 per cent of public offerings led to 30 per cent decline in the Shanghai index, losing around US$ 72.5 billion in value over four months. When information emerged that CSRC would shelve any plan for the sale of state share, the market rapidly responded with a 10 per cent increase in value. However, this argument is countered by the protagonists on the ground that trading of public enterprise shares in China will lead to crowding out of private sector as the private sector would have to compete for the same amount of resources with public sector. Although the Government has set up supervisory boards in public enterprises, the continuation of the old and sterile policy

---

[6] Woo, W T Hai, W Jin, Y B and Fan, G (1994) 'How successful has Chinese Enterprise reform been?', *Journal of Comparative Economics* 18: 410-437.

[7] Dollar, D (1990) 'Economic Reform and Allocative Efficiency in China's state-owned industries', *Economic Development and Cultural Change* 39: 89-105.

boards have neutralised the benefits of this change. Public reforms in China are also opposed on the ground of equity. It is said that disparities in incomes have increased since the onset of public enterprise reforms taking the shape of transparent or veiled privatisation. Chinese workers have expressed the fear of job losses in view of the Government's assertion that during 2006–11 each year about ten million people will lose jobs. Public enterprises accounted for 64.3 per cent laid off workers in 1966 and 68.4 per cent in 1997. This is in the backdrop of the fact that the rate of urban employment in China is more than three per cent.

4. A COMPARATIVE VIEW OF PUBLIC ENTERPRISE REFORM IN INDIA AND CHINA

Public enterprise reform in India started in 1990s. The sub national public enterprise reforms are a special feature of public enterprise reforms in India. The tempo of public enterprise reform has been far swifter in China as compared to India. Chinese reforms have come through the route of public law whereas the public enterprise reforms in India have taken the 'executive route'. The financial outcomes of Chinese public enterprise reforms have been amazing. The financial outcomes of the Indian public enterprise reforms taking the course of privatisation have been disappointing as the realisations have been about 50 per cent of the planned targets. Public enterprise reform in India has been found to be weak on the non-privatisation end. Chinese public enterprises reforms have transformed the left over public enterprises in terms of greater autonomy, low accountability and higher financial delegation. Public enterprise reforms in China have integrated the privatized enterprises with the foreign domestic investment sector, which has been a weak spot in the Indian context. Alienation of personnel in Chinese public enterprises from the rank and file of employees in Government has been a major success in the case of China. In India even in the case of reformed public enterprises the goal of achieving complete alienation has not been possible for the Government. However, in the case of both Chinese and Indian public enterprises, reforms have given rise to the problem of downsizing the workforce resulting in unemployment and inequity, a problem both the countries have not been able to solve due to inadequacy of social safety net.

To conclude, public enterprise reform in China has made a great headway. Small enterprises are being privatised first. Marketisation of public enterprises is catching up. The Government is minimising its interface with public enterprises. Non-privatised public enterprises are undergoing restructuring. However, public enterprise reform has hit the air pocket in terms of slow removal of entry barriers, continuation of the burden of social responsibility on public enterprises, lack of adequate progress on establishing sound corporate governance system and integration of public enterprises with domestic and international capital markets.

Industrialisation Dilemma and Civilisation Model Innovation under Resource and Environment Restrictions in Large Countries—A Review on the Industrial Civilisation of "Cost Externalisation" and an Idea of Ecological Civilisation

Zhang Xiaode

1. INDUSTRIALISATION DILEMMA UNDER RESOURCE AND ENVIRONMENT RESTRICTIONS IN BRICs

To say that the western-countries-belonged market economy and developing countries to industrialisation had been an issue puzzling the world after World War II. The vigorous development of Four Asian Tigers during 1970s to 1980s was demonstrated that industrialisation featuring the realisation of market economy in developing countries. Jim O'Neill, chief economist of Goldman Sachs, America, has turned the research and attention on BRIC from the successful realisation of market economy and industrialisation to how these four BRIC countries of high population will change and impact the global economic context hitherto led by western countries. Indeed the change of being countries worrying at how to transplant market economy from western countries to being countries eclipsing western countries' leadership in world industrialisation is a milestone of 21st century.

However, if constrained by resource and environment, we may find that, the vigorous development of four BRIC countries not only eclipses leading economic role of western countries' in the world, but also posts an issue that by what model and approach the four BRIC countries will realise industrialisation,. The earth does not sufficient resources and environment to support industrialisation of BRIC countries' in the western way of high energy-use and high pollution. Therefore, it is not the western countries' leading economic role in the world that suffers from the vigorous development of BRIC countries, but the western model of industrial civilisation itself that suffers.

Developed western countries, with only 11.2% population of the world and in more than 200 years' development have realised industrialisation. The essential difference between developing BRIC countries and western countries is that these four countries have huge population. The total population of seven western countries is 720-million or so, 11.2% of the world's population, 100-million per country. The total population of the four BRIC countries is 2.6-billion, 3.6 times that of seven western countries put together and 40.8% of the world's population, 700-million per country. As such industrialisation shall disable the earth's capability to provide the needed resources and retain its environmental. *Living Planet Report 2006* issued by WWF on October 24, 2006 pointed out that, the natural resource consumption speed by human beings has far exceeded the nature's regeneration capacity. Meanwhile other beings have more and more reduced living space. The earth's ecosystem shall collapse in the midst of this century if the current status continues. The *Report* shows that the increase of human population from 3-billion to 6.5-billion from 1961 to 2003 has increased natural resource consumption more than 3 times. From 1980s human beings' consumption of natural resources has had a speed exceeding their regeneration speed. Human "ecological footprint" has exceeded the Earth's ecological capacity by 25% to year 2003, in which the world "ecological footprint" per capita was 2.2 global hectares(gha), and the average biologically productive area per person worldwide was approximately 1.8 gha. Carbon dioxide emission, one "ecological footprint" calculator, contributes 48% to humanity's impact on Earth's ecosystem. Carbon dioxide emission has seen on the increase more than 9 times in the past 40 years or more. Stated by the *Report*, many developed countries of Europe and America have consumed a huge mass of resources to improve their life quality these 30 years. James P Leape, the WWF International Director General, said whole releasing the report, "We need five earths to meet our requirements if people worldwide live as Americans."

Information about BRIC Countries

	China	India	Russia	Brazil	Total	Percentage in World
Area (10-thousand)	960	320.8	1707.5	854.7	13381.6	28.70%
Population (100-million)	13	10	1.45	1.7	26.17	40.80%
GDP 2007(100-million$)	30100	9280	11400	9340	60120	12.5
GDP per capita($)	2280 6 T	830	8030 2	4930		2227

Source: National Bureau of Statistics of China

Currently the GDP of the four BRIC countries 6-trillion dollars, 12.5% of the world; average GDP per capita 222,7 dollars. The gross GDP of BRICs shall go to 26-trillion dollars if their average GDP per capita reaches 10-thousand dollars, approaching the gross GDP 29-trillion dollars of seven western countries. The gross GDP of BRICs shall go to 52-trillion dollars if their average GDP per capita reaches

20-thousand dollars, half of the average GDP per capita in seven western countries. International research and practice show that resource consumption per capita has close relation to increase of GDP per capita. Viewed worldwide, reaching GDP per capita of medium-developed countries, 10-thousand dollars, shall see rapid increase of resource consumption per capita, a value above 4-ton standard coal; thereafter increase of resource consumption shall slow down. When GDP per capita reached 10-thousand dollars, South Korea had resource consumption per capita 4.07-ton standard coal (1997), Japan 4.25-ton standard coal (1980), and America 8-ton standard coal (1960). At present resource consumption per capita of BRICs shall reach 12-billion-ton if to 4-ton per capita is taken into account, 80% of current global gross resource consumption. This means that BRICs shall almost double the load of the Earth's resource consumption in the future. At present humanity's "ecological footprint" has exceeded the Earth's ecological capacity by 25%. Therefore, in the upcoming 10 to 15 years, the four BRIC countries shall double the Earth's ecological load, not including not the other 40% world population achieving similar level of industrialisation.

Information about Seven Western Countries

	Population (10-thousand)	Area (10-thousand Km^2)	GDP (100-million $ 2007)	GDP per capita ($)
America	30053	982.66	139800	46280
Japan	12746	37.78	49113.62	38533
Germany	8242	35.70	28582.34	34679
England	6060	24.48	23413.71	38636
France	6088	54.70	21537.46	35377
Italy	5813	30.12	17839.59	30689
Canada	3310	998.47	10889.37	32898
Total	72312	2163.91	291176.09	
Percentage in world %	11.2	16.17	60.6	402660 (per capita)

Source: National Bureau of Statistics of China

Under such a background the four BRIC countries under such a background shall choose a new development approach and mode, different from the industrial civilisation model of western countries.

Industrial civilisation established by western world contains many good things worthy of our study and borrowing. However, we shall not wait for the end of the industrial civilisation to begin our exploration of new models of civilisation.

2. WESTERN INDUSTRIALISATION IS A MODEL CHARACTERISED BY COST EXTERNALISATION

Developed western countries countered constraints of resource and environment after industrialisation. Therefore, at beginning of the industrialisation model they did not take the required resource and environment costs into consideration. Western industrialisation model assumed that the supply of resources is infinite, and the environment has limitless self-purification capability. Perhaps this assumption was true at that time. But once the energy consumed and environment polluted by industrialisation exceeded the Earth's capacity, this assumption became false and dangerous. Energy consumption and environment pollution incurred were transferred to the cost endured by nature and society. From this view the industrialisation model of western countries is a kind of industrialisation by "cost externalisation".

3. WESTERN INDUSTRIALISATION PURSUES LIMITLESS EXPANSION OF PRODUCTION WITHOUT CONSTRAINTS OF CONSUMPTION

The whole industrial economic system, driven by market competition and technological innovations, has an ultimate goal to maximize output though minimum input. Directed by such a goal, the western industrialisation has an internal motor to inspire human desires of consumption and continuous expansion of production scale by expanding consumption. The essential and ultimate goal of human production at all times is to meet human beings' requirements for life. In the western model of industrialisation, consumption exists for production, and market dominates consumption. Industrialised production without constraints of consumption targets will grow and expand limitlessly. So it is a scene special to the times of industrial economy: Driven by competition, pursuing GDP growth and material consumption beyond physiological demand without limit becomes a global illness of civilisation that cannot be restrained.

In the modern industrial production system, on the one hand we are worrying over the crisis of resource and environment; on the other hand all our policies and mechanisms are making efforts to realise GDP growth to meet unlimited material demand. Such efforts of industrial economic system unconstrained by consumption targets are reasonable in developing countries that suffer poverty and hunger. However, the society of America shall be in horrified if economic growth is discovered to be slowing down, even though it has GDP per capita exceeding 40-thousand dollars. Almost all modern people are suffering from the sickness of economic growth desire. Pursuit of unlimited growth has already become a culture prevailing in modern industrial civilisation. Technical progress is insufficient unless industrialisation model is reformed radically.

4. WESTERN MODEL OF INDUSTRIALISATION CAN BE APPLIED ONLY TO A SMALL NUMBER OF PEOPLE OR COUNTRIES

The industrialisation model driven by market competition makes the strong stronger and the weak weaker. A periodic economic crisis caused by polarisation that is incurred by competition has been huge `obstacles to the economic and social development of developed western countries at the beginning of 20th century. The worldwide energy crisis spreading from America in 1929 to all developed western countries taught their governments to remedy and solve effectively the challenge of polarisation caused by competition through macro regulation and direction on public products supply management system. However, such macro regulation and public products supply management system exist only in individual countries. After World War the polarisation effects caused by market competition appeared worldwide following globalisation of economy and emergence of a world market, for many developing countries became independent and western market economy was penetrating the world. Consequently, developed industrial countries and developing countries become more polarized. Today only a small number of developed countries can enjoy the civilisation of industrialisation because they are unable to establish a global regulating system to remedy polarisation effects caused by global competition. These developed countries, enjoyers of industrialisation, by their competence have not only cornered too much energy of the world, but also transferred the cost of energy consumption and environment pollution to developing countries by industrial transfer. Developing countries can become industrialised western industrialisation in accordance with the model if the Earth's resource and environment have infinite capacity. However, the Earth does now allow new countries of market economy to carry out industrial transfer as developed western countries, because Earth's resource and environment are already in crisis.

Western mode of industrialisation can only meet the industrialisation requirements of a small number of countries. The current vigorously developing China aiming at industrialisation have 20% population of the world, which is almost double that of developed western countries. The largest difficulty challenging China's industrialisation is whether China has the ability to create an industrialisation model that most of its people can enjoy its fruits in contrast to a small number of western countries' enjoyment of western industrialisation. This difficulty challenges not only China's industrialisation, but also the evolution of human civilisation. Removal of this difficulty shall bless China's modernisation and also human civilisation.

5. WESTERN INDUSTRIALISATION RESTRAINS AND KILLS DIVERSIFIED DEVELOPMENT OF HUMAN CULTURE AND CIVILISATION, AND SEVERELY INJURES ECOSYSTEM OF HUMAN CULTURE AND CIVILISATION

The development of industrialisation featuring cost externalisation has not only damaged natural ecosystem, but also injured ecosystem of human culture and civilisation. Ancient society before appearance of industrialisation was an ecosystem containing diversified cultures and civilisations. The might of material and wealth productivity formed in western industrialisation by technical innovation and market competition disintegrated ancient production mode and production relationships. The replacement and disintegration of ancient production mode and production relationships by industrialisation was a necessary price paid for the progress of human civilisation. Nations scattered worldwide almost finished the evolution of agricultural civilisation in parallel, for they were separated by relatively enclosed environments. Industrial civilisation was born in the west, and then spread to the world. The western world quickly formed economic, cultural, and military competence by industrialisation and, the process of western industrialisation penetrating to the rest of the world had not only disintegrated ancient production mode, but damaged the diversified cultural ecosystem originated from ancient society. From 15th century to 19th century, aboriginals of Latin America and Africa and their culture suffered catastrophic damage because they lacked ability to protect themselves during western colonisation process. After World War, national cultures of developing countries, impacted by commodity economy and western life style, are being eclipsed and replaced under a relatively peaceful environment. Especially after the end of Cold War in 1970s, economic globalisation in fact is the popularisation of market economy worldwide. Western culture is prevailing around the world after the socialist alliance led by Soviet Union disintegrated.

Industrialisation at the cost of damaged cultural ecosystem featuring diversity, similar to the economic growth at the cost of damaged natural environment, shall draw our attention. We have been aware of the importance of biological diversity to the self-balancing and self-protect on of the natural ecosystem, and we shall be aware of the importance of human cultural diversity to the balancing of human cultural ecosystem. Human civilisation shall see its doomsday if the world only has one culture, and all the people are living in one style; the evolution of modern industrial civilisation shall bring us such a day. Human civilisation can never evolve further if human civilisation just means one kind of culture, for the evolution of Nature and the development of material world both require diversity for mutual progress. Singularity means deathly stillness.

6. DILEMMA OF WESTERN INDUSTRIALISATION IS THE DILEMMA OF MODERN HUMAN CIVILISATION AND INDUSTRIALISATION DILEMMA SHALL HAVE A SOLUTION DESIGNED BY A NEW CIVILIZED MODE RECONSTRUCTION

Civilized mode means the integration of economy, politics, and culture formed on the basis of specific production mode. Western industrialisation model of cost externalisation was formed in specific historical conditions and western cultural environment. This specific industrialisation model had arisen out of a specific philosophy, thinking style, cultural system, specific life style, and political mode. So we can see that the defects of western industrialisation model are not merely limited to industrialisation itself, but they are the defects of the whole civilisation. We shall with an eye on civilisation to review the western industrialisation model. We must review and innovate values, thinking style, cultural and life styles in addition to the removal of economic dilemma.

"External Management Mode" cannot solve the dilemma of industrial civilisation mode

Viewed worldwide, problems of environment and resource have been well dealt with in developed countries, and developing countries aiming at industrialisation become disaster areas of such problems. This makes us think that the constraints of environment and resource are no longer a problem in developed western countries, and these countries have already turned from industrialisation of cost externalisation to industrialisation of cost internalisation. We shall not deny that, from 1970s, developed western countries have by a series of measures for reinforcing environmental monitoring and increasing investment on techniques of environmental protection reduced energy consumption and improved environment under the regulation of government policies for environmental protection. However, we cannot say that environment and energy no longer are problems in developed western countries, for such regulation is "external management mode" without changing the existing industrialisation mode. This external management has two major aspects:

Industrialised western countries established external management system for industrialized production system by economic surplus to assimilate external cost caused by industrialisation. These countries did not internalize industrialisation cost by changing consumption mode and economic operation flow. On the one hand, these countries invested in environmental protection capital and techniques to maximize clean production without changing the original life style. On the other hand, absolute energy consumption volume is still increasing, and the production is still expanding without limit. America's GDP was 5.4-trillion dollars in 1990, and increased to 13.9-trillion dollars in 2007, an increase of 2.5 times. GDP per capita was 22,380 dollars in 1990, and reached 46,280 dollars in 2007, an increase more than 2 times. During the same period the gross trade amount of America was increased from 396.3-billion dollars of 1990 to 3,649.9-billion dollars of 2006, an increase more than 9 times. These data showed that America rapidly accumulated wealth by developing high-tech products with high added-value, and by the wealth of added-value service industry America harvested commodities for high energy-use through international trade. A great deal of data show that the absolute energy amount consumed by developed western countries has been increasing, not decreasing.

Countries	Gross energy consumption 2006 (10-thousand-ton standard coal)	Gross GDP energy consumption (ton standard coal/10-thousand dollars)	Energy consumption per capita (ton standard coal)	GDP per capita (dollars)	Rank of GDP per capita	GDP energy consumption per capita (ton standard coal/dollars)
Japan	74332	20373	5.8245	36486	10	1.60
Germany	46929	14178	5.6918	33099	17	1.72
America	331037	78693	11.0085	42067	4	2.62
Philippines	3594	33152	0.4017	1084	118	3.71
Brazil	29504	89109	1.5687	3311	77	4.74
Indonesia	16335	149452	0.6655	1093	117	6.09
India	60456	927233	0.5519	652	133	8.47
Egypt	8396	75095	1.0642	1118	116	9.52
China	242549	1794003	1.8339	1352	112	13.56
World	1552786		23.789			

Source: BP, National Bureau of Statistics of China.

Developed western countries by industrial transfer have externalised energy consumption and environmental pollution to assimilate costs beyond endurance of their industrialisation system. In 2006 Japan, Germany, and America with 7.6% population of the world have produced 43% GDP and consumed 30% energy consumption of the world. We know from the above table that China, India, and Brazil with high populations also have become countries of high energy-use. Especially China's gross energy consumption reached 15% of the world. However, a part of China's energy consumption was transferred from developed western countries by trade. In the period 1990s America was transformed from economy of manufacturing model into knowledge economy, and during this period America saw fastest growth of foreign trade. America harvested rapid growth at trades of commodities and services in the past 10 years. America's gross value of commodity import and export trade grew from 907.9-billion dollars of 1991 to 1996-billion dollars of 2000, increasing by 2.2 times. Import value was increased by 149%; export value 85%, and commodity trade deficit by 6.7 times. During 1992 to 1999, America saw average annual increase of 6.5% in service export. In year 2000, service trade at least occupied 38% of export value in America. America mainly imports energy resources and products of high energy-use. Imported oil is the largest commodity contributing to America trade deficit. America consumes about 30% of the world's gross resource output. America needs to import a great deal of resources from Middle East, Africa, and other places. Fifteen of top 20 oil suppliers to America are members of top 35 trade deficit countries vis-à-vis America. Meanwhile America imported a mass of labour-intensive products to meet its populace's demand on basic consumables and domestic economy's demand of some means of production. China's exported products to developed countries have a percentage of 50% belonging to high energy-use and high pollution types. Bo Xilai, the former minister of the Ministry of Commerce of PRC, had lamented that China exports 800-million shirts in exchange for one Boeing plane. Most large commodities contributing to China's trade surplus are products of low added-value, high energy-use, and high pollution.

6.1 Eco-friendly Civilisation Mode Featuring Cost Internalisation

"Cost internalisation" eco-friendly civilisation mode means that, directed by the eco-friendly idea of balanced co-existence of man and nature, to establish a new and healthy civilisation mode worldwide featuring diversified cultures, shared civilisations, happy life, through eco-friendly life of low energy use and innovative production mode by measures of techniques and intellectual innovations in a circular mechanism balancing man and nature, consumption and production, and competition and co-existence. This idea can be detailed as follows:

1. **Establish a new wealth-producing system driven by consumption; production serves life, while being constrained and balanced by consumption:** Traditional industrialised production system aims at maximizing the output of material wealth. It stimulates consumption demand to maximize production output, making consumption serve production and push forward industrial production system. This production system pursues limitless growth without constraints of consumption, and it just produces products as it wills, continuously consumes energy, and is self-expanding always. No clean production can give a radical solution to high energy-use if this production system remains the same.

   The internal drive mechanism that is stimulating the production system's expansion always shall be changed first before altering the production system of limitless expansion. The new modern eco-friendly production system shall produce wealth while maintaining eco-friendly civilisation and happy life.

2. **Three innovations for the new wealth production system:** Firstly realize innovation of economics research. Economics of industrial civilisation aims to maximise output by minimum input. Economics of eco-friendly civilisation times shall maximise life happiness by minimum energy use, that it shall re-design the modern production in accordance with human pursuit for happiness and comprehensive development, maximise output without waste and balance consumption and production.

Secondly find a new technical innovation of eco-friendly civilisation to meet the demand for eco-friendly and happiness. Traditional technical innovation system was established for maximising production output. Technology in traditional production systems has two edges: technical innovation reduces energy use; and techniques are measures and drivers for limitless expansion of production. Eco-friendly civilisation means, directed by the idea of harmony between man and nature, to reconstruct the modern scientific and technical innovation system aiming at low energy use, circular, and self-purification life and residence.

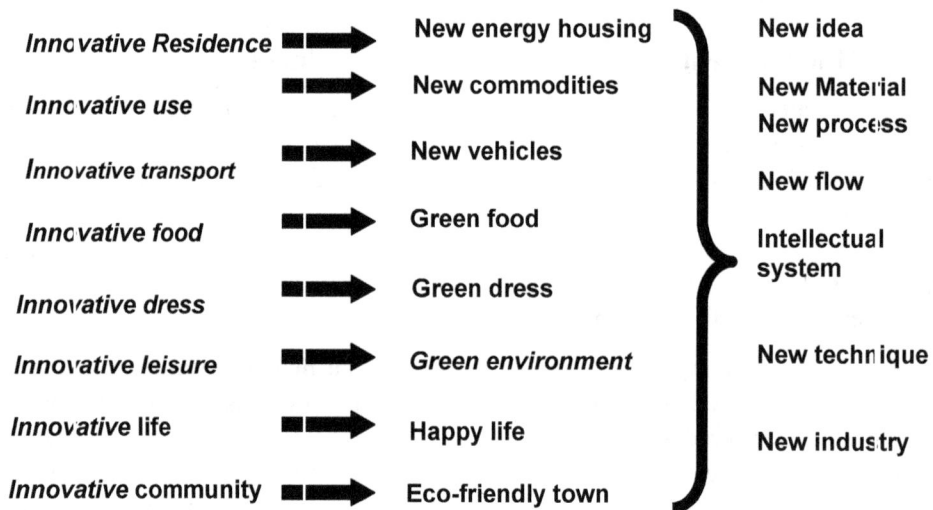

Innovative Residence ■■➡	New energy housing	New idea
Innovative use ■■➡	New commodities	New Material
		New process
Innovative transport ■■➡	New vehicles	
		New flow
Innovative food ■■➡	Green food	
		Intellectual
		system
Innovative dress ■■➡	Green dress	
Innovative leisure ■■➡	Green environment	New technique
Innovative life ■■➡	Happy life	
		New industry
Innovative community ■■➡	Eco-friendly town	

Industrialised economic system has no demand on low energy use, eco-friendly target, and maximisation happiness. It contains conflicts between high-efficiency production and high energy-use life. For example the currently popular buildings with large-area glass-curtain wall shall have energy consumed by air conditioning three times higher than that of general buildings. Investigation of Tsinghua University shows that China's large public buildings consume energy 10 to 20 times that of civil buildings. The Europe Union had statistics showing that buildings in post-industrialisation society consume 50% energy of the whole society, occupying 48% of plantation coverage, 50% of total greenhouse gas emission, over 48% of total pollution exhaust, and 42% of total water resource consumption.

In Germany heating consumes about 1/3 of the gross energy use. The new energy saving regulation issued by German government in February 2001 a provides that new buildings shall meet the criterion of "7-liter" (i.e., oil consumed by hefating shall not exceed 7 liter, or 10.5-kilogram coal equivalent). The world leading chemical German company BASF started a project to rebuild old houses, altering an old building of 70 years into "3-liter house" with energy saving effects far better than that specified in national standard of Germany. Compared to the original building, the rebuilt house reduced the original 20-liter of oil consumed for heating to 3-liter, just 15% of the original consumption. Meanwhile the CO_2 emission was reduced to 1/7 of the original. This case explains that the change of the target application of innovative modern technology shall see huge prospect of energy saving.

Thirdly establish a new wealth creation system balancing material production and spiritual production for maximising the benefits of eco-friendly, healthy, and happy life. Another approach to reduce pollution is to control scale of material and energy use, for pollution and resource consumption are positively correlated to economic scale. To control the thirst for more materials shall replace human material consumption by furnishing elements of spirit and culture. New life of higher quality shall comprise materials, spirit, culture, and art.

3. **Establish circular economic system and life system of cost internalisation and self-purification ecological cycle.** Circular economy focuses on high-efficiency utilisation and circular use of resources by "3R" principles (Reduce, Reuse, Recycle), and features low energy use, low emission, and high efficiency. Its carrier is the eco-industry chain, its important measure clean production, aiming at effective use of material resources and sustainable development of economy and ecology. At present four BRICs countries are at the initial stage of industrialisation, so it shall be a good choice to import circular economy before the completion of the infrastructure construction.

4. **Constrained by resource and environment:** To balancing the always-expanding industrialised production by life direction; by innovative ecological techniques to establish life mode of low energy use and ecological nature; by circular economy of low energy use, self-purification, and reuse; finally by assistance from new value, new culture, and new economics to build ecological civilisation of low energy use, by moving closer to harmony between man and nature, and by such a civilisation model four BRIC countries have no need to live in western-style modern life by GDP per capita 40-thousand dollars and

environmental pollution. GDP per capita 5-thousand dollars or less shall enable people of BRICs to live a more civilized, more civil, happier, and healthier life. Such a new civilisation will not extort from nature its environment, nor will it kill the benefits of other countries. Such a civilisation shall benefit world peace and, all the people around the world.

5. **Under such a context four BRIC countries** shall adjust their existing development strategies to transform the strategies followed by developed western countries into an innovative strategy aiming at building ecological civilisation. In four BRIC countries China, India, and Russia are of oriental culture. Especially China and India had been two members of the four great ancient civilisations, and they two are representatives of oriental civilisation and culture. Indian culture emphasises meditation and spiritual construction, and pursues harmony between man and heaven. Chinese culture holds merits the most important and peace the best, and thinks that human, earth and heaven are in harmony in a dialectical way. These two cultures contain values of ecological civilisation. China and India shall cultivate and catalyse ecological civilisation. China and India had lagged behind at the beginning of industrialisation 500 years ago. Nowadays China and India are at the beginning of large scale industrialisation. They shall not follow their western counterparts, but shall adapt industrialisation and innovation to civilisation by making most out of subsequent advantages of new market economies and oriental culture by learning from the western industrialisation experience.

REFERENCES

[1] Goldman Sachs' opinion on BRICs: China will be the world's largest economy in 2035, *Beijing Morning Post*, May 24, 2006.

[2] Zhang Xiaode: To Establish Sustainable Development Mode of Cost Internalisation, China National School of Administration, Issue No.1, 2001.

[3] Song Yuhua: Analysis into America's Enormous Trade Deficit, *World Economics and Politics*, Issue No.11, 2002.

[4] BP World Energy Statistics 2007.

China and India: Economic Perspectives

Dong Xiaojun

1. AN OVERVIEW OF CHINA AND INDIA'S ECONOMY

As the BRICs[1], both China and India have enjoyed rapid economic growth and established themselves as world's largest emerging economies. The recent years have seen more accomplishments of economic reforms in both countries. Since China started its economic reform and opening to the world in 1978, it has enjoyed world's fastest economic growth rate and is playing an increasingly important role in the overall economic growth of Asia. China's economic growth per capita is rising by 9.5 per cent annually. India's economic growth per capita was now rising by 7.5 per cent annually, since India started its economic reforms in 1991.The faster growth, the OECD said, had resulted in China becoming the second-largest economy in the world in 2006 in purchasing power parity terms behind only the US and India is the third. The sustained and fast economic growth of China and India in recent years has attracted universal attention.

All the talk about China and India being the fastest growing economy today, while certainly true, requires a somewhat broader historical perspective. For most of the past two millennia, China was the world's economic superpower–in 1820 it contributed about a third of global gross domestic product. Then it slid into more than a century of decline. As Table 1 shows, in 1820 China was not only the biggest country in terms of population but also the biggest in terms of GDP. At that time, India was the second biggest country in terms of both population and GDP. This was mainly due to the agricultural sector being the major contributor to employment and GDP as a result of the still rudimentary state of technological development. The Industrial Revolution changed things quite dramatically around the world. It hanged the ways how the world produced its goods. It also changed our societies from a mainly agricultural society to those in which industry and manufacturing enjoyed primacy. China missed the industrial revolution, turned in upon itself and fell prey to warlordism and opium addiction. By 1949, its share of the global economy had fallen to 5 per cent China's remarkable transformation in the past 20 years has encouraged

---

[1] **BRIC** or **BRICs** are terms used in economics to refer to the combination of **Brazil**, **Russia**, **India**, and **China**. General consensus is that the term was first prominently used in a thesis of the Goldman Sachs investment bank. because of the popularity of the Goldman Sachs thesis "BRIC" and "BRIMC"have become more generic marketing terms to refer to these emerging markets.

hopes of its regaining its historical pre-eminence. China has an average annual growth rate of 9.7 per cent from 1980 to 2007.Bookshelves are full of titles predicting the emergence of China as Number One, the onset of The Chinese Century and its metamorphosis into a Big Dragon to challenge the US.

Table 1: 1820 and 2006 Top 10 Leading Economies[2]

Rank	1820 (in percent), Share of world total			2006 (in percent) , Share of world total		
	Country	GDP	Population	Country	GDP	Population
1.	China	28.7	35.7	United States	19.9	4.6
2.	India	16.0	19.6	China	15.4	2.0
3.	France	5.4	2.9	Japan	6.4	1.3
4.	United Kingdom	5.2	2.0	India	6.3	20.2
5.	Prussia	4.9	4.2	Germany	4	0.9
6.	Japan	3.1	2.9	United Kingdom	3	0.9
7.	Austria Hungary	1.9	1.3	France	2.9	0.9
8.	Spain	1.9	1.1	Italy	2.7	0.7
9.	United States	1.8	0.9	Russia	2.6	0.5
10.	Russia	1.7	1.1	Brazil	2.5	0.7
	Top ten total	70.6	71.7	Top ten total	65.7	32.7

India once is the biggest country of textile industry. From the very beginning, the Industrial Revolution relied upon trade. India is the colony of England. England loots the India and can explain the Industrial Revolution affect to the colony. Before 1850, South America, chiefly Brazil, served as the largest single market for British textiles. After the beginning of the Great Depression in 1873, India became the largest single market for British textiles. Something possible because Britain had earlier destroyed India's textile industry. Through several decades of efforts, India has established a relatively integrated national economic structure and considerably improved the livelihood of its people. Since independence, though its economy has not grown as fast as China's, India's development has been relatively steady and balanced with no roll-coastering. India solves the food supply through "green revolution" in agriculture, by "white revolution" in the milk industry etc. increase farmer income, built up the industry system, have the certain international competition. India acquired The economy development of India obtain achievement. Since its economic reform in 1991, India has also registered one of the fastest growth rates in the world, and has become an increasingly significant economic presence. India has an average annual growth rate of 8 per cent from 1980 to 2006. Now, India is endowed with a

---

[2] Source: World Economic Outlook, the International Monetary Fund for 2006 data and Angus Maddison, The World Economy: Volume 1: A Millennial Perspective and Volume 2: Historical Statistics, OECD, 2001 and 2003, for 1820 data.

unique advantage because of its cultural richness, abundant national resources, and the steady mentality of its people.

China and India are often believed to be the most competitive economies in the world – a threat to advanced economies with low-cost manufacturing and services, but also an opportunity with huge markets and combined populations of more than 2bn.

2. COMPARISON OF CHINA AND INDIA'S ECONOMIC DEVELOPMENT MODES

Without a doubt, China and India's gradual shift away towards a more market-based economy had yielded undeniable benefits. The development models of China and India.

China's model follows that of other East Asian economies and pursues income expansion through maximizing trade and investment. Government policies aimed at incentivising export production and capital accumulation are at the heart of this model. China's public sector leads its economic development. China started reform and opening to the world in 1978, then the government owned everything and there was no domestic business class to lobby against opening up or government exercising its power. China's infrastructure is far more developed than that of India. For example, the mileage of China's expressways has reached tens of thousands kilometers. China' investment environment is good, too. This is why China has gone further than other East Asian economies in export/investment model.

India's economic reform chose another model: India did not undertake the extensive manufacturing industry revolution, but development the servicing business to push the economic growth, which rounds the disadvantage factors such as low saving rate, poor manufacturing industry and FDI not enough etc. On the contrary, India has three greatest advantages—high educational background, the information science and technology and competence in English. India's private sector leads its economic development. India's economy reform began more than 10 years later. India is very experienced in the structuring of market economy. Although India introduced some elements of planned economy after its Independence, the private sector has remained very viable. In India, the private sector had 92% of total employment in whole country; but the state-owned section shared 8%. S the private sector accounts for a great proportion, most cities, including its capital city New Delhi, have no tall buildings except in Bombay. As for the superhighways and the subway construction is also meagre. Experts say that India's infrastructure falls behind than for China by ten to fifteen years. Under its democratic system, balance of interests and income distribution dominate the government's policies. India has been leaning towards growth through liberalisation of trade and domestic market in the past two decades or so, though at a slower pace than China. In particular, its domestic business community has a powerful voice on how fast to open up domestic markets to foreign capital. Furthermore, its trade is much smaller than China's and, hence, India is less vulnerable to international pressure in opening up its domestic markets.

India has an Anglo-Saxon style financial system, radically different from China's government-controlled financial system. The transmission from capital inflow into demand is very similar to that in Anglo-Saxon economies. India's aggregate debt to GDP ratio has increased by 28 percentage points in the past five years, largely to fund growth in household and government demand. India's economic momentum, therefore, depends on capital inflow that sustains credit growth that sustains demand growth. India stock market promotes the capital and saving in a very long period.This has made India's capital markets more sensitive to global liquidity cycle than China. This is the main reason that global liquidity, though supporting India's capital markets, has become the engine of India's growth now.

Table 2: Financial System Composition 2005

Particulars	China	India
Bank assets	73%	41%
Stock market capitalisation	14%	35%
Government bond	7%	22%
Corporate bond	6%	2%

In terms of the financial system composition, in total financial assets the bank property of China has 73%, but India only have 41%;The capital market of India is more flourishing than China, the stock market capitalisation has 35%, but China only have 14%.Unlike China, India's financial system is still small relative to the economy

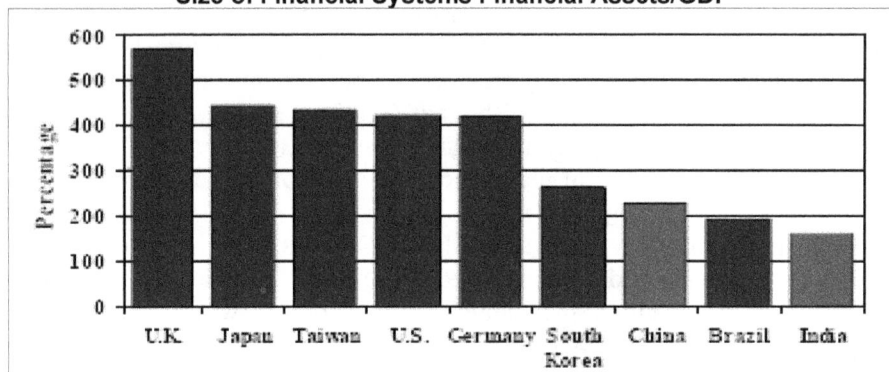

Size of Financial Systems Financial Assets/GDP

Chart 1: Distribution of World's Financial Assets[3]

---

[3] Source: International Financial Statistics, International Monetary Fund; *Emerging Market Fact Book*, Standard and Poor's; and *Quarterly Review*, the Bank for International Settlements.

Table 3: Comparative Financial Systems

		China (%)	India (%)
GDP	$44 trillion	5.0	1.7
Population	$6.5 billion	20.2	17.0
Total Financial Assets	$152 trillion	3.3	0.8

Table 3 provides a broader perspective of China and India by comparing them to select countries in terms of shares of world total financial assets (including bank assets, bonds outstanding and stock market capitalisation). It is clear that the world's income and financial assets are not distributed among these countries on the basis of their share of world population. Indeed, China accounts for 20 percent of the world's population but only 5 percent of the world's GDP and 3 percent of the world's financial assets. India is in even a worse comparatively, accounting for 17 percent of the world's population but less than 2 percent of the world's GDP and less than 1 percent of the world's financial assets.

India's banks are dwarfed by many of their international peers, in spite of their vast potential market in India and overseas. Industrial and Commercial Bank of China, China's largest bank, has a market capitalisation of about $55bn compared with SBI's $30bn.Although the total financial assets in China is larger than India's, India's financial system is operating quite healthily and non-performing loans are in low rate.It is a big trouble of financial industry in our country that most of the banks in China have been sticking to a lot of nonperforming Loans.

Encouragingly, as a result of these efforts the NPL ratios (i.e., nonperforming loans to total loans) of each of the Big Four have declined sharply from 2002 to 2006, as may be seen in chart .By September 2006, non-performing loans (NPLs) in the "big four" announted for 7.5 percent. By comparison, China operations of foreign banks had fewer non-performing loans. City Bank and the Hong Kong and Shanghai Banking Corp (HSBC) registered NPL ratio of 2.7 percent and 3 percent, respectively. The massive NPLs weigh on Chinese banks, especially the four state-owned commercial banks, and weaken their competitiveness in the market.

These differences have led to a very different mix of demand growth in this cycle between the two economies. Production for export and construction drives China's economy in the current cycle, while India's consumption, funded by credit, is driving its demand.

(Percentages, end of year)

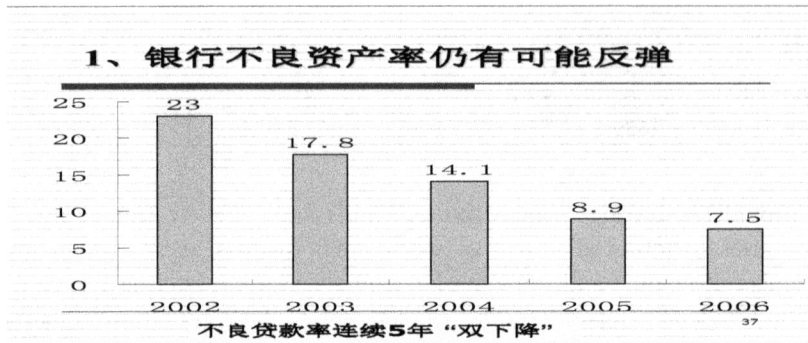

1、银行不良资产率仍有可能反弹

不良贷款率连续5年"双下降"

Chart 2: China's Reported Nonperforming Loans to Total Loans of the Big Four (2002-2006)

3. THE PERSPECTIVE AND WORRIES OF CHINA AND INDIA'S ECONOMY

3.1 How about the Perspective of China and India's Economy?

If China and India's Rapid Growth Continues. China and India's GDPs would exceed today's rich countries. A prediction by Goldman Sachs as to exactly when this will happen is provided in Chart 3[4]

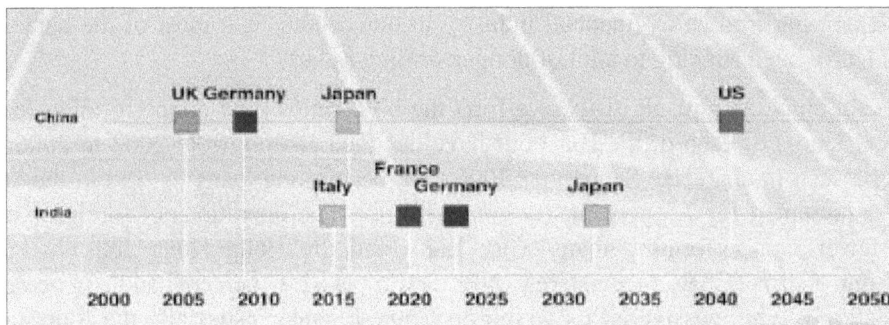

Chart 3: When China's and India's GDPs would Exceed Today's Rich Countries

Goldman Sachs argues that the economic potential of <u>Brazil</u>, <u>Russia</u>, <u>India</u>, and <u>China</u> is such that they may become among the four most dominant economies by the year 2050. As may be seen, China is expected to pass the United States in 2040 and India to pass Japan in 2030. The BRIC thesis (defended in the paper *Dreaming with BRICs: The Path to 2050*) recognizes that Brazil, Russia, India and China have

---

[4] Source: Goldman Sachs ,Global Economics Paper No: 99, October 2003.

changed their political systems to embrace global <u>capitalism</u>. He predicts China and India, respectively, to be the dominant global suppliers of <u>manufactured goods</u> and <u>services</u> while Brazil and Russia would become similarly dominant as suppliers of raw materials. The world's two largest emerging economies, China and India, are the key players in the current round of globalisation. It is now widely believed in the world that China and India would become economic powers standing in the forefront of the world.

The US Government Accountability Office estimates, reported this year that China's economy in PPP terms would be larger than the US by 2012.

For all the awe that their economies create, China and India rank 34th and 48th respectively in the World Economic Forum's global competitiveness index. Their low ranking reflects the need for these economies to improve many aspects of their markets and average living standards before they can be compared with advanced economies. In fact, the question perse is not so relevant. Prospects of China's and India's economic growth would depend on many unpredictable factors. China and India face economic, financial landmines just like any other emerging market.

Where is the risk for China and India's Economy? US economic imbalances posed a threat to its productivity and the global economy. Higher inflation has recently triggered popular reaction in Asia. Rising Asian inflation would be "a really serious issue this year. "Keeping inflation under control will be one of the major challenges in 2008-09.

For the moment, the slowdown in the US is starting to affect China and India. India's government admitted its economy was coming off the boil and faced big challenges to achieve its growth goals in the coming years. Mr Chidambaram forecast growth of 8.7 per cent in the financial year ending March 31, down from 9.6 per cent the previous year, and warned of a possible resurgence of inflation.

Sales of motorcycles, cars and other expensive consumer goods fell sharply last year as the central bank tightened monetary policy to curb inflation. The slowdown means India is falling behind in its goal of sustaining an average growth rate of 9 per cent in its latest five-year plan, which covers the period from 2007-08 to 2011-12, and forecasts Chinese-style double-digit growth in its final year. India must push through further reforms if it is to achieve the government's objective of double-digit economic growth by 2011 (Indian Government set the economic growth rate is to be up to 8% - 10%), the Organisation for Economic Co-operation and Development warned in 2007/10/10.

In China, inflation had reached an 11-year high at 6.9 per cent, boosted by a 18.2 per cent jump in food prices. A level that will harden Beijing's resolve to tighten monetary policy. The government is concerned that inflation, which has so far been confined to food, could spill over into other sectors. At present, China has announced it has shifted its monetary policy stance from "prudent" to "tightening".

China has lifted interest rates five times and reserve ratios 10 times last year, with little impact so far on either the pace of economic growth or inflation. Beijing is reining in credit, in part by ordering banks to lend less. The battle against inflation has been made harder by the US Federal Reserve's rapid-fire round of interest rate cuts. Raising rates in China, thus further widening the differential with the US, runs the risk of attracting more inflows of "hot" money.

I suggest that the PBoC needs to tighten monetary policy to keep a lid on inflation but its options are limited. It can raise reserve requirements for banks, but there is a limit to how far it can do so without undermining their profitability. It can raise interest rates, but that would make the dollar reserve problem even more acute.

China's remarkable resilience to both the 2001 global recession and the 1997-98 Asian financial crisis have convinced almost everyone that another year of double-digit growth is all but inevitable. But should we be so sanguine? In fact, the odds of a significant growth recession in China (at least one year of sub-6 per cent growth) during the next couple of years are 50 per cent. With Chinese inflation spiking, notable back-pedalling on market reforms and falling export demand, 2008 could be particularly challenging.

Next, we analyse the differences in risk realm in China and India.

4. CHINA FACES TWO STRONG RISKS: THE NON-PERFORMING LOANS RISING AND FINANCIAL SYSTEMS LOSE CONTROL

Although official figures for non-performing loans look encouraging, the banks are still in poor shape. A deserves concern of phenomenon: New macro control will bring how much of non-performing loans (NPLs)?

Maybe, the third high peak period of the non-performing loans are in formation currently. Review the past, the non-performing loans had two high peak periods. The first is during 1991-1993, the non-performing loans rate of four state-owned commercial banks are from 1990 of 10% to 20% of 1993 or so because of the economy growing too rapidly. The second is 1997-1998 years, after the financial crisis in Asia, the non-performing loans rate hiked to 20%. Through several years of macro-control, a large share of lending from the boom of 2001-07 could turn into bad debt, which may be the third high peak of the non-performing loans rate. For China and India, it is difficult to disaggregate the possible effect of slowing credit growth, as a result of a slower mainland economy, from any possible impact of a sub prime or other global issues. The Experts estimate that it is inevitable that the problem will come up in 2 or3 years or so. The optimistic evaluation is about 3%, the conservative evaluation is about 5% and the pessimism evaluation is about 8%.If China fails to deal with these, it could find itself going through the same experience as Japan in the 1990s, when bad loans led to a credit crunch and a long economic slowdown.

As the financial market is continuously opening, foreign financial organisations will rush into and bring enormous shocks to our domestic financial industry. So far, just a dozen are incorporated in China. Western banks that have done so, including Citigroup, are rolling out more branches, but high start-up costs aside, foreign banks are enjoying something of a sweet spot. In the first five months of last year, overseas banks' profits in the country grew by an annualised 43 per cent, according to regulators; the total is just $400m shared among 75 banks.

Besides, in advance of their listings, the banks have also been selling strategic stakes to foreign financial institutions (foreign ownership of banks is capped at 25%). I still regards state ownership of the banks as a vital bulwark against financial instability. It knows that this often leads to unproductive investments. But it also shores up public confidence in the banking system, which is essential for maintaining the flow of savings and foreign investment. I worry that the foreign capital contest will cause our country inevitably lose control over banking.

5. INDIA FACES RISKS: GLOBAL LIQUIDITY AND INFLATION COULD BE HEADWINDS

India's stock market has become critical to its economic performance. The foreign inflow into its stock market is a major source of liquidity for funding its current account deficit, keeping interest rates low, and sustaining credit growth necessary for its demand growth. But the short-term outlook for India, hence, depends very much on global liquidity. The overall background of global liquidity will likely decide the momentum of the Indian stock market and its economic momentum. Betting on India's stock market is equivalent to betting on sustained global liquidity boom, I believe.

I worry, once the Global liquidity and inflation become the headwinds, Indian economy will be inflicted by heavily losses. All crises are different. But many have shared common features. They begin with capital inflows from foreigners seduced by tales of an economic El Dorado. This generates low real interest rates and a widening current account deficit. Domestic borrowing and spending surge, particularly investment in property. Asset prices soar, borrowing increases and the capital inflow grows. Finally, the bubble bursts, capital floods out and the banking system, burdened with mountains of bad debt, implodes.

As the stock market is so important to the economy, the government is likely to take actions and provide rhetorical support to sustain the momentum in the market. But at present, stock markets across the region have continued to lose ground since the beginning of January. The MSCI Far East ex-Japan index has fallen by some 12 per cent in dollar terms and mutual funds sales across Asia have struggled as investors have taken on board both a slowing US economy and mounting uncertainty in the financial sector. When both illiquidity and insolvency emerge in the financial system, credit growth slows, or even goes negative, and spending, particularly on investment, weakens. Most crisis-hit emerging economies experienced huge recessions and a tidal wave of insolvencies. Indonesia's gross domestic product fell more than 13 per cent between 1997 and 1998. Sometimes the fiscal cost has been over 40 per cent of GDP. Stock market correlations between Asia and the US (and Europe) are at 30-year highs, mounting risks for emerging markets. The excess liquidity in India's banking system has vanished recently. If global liquidity dries up, the Indian economy would slow down substantially. So, the IMF thinks that global imbalances and the management of capital inflows into emerging economies as sources of risk.

Corporate Governance in China

Geeta Rani

Corporate governance practices in many countries have displayed some convergence towards Western standards in recent years (often emulating Britain's 1992 Cadbury Code and the United States 2003 Sarbanes-Oxley Act), but countries generally retain a set of distinct practices. In building its own system, China has been no exception. Four distinctive features of Chinese corporate governance in the late 2000s are particularly notable: 1) highly concentrated ownership; 2) strong state ownership; 3) pyramid ownership structures; 4) weak markets for corporate control.

1. HIGHLY CONCENTRATED OWNERSHIP

Company ownership is normally is generally diffuse in the United Kingdom, United States and other Western economies, with relatively few shareholders controlling more than a few per cent of the shares of any given firm. B contrast, ownership in China's listed firms is highly concentrated. Of the 1,602 companies listed on the Shanghai and Shenzhen stock exchanges in August 2008, the single largest owner held 36 percent of an average company's shares, the top three owned 49 per cent and the biggest five controlled 52 per cent. The high degree of concentrated ownership has remained relatively to exercise more control over Chinese companies than is common among their Western counterparts.

2. STRONG STATE OWNERSHIP

Despite a long-running process of privatization of state-owned enterprises, government agencies have maintained a high level of ownership and thus strong influence over many of the country's publicly listed firms. State-owned or state-controlled enterprises were responsible for 31 per cent of China's GDP in 2007, but the Shanghai Stock Exchange reported that the government held 51 per cent of its listed shares. Government officials overseeing the state's ownership stakes are not immune to political considerations; members of the Communist Party are often appointed to company boards, and Chinese regulations require that publicly listed companies provide necessary support for the functioning of the Communist Party within their firms.

3. PYRAMID OWNERSHIP STRUCTURES

Most major British and US publicly traded companies are owned and operated as stand-alone entities that work independently of one another to optimize investor returns. Many listed Chinese firms, by contrast are owned or controlled boy an unlisted parent company, and many of the listed firms, by contrast are owned or contributed by an unlisted parent company, and many of the listed firms in turn control other listed companies. The resulting pyramid ownership structure has opened the way for the malfeasance of tunneling, in which a controlling firm extracts resources from other firms in its pyramid whose minority owners would disapprove if the transfer came to light. A 2006 study by the Shanghai Stock Exchange revealed that such practices had become widespread: of the 1,377 firms studied, 35 per cent had misappropriated to their parent companies funds totaling RMB 48 billion. As a sign of the breadth of the problem, in 2006 China added pyramid misappropriation to its criminal code.

4. WEAK MARKETS FOR CORPORATE CONTROL

Because two-thirds of a typical firm's shares were held by the state and the companies themselves, and were untradeable before 2005, the market for corporate control in which companies and investors compete for control of other firms has been virtually non-existent. With formal movement of untraded shares on to the open market completed by 2007, active contests for control became more feasible. Yet even then, large blocks of a company's shares – often a third, half or even more – remained in the hands of public agencies. Unlike private investors, state organizations are concerned with a host of factors in addition to optimizing shareholder value, and few of the newly 'tradable' shares were actually traded in any case. A CSRC Study in 2008 found that among the 10 largest market-cap companies on the exchanges, 8 of them had fewer than 10 per cent of their shares to active trading, and the other 2 had less than a third actively traded. As a result, mergers and acquisitions were achieved through negotiation, and most required state approved as well. A hostile takeover bid for a financially underperforming company – the most prominent weapon in the western arsenal for corporate control would rarely attract the shares required or win government approval. More entrenched management at poorly performing companies had been one result.

5. THE CHINESE GOVERNING BOARD

As the Chinese public equity market matured, the organization, composition and practices of boards of directors of some publicly listed companies in China came to acquire some features similar to those of Anglo-American firms. The personal computer maker Lenovo, for instance, brought several independent directors on to its boards after it acquired the IBM personal computer division in 2005. Chinese governing boards have nonetheless followed a distinctive path in the area of 1) board structure, 2) shareholder rights, 3) disclosure and transparency, 4) corporate social responsibility, 5) the role of directors, and 6) executive compensation.

5.1 Board Structure

China has adopted a two-tier board structure similar to the German convention of having a supervisory board overseeing a board of directors. Chinese supervisory boards are required to have at least three members, and a third of the member must be employee representatives. In principle the supervisory board monitors the directors and the management, but in practice virtually all supervisory board members are from inside the firm, and the supervisory board largely rubber-stamps the decisions of directors and management.

The board of directors in the Anglo-American system sits at the hub of company governance, while in China the annual shareholders' meeting has emerged more to the front of the centre. Chinese company law endows the shareholders' meeting with power normally reserved for the board in the United Kingdom and United States. The board of directors in China, for instance, is required to 'develop and formulate' the company's annual budget and investment plan, but not approve the budget and plan, as is common in the Anglo-American world. Still, given that those attending the annual shareholders' meeting cannot effectively exercise discretionary authority in that venue, most of the real decision-making power remains in the hands of the directors and management.

Chinese regulations require a firm to designate one individual as 'legal person representative' to act on behalf of the firm. This position is normally assumed by the chairman of the board, and this rule has had the effect of investing greater power in the board chair than is common among British or American companies when the chair and CEO roles are separated.

5.2 Shareholder Rights

China's company law, revised in 2006, requires greater disclosure of information to stockholders than is common in the West. Shareholders elect directors and vote at shareholder meetings, but they also have access to company charters, shareholder lists and the minutes of meetings of both the supervisory boards and the board of directors.

To protect minority shareholders at companies where ownership is concentrated and pyramids prevail, companies are required to follow formal procedures for entering into related-party financial transactions. It is now mandatory for instance, that shareholders approve a company's transactions with a controlling company and the controlling company cannot vote its shares on such transactions. Minority shareholders have the right to introduce motions at, and to converge or even preside over, shareholders' meetings, and they can adopt a cumulative voting system for electing directors and supervisors.

5.3 Corporate Responsibility

China has placed formal emphasis on corporate social responsibility, more so than is common in many Western economies. The company law of 2006, for instance, has required that a company observe social norms and business ethics standards, operate honestly, accept monitoring by government and the general public, and assume its social responsibility.

The exchanges have gone even further, Shenzhen demands of its listed companies that in the process of maximizing shareholders value, they must also 'consider' the interests of their creditors, must not sacrifice creditors' interest for the sale of shareholder value and must provide creditors with access to financial and operational data. Shenzhen companies must also 'commit themselves to social welfare services like environmental protection and community development in order to achieve social harmony.'

5.4 The Role of the Director

Prior to 2001, no law or regulation required that any directors be independent of management. The China Securities Regulatory Commission (CSRC) now requires that a third of the seats on a publicly listed company board be held by independent directors, and many companies have reached that threshold. A 2004 study by the Shanghai Stock Exchange found that independent directors constitutes nearly a third of the board members, and on occasion have exercised a very independent role. In one widely publicized incident, for example, an independent director challenged related-party transaction by the board chair of a prominent food maker, and upon CSRC investigation the company ousted its chairman.

The 2006 Company Law strengthened the obligations of directors to include both 'duty of loyalty' and 'duty of care' though neither is defined very clearly. It did state that the loyalty obligations included forbidding the use of company funds for personal use, the making of loans to others without authorization, the disclosure of proprietary information, self-dealing and bribes. It also held directors personally liable if director decisions violated state regulations or the company charter.

5.5 Executive Compensation

When compared to the West, the executive compensation has been substantially lower, though it has been substantially rising. According to the survey conducted by the Shanghai Stock Exchange the highest-paid executive of listed firms in 2003 was close to RMB 200,000 (£ 16,800), but just two years later the average had jumped to RMB 300,000 (£25,200). The highest-paid executive in 2005 received compensation of RMB 6 million (£ 500,000), but three years later the largest executive pay cheque had soared to RMB 66 million (£ 5.5 million). Not surprisingly, executive compensation in state-owned enterprises remained far below that in privately held corporations.

In spite, of the rapid rise of executive compensation, most pay remained fixed, rather than varying with performance. In many US and British listed firms the great majority of top executive compensation is variable, while in Chinese listed firms, according to a study in 2006, fully 97 per cent was still paid in the form of a fixed salary. Only a tenth of the firms used stock options at all. In 2006 the CSRC gave its blessing for more, though it declared that no more than 1 per cent of a company's shares can be used as options for the top executive, and no more than 10 per cent for all of the executives combined.

5.6 Chinese Governance

China has created one of the largest markets for publicly listed companies in the world. The total market capitalization of the two Chinese stock exchanges ranked below only those of the United States, Japan, Europe and the United Kingdom in 2008, up from no market capitalization at all less than three decades earlier.

China's regulatory regime has come to include everything from prohibitions against self-dealing and tunneling to prescriptions for independent directors and contingent compensation. Though some features of Chinese corporate governance are akin to those found in most Western economies, several features remain distinctive, including highly concentrated ownership, much of it by the state, and a relatively weak market for corporate control. Likewise, though certain aspects of the governing boards of Chinese publicly traded companies are similar to those elsewhere, distinct features are evident here too, including less influential boards, weaker disclosure enforcement, greater social responsibility and less contingent compensation.

A REPORT

Economic Reforms in India and China

Prelude

China and India are two largest countries of the world in terms of population. The two countries are considered as two powerful engines that will lead the world to the Asian Century. Both the countries are booming with a very high rate of economic growth and face the social and political challenges of consolidation. China and India are engaged in re-writing their economic history and creating a great economic future by transforming their respective economies and societies. They have been doing so for the last three decades. The two countries could further add to their socio-economic and political mite by understanding the dynamics of economic reforms through exchange of experiences and confabulations on the future strategies to lift the rate of growth and at the same time remove social dissentions.

Ever since the achievement of independence in India in 1947, and of liberation in China in 1949, there has been intense interest in the comparative economic performance of the two Asian giants. In the early phase, the interest was anticipatory; would the socialistic economy with a democratic polity match up in its economic performance with the socialist economy and its revolutionary socialist system? China showcased socialism; India aspired to a "socialistic pattern of society" and boasted a parliamentary democracy. In the charged post-colonialism, the eyes of the many nations were on this race. The two great powers were also in the stands, with more than just a gambling of voyeuristic interest and stake in the outcome – it was no ordinary day at the races.

Both countries, wanted to modernize their systems and achieve rapid long term growth with equity. However, it is arguable that in their own perceptions, the two horses were running different, independent, races. India mostly compared its performance with its own past, demonstrating the achievements of the new proud independent nation with the stagnation and mass deprivation of the colonial era. This was not a difficult race to win. A second yardstick was again the internal comparison with its own adopted plan targets – had they been achieved, and usually of course they had not. China, on the other hand, never seriously compared its own performance with its Himalayan neighbour. Doing better than India was not the issue: the challenge was to catch up with the West. In 1958, the Chinese Communist Party launched the campaign to "Catch up with Great Britain in Fifteen Years". China had set itself targets on a truly Himalayan scale.

What happened? In terms of comparative performance since 1950 with respect to a full range of material, economic and social indicators, there can be no argument that China has performed emphatically better than India. Starting from a virtually identical position in 1950, China's per capita income stands at twice the level of India in 2003; it has a much lower incidence of headcount poverty regardless of the specific methodologies uses; its life expectancy at 71 is 6 years more than that of the average Indian; its adult literacy rate is 91% compared to 65% for India; it has more than twice as many physicians per head of population than India; only 8% of its under-fives suffer are moderately underweight and none are severely so, whereas for India, as many as 47% are moderately or severely underweight; only 14% of these children suffer from moderate or severe stunting in China, but as many as 46% do in India. On other comparisons, Chinese electricity consumption per capita, a crucial indicator, is 893 Kwh in China, compared with just 379 in India; cement production is 650 m tons per year in China, and 109 in India; steel production 163 m tons in China and 29 m tons in India. In China, as much as 53% of the GDP comes from industry, in India only 26%. Of course, in comparison, India obtains 52% of its GDP from services, while the percentage for China is only 32% - though it is questionable if this comparison fully reflects a mature, or a partially residual services sector. Regardless of this, the Chinese growth rates in agriculture, industry and services are all above the Indian ones. And for those who might point to India's sterling IT sector performance, it is growth noting that the fixed line and mobile phone subscribers per 1000 people in China were 424 in 2003, as against just 71 in India; that internet users per 1000 people in China were 63 against 17 in India, and that personal computers per 1000 persons were 28 in China (in 2002) compared with 7 in India. The answer to the question, who won, is not much in doubt. Indeed the margin of the victory is quite astonishing.

More significant is the question of how this was achieved. How did China do it? Most often, observers point to the impact of the Chinese economic reforms after 1978, and to the fact that the reforms started rather later in India. However, a crucial fact is that the differential performance was already observable in full measure by 1978. This calls for a careful assessment of the relationship between the achievements of the collectivist development period in China, and its potential and real contributions to post-1978 economic performance. We argue that in this, a vital role was played by institutional factors. While the institutional framework served as a contextual rigidity and as a development constraint in India, in contrast, the Chinese socialist development state was able to address the institutional framework as a prime target variable, to be refashioned instrumentally as deemed optimal functionally with respect to accelerating the growth process. This dimension provides an underlying unifying leitmotif over the entire period since 1949 in China.

In the past decade, the Indian economy has posted high growth rates, sparking the question: Is India catching up with China? Is there a convergence? This higher growth rate does seem to suggest that the rates of change are getting closer, but the levels of the growth rates remain higher for China, implying that in terms of absolute level of achievements, there is little likelihood of India catching up, or overtaking China

THE THOUGHT EVOLUTION

It was in 2003-04, the idea of the seminar was mooted by Prof R.K. Mishra during his discussions with his counterparts in China which country he traveled on the invitation of the Asian Development Bank. This was further discussed in February 2005 at the Lee Kuan Yew School of Public Policy, National University of Singapore and later at INTAN, Malaysia in December of the same year. The China National School of Administration (CNSA) and Institute of Public Enterprise (IPE) further discussed the proposal in July 2007 at Abu Dhabi where broad agreement on the areas of discussion and the modalities of the presentations were finalized. This followed a spate of telecons and exchange of mails regarding the thrust and methodology of the seminar. Finally, it was agreed to hold the first part of the seminar in Beijing in June 2008 and the return seminar at Hyderabad in January 2009. It was further agreed to bring out the papers and proceedings of the seminar in two volumes under the joint co-editorship of Prof R K Mishra and Prof Wang Jian to be assisted by two colleagues on each side to be identified later.

BACKGROUND OF THE VISIT

China and India are the two largest countries of the world in terms of population. The two countries are considered as powerful engines that will lead the world to the Asian Century. Both the countries are booming with high rate of economic growth and face the social and political challenges of consolidation. China and India are engaged in re-writing their economic history and creating a great economic future by transforming their respective economies and societies. Both the countries are engaged in modernizing their socio-economic systems and are actively involved in achieving rapid long term growth with equity. In this backdrop, the Institute imitative of a dialogue with the China National School of Administration (CNSA), Beijing during the period 2004-2007 translated itself into an agreement of organizing a two-way seminar on "Economics Reforms in India and China". The first part of the seminar was conducted from 2–4 June, 2008 at the CNSA which also organized visits from 5-6 June, 2008 to neighboring Shijingshan District (Training Base), Tianjin Institute of Public Administration and Shanghai Institute of Public Administration covering some major economic institutions. The seminar had participation from 30 participants from India and China.

Detailed Summary of Inaugural, Technical and Valedictory Sessions

MONDAY 2ND JUNE 2008

The two day seminar started with the welcome address by Prof Zhou Shaopeng, Department of Economics, CNSA highlighting the developmental issues in both the countries which started the reforms during the same period.

Prof Wang Jian, Director–General, Department of Economics, CNSA pointed out that China was busy with rescue operations due to the unfortunate earthquake and also hosting the Olympic Games. He also added that the expectations of the world from dragon and elephant are manifold in the economic reforms front since China and India both the fastest growing economies face similar challenges and problems. By providing a common forum for discussion and exchange of views on various issues relating to the development will help these two countries in improving their performance. He wished the seminar a great success.

KEYNOTE SPEECH 1

Prof Wang Jian, delivered the first keynote address titled 'An Overview of years of Economic Reforms and Opening up in China'. Prof Jian observed that the economic reforms not only resulted in the unprecedented development but also brought in a number of problems. He detailed six major stages (1978-2007) of macro economic changes in China transforming the planned economy of China into a market economy. The six stages include:

(a) Macro Regulation

(b) Boost tight economy

(c) Hard landing macro regulation

(d) Soft landing macro regulation

(e) Deflation.

(f) Controlling rate of inflation. The period 2003-07 was the first phase directed to control the rate of inflation. The inflation growth was halted during this period. Since August 2007, the open economy phase known as second phase has begun raising the head of ugly inflation and overheating of the economy. All efforts are getting directed to control the inflation.

KEYNOTE SPEECH 2

Prof R.K. Mishra, delivered the second keynote address titled 'An Overview of Economic Reforms in India'. He pointed out that India initiated the economic reforms by ushering in economic liberalization in 1985 and had to carry the exercise to the logical culmination by giving way to the economic reforms as the fiscal deficit was soaring, revenue imbalance, inflation was galloping, unemployment was increasing, and agriculture was in a bad shape and trade deficit increased beyond the limits. India took resort to stabilization and structural adjustments programme which was very difficult from the approach followed by China. Sounding a note of caution, he urged on both the countries that economic growth should not be fastened at the cost of damaging environment He suggested that the culture of innovation should permeate the socio-economic systems in the two countries resulting in competition and higher productivity. Prof Mishra said that India has come out of the low growth trap – the Hindu Rate of Growth of 3 per cent to ascend to the high growth zone of 9 per cent per annum.

FIRST PLENARY SESSION

The first plenary session on Economic Reforms, was Chaired by Prof Li Xuefeng, Department of Economics, CNSA. There were five speakers in the session. Their contribution is detailed below:

1. **Prof Wang Haibo, Academician, Chinese Academy of Social Science, 'Prospect of the Economic Development between 2008 and 2020'.**

   Prof Haibo presented the practical and theoretical dimensions of economic development in China which respectively mean deploying factors of production without causing inflation and increasing the growth rate. During the period 2008-2020 the Chinese economy is expected to constantly grow at nine per cent per annum with minor fluctuations, volatility and some structural problems.

2. **Prof Naresh Sharma, Department of Economics, University of Hyderabad, 'Economic Reforms in Agriculture Sector in India'**

   Agriculture is the mainstay of Indian economy. It provides employment to 65 per cent of the Indian people. Agriculture contributes about 18 per cent to the country's total GDP. He examined both economic reforms specific to agriculture and also economic reforms in general.

3. **Prof Huang Hengxue, School of Government Management, Peking University, 'Economic Reforms in China'**

   The four ways of economic diversification in China are (i) recycling economy, (ii) Optimum input-output usage, (iii) energy conservation and eco friendly economic development, and (iv) sustainable development. Economic development in China will be achieved two pillars: technical innovation and market economy.

4. **Prof R.K. Mishra, Director, IPE, 'Second Generation Reforms in India'**

   India completed the first decade of economic reforms in 2001. The agenda for economic reforms was preceded with two tasks viz. the country would undertake widening and deepening of economic reforms which were initiated in the first flush and the economic reforms would transfer from the center to the states for their wider and deepening of economic reforms and traverse from the center to the states for their wider acceptance and producing lasting impact on the Indian economy. Besides discussing the widening and deepening of reforms and their journey from the center to the states, he explained the institutional dimensions and the impact of economic reforms with regard to the socio-economic goals laid down in the planned approach in Indian constitution.

5. **Prof Zhang Zhanbin, Department of Economics, CNSA, 'Development Approach Similarity between China and India and their strategic choices'**

   As two large counties in the world, China and India share similar development approaches. By mid 21st Century, Europe, China, the US, and India will become the largest four economies of the world. The new emerging eastern markets will act as the engines of the global economy and the world's economic order will undergo tremendous change. Long-term economic growth will support the nation's manpower. The 11th Five year plan of China divides the entire land area into Optimum Development Area, Limited Development Area and Restricted Development Area. The concept of Industrial clusters was introduced as the restructuring device.

SECOND PLENARY SESSION

The Second plenary session on Public Enterprise Reforms, was Chaired by Prof R.K. Mishra, Director, IPE. They were four speakers in the session. Their presentations are given below:

6. **Ms Janaswamy Kiranmai, Assistant Professor, IPE, 'Performance of Public Enterprises in the Era of Economic Liberalization'**

   The economic liberalization has brought about a radical transformation in PE policy issues. The PE policy leans towards a balanced approach. The behaviour of the Government at times has been inconsistent with the professed policy. During the period 1999-2004, PE privatization and disinvestment was attempted on imprudent basis. The sale of Bharat Aluminum Company Limited (BALCO) and the transfer of property of the Hotel Airport, Mumbai are the cases in point. The sales were transacted at un-remunerative prices to the Government without a proper social safety net to the employees and disregarding the well established principles of preventing the creation of monopoly. The Airport privatization has been opposed not only by the labour unions and the Left but also by a bidder on the ground of administrative sanctity. She focused on the analysis of performance of CPSEs with reference to some important ratios such as profit before interest and tax to capital employed, sales to capital employed. In conclusion PEs in the era of economic liberalization have done extremely well.

7. **Mr D Venkateswara Rao, IAS, Principal Secretary, Department of Public Enterprise, Government of Karnataka, Bangalore 'Political Economy of state Level Public Enterprise reforms in India: Special Reference to Karnataka'.**

The arena of fiscal federalism in India, which had been a minefield of political conflicts even in the pre-reform era, has been showing signs of becoming a full-fledged battlefield in the wake of the economic reform programme initiated in 1991. The experience of federal governance in different parts of the world has been one of persisting tensions and conflicts of various types between the central and sub central governments. It is observed that the performance of the public sectors have improved for the past 3-4 years and turnaround into considerable profits, which is satisfactory.

8. **Prof Li Xuefeng, Department of Economics, CNSA 'An Analysis on Mainland China's Economic Growth and Policy between 1992 and 2006'.**

In 1992, China announced its aim of building up a socialist market economy. The entire economic growth in China had four aspects: economic development, economic policies, institutional reforms, cultural and political factors. During the period of economic reforms, various policies like new fiscal and market systems, new banking system, financial regulations have been introduced. By introducing various institutional reforms, the productivity of Chinese economy has gone up.

THIRD PLENARY SESSION

The third plenary session on Prospects and Challenges was chaired by Dr. Hui Shuangmin, Department of Economics, CNSA. They were four speakers in the sessions:

9. **Prof Zhang Xiaode, Department of Economics, CNSA, 'Industrialization Dilemma and Civilization Model Innovation under Resource and Environment Restrictions in Large Countries'**

The real challenge posed by the vigorous development of BRICs (Brazil, Russia, India and China) to their western counterparts is not to eclipse their leading economic role in the world; instead, it has challenged the industrial civilization model of western countries. The industrial civilization model chosen by western countries that is described as 'cost externalization' only applies to a small number of countries. However, as the countries constituting 40% of all population in the world, the BRICs need to establish a new eco-friendly model given the resource and environment constraints. The model called 'cost internalization' is characterized by low energy consumption and high self purification capacity and it applies to all countries in the world. Public Service Delivery issues were discussed in this session. Social welfare system was started in rural areas. Various reasons for regional imbalances were discussed at length.

10. **Prof Dong Xiaojun, Department of Economics, CNSA, 'China and India: Economic Prospects Vs Challenges'.**

In this session various development issues in relation to China and India were discussed. It was observed that both India and China are strong in agriculture. In China public sector plays an important role where as in India public private partnership gained momentum. Capital markets are playing dominant role in the financial sector.

11. **Dr Suri Subrahmanyam Suribohtla, Associate Professor, IPE, Ms Lalitha Shanth Kumar, Senior Administrative Officer (Research), IPE, 'Technology Reforms: A Case Study of E-Governance in India'.**

The successful governance in the country requires a direct dialogue between people and government. The governance has to be simple, moral, accountable, responsive and transparent (SMART). The e-Government sought primarily with a view in cutting the cost of governance in the developed world. Though this has been stated as one of the reasons for developing nations too, it would appear to be lower down the order of priority with savings in cost accruing primarily form process *optimization and* labour costs in India. E-Governance is emerging as a new tool to establish SMART governance paving the way for the socio-economic transformation of the country, its modernization and integration with the rest of the world. The paper highlights centralization vs. decentralization dimensions in relation to e-Governance and incorporates case studies on e-Governance in Andhra Pradesh which is recognized as the *change leader in the country*. In conclusion he has highlighted that the corporate sector in India has demonstrated very strongly as to how e-Governance helps it in improving its profits through better cost and effective customer service management. e-Democracy has taken off well in India with the limitations of human bias afflicting the polling teams stationed at the polling booths.

12. **Prof Zhang Qing, Department of Economics, CNSA, 'Consummating National Commodity Reserve System and Enhancing Stabilization of Macro Economy',**

In this session, the Chinese National Major Commodities Reserve System was discussed. It was stated that it is an inevitable choice to the Chinese government to improve the national major commodities system. It was further discussed that this system is a remedy to the limitations of fiscal policy and monetary policy in the new circumstance of mercerization and globalization.

FOURTH PLENARY SESSION

The fourth plenary session on Capital Market and Monetary Policy was Chaired by Prof. Naresh Sharma, Department of Economics, University of Hyderabad. They were four speakers in the session:

13. **Prof R.K. Mishra, Director, IPE, 'Financial Sector Reforms and Fiscal Policy Reforms in India',**

This paper was discussed in detail on financial sector and fiscal policy reforms. Major issues like prudential norms, asset liability mach, bank supervision, technolisization, productivity of banking system, competition, regulation and portfolio transformation were discussed in detail.

14. **Dr Ma Xiaofang, Associate Professor, Department of Economics, CNSA, 'The Impact of Subprime Mortgage Crisis on Chinese Economy'**

This paper discussed in detail the impact of sub prime mortgage crisis on Chinese economy. Most of the economists think that if the crisis continues, it will have great impact on global financial markets, and the US economy and the world economy will fall into recession. Three risk links were discussed in this financial accident: the prosperity of property market enhances the standard release of the mortgage loan and innovation in the products of mortgage loan; securitization leads to credit risk transfer from property financial institutions to capital markets; the increase of benchmark interest rate and the weakness of property market become the main fuse.

15. **Dr Xu Jie, Associate Professor, Department of Economics, CNSA, 'Changes of Monetary Policy in China'**

This paper dealt with as to how monetary policy is implemented in the Chinese economic. After July 2005, the foreign exchange regime shifted from fixed exchange rate to flexible exchange rate. It was further stated that the economy experienced imbalance between urban and rural areas and also between agriculture and industries. Issues like fixed exchange rate, capital flow in relation to monetary policy were discussed.

TUESDAY 3RD JUNE 2008

FIFTH PLENARY SESSION

The fifth plenary session on Social Sector Reforms was Chaired by Prof Zhang Qing, Department of Economics, CNSA. They were five speakers in the session:

16. **Prof Xu Zhengzhong, Department of economics, CNSA, 'Building Up a Universal social service system, promoting comprehensive modernization of economic society'**

    Various issues like economic and social development in China, opportunities and challenges facing Chinese social development, were discussed. In the world GDP, China moved from 8th rank to 4th rank. In case of trade, China shifted from 27th rank to 3rd rank. It was stated that research and development registered high place in industrialization. The Chinese economy shifted from tri-dimensional hierarchical type to flat network type using information technology. A gradual shift from closed society to outward society, industrial pursuance to industrial innovation, linear economy to circulating economy and survival culture to developing culture were discussed in detail.

17. **Ms Lakshmi Kumari, Chintalapudi, Ms.Lalitha Shanth Kumar, Senior Administrative Officer (Research), IPE, 'Social Sector Reforms'**

    Discussion was made on the poverty estimates in India, methods of measurement of poverty and the broad features of poverty and exclusion in India such as rural and urban poverty, agricultural poverty etc. The presentation concluded with suggestions for the elimination of poverty from the Indian society.

18. **Prof Shi Hongxiu, Department of Economics, CNSA, Fiscal Competition and Fiscal Accountability: Evidence from Unitary and Federal Countries**

    The paper asserted that market economy is the driving force for Chinese economic transformation. Supply and demand are the factors that determine competition. It was explained that public and non-public sector division can be made for greater accountability.

19. **Prof. R.K. Mishra, Director, IPE, 'Power Sector Reforms in India', Prof.Zhang Zhanbin, Department of Economics, CNSA, 'Development Approach Similarity Between China and India and Their Strategic Choices'**

    This paper brought out similarities and divergences in the development process of India and China. It was stated that both the countries concentrated on Heavy industries development and neglected agriculture and light industries. In both the countries Five year plan approach was followed. Economic Reforms was started in 1970 in China and 1990 in India. In China concentration was more on manufacturing sector where as in India importance was given to IT and service sectors.

VALEDICTORY ADDRESS

Prof Wang Jian, Director-General, Department of Economics, CNSA delivered the valedictory address. He stated that Prof Mishra's speech on power sector reforms, financial and fiscal sector reforms was very well received by the audience. He further said that the relations will continue for a longer period. We welcome more Indians to China to share their rich experience. We see deep cooperation between CNSA and IPE in the future to provide valuable proposals to both the governments. Co-operation between Dragon and Elephant should be continued in future. He stated that we have come to the end of the programme but the interaction with Indians have not come to an end.

Summary of Papers

Rapid Development of Capital Market and New Features and Strategies of Macro Economy

Prof. Wang Jian, Director-General, Department of Economics, CNSA

The capital Market in China has made great strides in recent years and gradually it has exerted more important impact on China's macro economy where new features have been shown, such as the co-existence of high securitization rate and high indirect financing rate, the inflow of international mobility attracted by the development of capital market, the co-existence of inflation and appreciation of RMB, the seesaw between stock market and real estate market as well as the co-existence of over-mobility and capital outflow. Based on the above-mentioned features, the following countermeasures should be adopted in order to achieve the continued growth of macro economy. Firstly, we should make the development of the capital market an impetus for the growth of the tangible economy; secondly, the balanced fiscal policy should be enforced; thirdly, flexible monetary policy should be adopted; fourthly, we must increase the minimum salary and perfect social security system; last but not least, performance assessment indicators for government should be improved.

Prospect of the Economic Development between 2008 and 2020

Prof. Wang Haibo, Academician, Chinese Academy of Social Sciences

Chinese economy achieved continued and rapid growth between 1978 and 2007. If there are no major domestic and international barriers, Chinese economy is still expected to develop continuously and rapidly between 2008 and 2020. If the prospect becomes true, China will create a unique miracle of economic development in the world. In order to justify the prospect, we have to analyze the special domestic and international circumstances China is faced with. Firstly, compared with its large economic power status in the history, China has now tremendous room for economic development. Secondly, although the potential for economic growth contained in the planned economy has been largely released ever since the reform and opening up, China still gets huge potential for economic growth. Thirdly and more importantly, China is endowed with a lot of favorable circumstances for economic growth. These are mainly the effect of further reform and opening up brought by globalization, the technological progress brought by knowledge economy, the higher development level of industrialization, the large population and large economy, the all-round macro-economic regulation that is adaptable to Chinese market economy, the long-term stable political situation and the relatively long term of peaceful international environment China is able to enjoy. In conclusion, although Chinese economy is still faced with various difficulties, it is expected to make long-term continued and rapid progress.

Economic Reforms in Agriculture Sector in India

Prof. Naresh Sharma, Department of *Economics, University* of *Hyderabad*

Agriculture is the mainstay of Indian Economy. It provides employment to 65% of the Indian people. However, at present it contributes only about 18% to the Gross Domestic Product (GDP) of India. Since Independence, Indian Agriculture has revolutionized itself in terms of ensuring adequate food grains by ushering the green revolution from late 1960s. However, now the Indian agriculture is in the throes of deep crises. The food grains output is almost static, the agricultural productivity is stagnant, the production of oil seeds and pulses is not increasing, investment in agriculture has encountered a steep fall, credit delivery to agriculture is not adequate, globalization is giving rise to self-sufficiency in agriculture, agricultural prices are not farmer friendly and a scissors crises like situation has engulfed the Indian agriculture. The present paper makes an intensive study of agricultural scenario in India, the reform measures over the past decade and a half and its relation to the performance of agriculture sector including the present scenario of agriculture crisis. The paper examines, for this purpose, both economic reforms specific to agriculture and also economic reforms in general.

Second Generation Reforms in India

Dr. Seeta Mishra, Assistant Professor, Post Graduate A. V. *College*

India completed the first decade of economic reforms in 2001. The agenda of economic reforms remained yet to be completed by that time. It was realized that there was no going back on economic reforms and that the country was committed to complete the unfinished agenda of economic reforms. It was decided to proceed with the task in two ways: one, the country would undertake the widening and deepening of economic reforms which were initiated in the first flush and, two, the economic reforms would traverse from the center to the states for their wider acceptance and producing lasting impact on the Indian economy. Besides discussing the widening and deepening of economic reforms and their journey from the center to the states, this paper would critically examine the institutional dimensions and the impact of economic reforms with regard to the socio-economic goals laid down in the planned approach and the Indian Constitution.

Development Approach Similarity between China and India and Their Strategic Choices

Prof. Zhang Zhanbin, Department of Economics, CNSA

As two large countries in the world, China and India share similarity between development approaches. The rapid development of China and India in the last 30 and 20 years has attracted significant attention from all over the world. Between these two countries, India is gradually catching up with and surpassing China. So China needs to learn from India's experience. By mid 21st century, Europe, China, US and India will become the largest four economies of the world, the new emerging eastern markets will act as the engines of the global economy and the world's economic order will undergo tremendous changes. However, there is still long way to go before China and India become the real strong countries. In order to become the real strong powers in the world, the two countries will need to adopt their own development strategies which aim at realizing the balanced development between urban and rural areas, social justice and conservation culture and enabling government reform. The strategies should help to amplify the two countries' strengths and lessen their weaknesses.

Performance of Public Enterprises in the Era of Economic Liberalization

Prof. R.K. Mishra, Director, IPE

This paper proposes to analyze the performance of the Public Enterprises (PEs) in the era of economic liberalization against the backdrop of trenchant criticism of their non-performance and argument about their folding up in the wake of the development of private sector and private initiative. In doing so, the paper portrays the Government policy on PEs, performance of PEs during the era of economic liberalization, salient features of functioning of PEs, and the scope for improvement in their future performance.

The Reform of State-Owned Enterprises and Nonpublic Sector of the Economy in China

Prof. Zhou Shaopeng, Department of Economics, CNSA

SOEs reform in China has undergone the stages of expanding rights and sharing interests within the basic framework of planned economy and innovating on systems in market economy. It is now entering a new phase of establishing and improving modern enterprise system marked with accelerating the development of listed companies. While strengthening SOEs reform, the non public sector of the economy is developing very rapidly. In the new historical era, efforts should be made to further the strategic restructuring of the state sector of the economy in order to adapt to the irresistible trend of the gradual integration between the state and nonpublic sectors of the economy. We must reform the single stockholding system and the unreasonable structure existing in Chinese SOEs including enterprises solely funded by the state and state-holding enterprises, especially those large and medium sized SOEs. We should actively develop the stockholding system reform and generally promote listed SOEs. Domestic and foreign strategic investors should be involved in the stockholding system reform of SOEs. Meanwhile, continuous efforts must be made to further develop the nonpublic sector of the economy. All these efforts will create a higher development level of the diversified ownerships of the economy.

Scenario of Public Enterprises in Karantaka

Prof. R.K. Mishra, Director, IPE & Dr. J. Kiranmai, Assistant Professor , IPE, Shri Venkateswara Rao, IAS, Government of Karnataka, Bangalore

The State Level Public Enterprises (SLPEs) are an important component of the public enterprise system in India. As per the Institute of Public Enterprise (IPE) database, there were 1,129 SLPEs as on March 31, 2005 with an investment of ₹ 2,59,184 crore. The contribution of the SLPEs to the Gross State Domestic Product (GDP) is about 5 per cent as compared to 10 per cent by the Central Public Enterprises (CPEs). The role of SLPEs can be assessed from the total turnover as a percentage of the GDP. There was no consistent pattern among states and this percentage generally varied from 1 to17 percent of the Gross State Domestic Product, with most states falling in the range of 6 to15 percent. Although, the SLPEs constitute 80 per cent of the total investment of the CPEs, they are more than four times the number of the CPEs. The average investment in an SLPE is 15 per cent of a CPE. However, the SLPEs in terms of the resource use and control depict a different picture as compared to their counterparts in the central sector in that they directly impact the functioning of the state economies and have a greater exposure to the state political systems. The SLPEs are characterized by weak middle management systems as they do not have on their rolls the requisite number of professionally qualified mangers. The top management in these enterprises comprises mostly an IAS CEO and nominees of the state governments drawn from civil services, defeated politicians and political party in power. The financial performance of the SLPEs bears the brunt of these shortcomings. Between 1990-91 and 2004-05, the SLPEs continued to incur net losses and showed the chronic tendency of accumulating losses. The macro analysis provides in the beginning an overview of the SLPEs in India in terms of various financial parameters followed by the general scenario in regard to their privatisation.

The differentiating features of privatisation of the SLPEs vis-a-vis the CPEs have been outlined to bring out the challenges that the various state governments have to meet in reconsidering the retention of their portfolios of the SLPEs. The summing up provides the conclusions to formulate an appropriate policy in this regard. In other words, the paper makes an attempt to focus the political economy of economic reforms in the SLPEs and the lessons that these enterprises could draw from such an analysis for their efficient functioning in future.

An Analysis on Mainland China's Economic Growth and Policy Between 1992 and 2006

Prof. Li Xuefeng, Department of *Economics, CNSA*

In 1992, China announced its aim of building up a socialist market economy. From then on, its economic growth revealed to be unprecedented scenery in its history and aroused the attention of the world. What really happened in the last fifteen years? What should the Chinese government do to sustain its economic growth in the future? This paper analyzes the key issues of China' economic growth: the initial circumstances, the economic growth performance, the economic policy, the institutional reform, the related cultural and political evolution. The last part of the paper raises suggestions for future growth policies.

Policy Restructuring for Industrial Cluster Upgrade in China

Dr. Li Jiangtao, Associate Professor, Department of *Economics, CNSA*

One challenge facing Chinese economy is to upgrade the industrial clusters. An important factor causing the challenge is the lack of appropriate policy system. Therefore, policy restructuring has become an urgent task for industrial cluster upgrade. Ever since the reform and opening up to the outside world, the industrial clusters, as a modern organization mode of industrial economy, have played an essential role in the continued growth of Chinese economy. Having experienced the embryonic, growing and partially mature stages, the industrial clusters are now entering an important turning point of how to further develop. Recently, the large-scale retreat of Hong Kong and Taiwan enterprises from Pearl River Delta has exemplified the challenge facing the current industrial clusters. The question is whether China is able to further industrial cluster upgrade. If the answer is yes, the industrial clusters will enter a new stage of qualitative change by technological and institutional innovation; if the answer is no, the industrial clusters will gradually weaken and finally disappear in the economic development process. As a matter of fact, the industrial clusters have proved its effectiveness in promoting industrial upgrade and economic growth through the economic practice in developed countries. The relatively low development level of Chinese industrial clusters has been caused by many factors. Among them, the lagging government policy is an important one. It was the major constraining force for the development of Chinese industrial clusters in the past, and whether government policy will be restructured directly determines the long-term economic growth when Chinese economy enters a new development period.

Industrialization Dilemma and Civilization Model Innovation under Resource and Environment Restrictions in Large Countries

Prof. Zhang Xiaode, Department of *Economics, CNSA*

The real challenge posed by the vigorous development of BRICs to their western counterparts is not to eclipse their leading economic role in the world; instead, it has challenged the industrial civilization model of western countries. The industrial civilization model chosen by western countries that is described as "cost externalization" only applies to a small number of countries. However, as the countries constituting 40% of all population in the world, the BRICs need to establish a new eco-friendly model given the resource and environment constraints. The model called "cost internalization" is characterized by low energy consumption and high self-purification capacity and it applies to all countries in the world.

China and India: Economic Prospects vs. Challenges

Prof. Dong Xiaojun, Department of *Economics, CNSA*

As the BRICs, both China and India have enjoyed rapid economic growth and established themselves as the world's largest emerging economies. Without any doubt, China and India's gradual shift away towards a more market-based economy has yielded undeniable benefits. The development models of China and India's are very different. China's model follows that of other East Asian economies and pursues income expansion through maximizing trade and investment. Government policies aimed at promoting export production and capital accumulation are at the heart of this model. India's economic reform chooses another model: India did not take place the extensive manufacturing industry revolution, but development the servicing business to push the economic growth. India has an Anglo-Saxon style financial system, radically different from China's government-controlled financial system. This has made India's capital markets more sensitive to global liquidity cycle than China. This is the main reason that global liquidity, though supporting India's capital markets, has become the engine of India's growth now. In terms of the financial system composition, China's bank property take more proportion than India's in total financial assets, but India's capital market is more flourishing than China's. Unlike China, India's financial system is still small relative to the economy although the total financial assets in China is larger then India's, but India's financial system is operating quite healthily and non-performing loans are in low rate. It is a big trouble of financial industry in our country that most of the banks in China have to deal with a lot of non-performing loans. These differences have led to a very different mix of demand growth in this cycle between the two economics. Production for export and construction drivers China's economy in the current cycle, while India's consumption, funded by credit, is driving its demand.

What is the prospect of China and India's economy if the rapid growth continues? China and India's GDPs would exceed today's rich countries. But the question perhaps is not so relevant. Prospects of China and India's economic growth would depend on many unpredictable factors. China and India face economic, financial landmines just like any other emerging market. On the other hand, we have the same risk. The US economic imbalances posed a threeat to its productivity and the global economy. "Keeping inflation under control will be one of the major challenges in 2008-09. China faces two strong risks:

(1) New macro adjustments to control may cause the non-performing loans rising rapidly.

(2) The financial market opening may not be controlled. India faces risks such as global.

Liquidity and inflation could be a headwind, which once happens, Indian economy will be inflicted losses heavily.

Technology Reforms: A Case Study of E-Governance in India

Dr. Suri Subrahmanyam Suribohtla, Associate Professor, IPE & Dr. Lalitha Shanth Kumar, Senior Administrative Officer (Research), IPE

Technology reforms are key to the growth and development of any economy. The history of growth and development of the last 250 year points out that the countries with an advantage in technology had also economic predominance and social advantage. Technology is an omnibus term including in its ambit the technologies ranging from most traditional to the most modern technologies pervading defence, rocket science, bio-technology, nanotechnology, computer and information technology, etc. The e-Governance, an off-shoot of the computer and information technology, provides a connect between science and people and enhances the welfare of the later through rapidity in transactions and savings in time and space.

The successful governance in the country requires a direct dialogue between people and government. The governance has to be simple, moral, accountable, responsive and transparent (SMART). The e-Government sought primarily with a view in cutting the cost of governance in the developed world. Though this has been stated as one of the reasons for developing nations too, it would appear to be lower down the order of priority with savings in cost accruing primarily form process *optimization and* labour costs in India. E-Governance is emerging as a new tool to establish SMART governance paving the way for the socio-economic transformation of the country, its modernization and integration with the rest of the world. The paper highlights centralization vs. decentralization dimensions in relation to e-Governance and incorporates case studies on e-Governance in Andhra Pradesh which is recognized as the *change leader in the country.*

Consummating National Commodity Reserve System and Enhancing Stabilization of Macro Economy

Prof. Zhang Qing, Department of Economics, CNSA

National Commodity Reserve" is to reserve all kinds of commodities by states. It is the general name of reserve of grain, cotton, sugar, oil and other important agricultural products, industry materials and fuels. "National Commodity Reserve System" is the system established for reserving important commodities for a country in different period of economic development. It is for the national interests, not only the reserved commodities is belong to "public goods", but also the mechanism of adjustment and controlling of national commodities reserve system as one of instruments using by government to intervene economy is of "public goods" in true nature. The purposes of national commodities should be insuring the national security, domestic market stability and the healthy and steady development of national economy. What's the problem of the current national commodity reserve system? There are several problems which need to be resolved, such as lacking of coordination between a administrative agencies, unclear rights and responsibilities; lacking of legal safeguard; not suitable to new changing of mercerization and globalization; the health development of reserve corporations is restricted by the lacking of distinction of function; there is not a mechanism against market risk and the risks could not be transferred. What are the roles of market and government for the economic development? National major commodities reserve system is an important instrument for government intervene the economy and important supplemental should be an inevitable choice for Chinese government to improve the national major commodities system in order to remedy the limitations of fiscal policy and monetary policy in the new circumstance of mercerization and globalization. National defense security is the basis and safeguards of national security and the national economic security has widespread meaning under the new trend of globalization. National commodities reserve is an important instrument to insure the national defense and resources security.

In future, it is necessary to establish a high efficient and coordinated adjustment mechanism, to separate the government and enterprises, management at several levels, reserving according the laws, to insure the achievement of target of national security and macroeconomic adjustment and the increasing of state assets of national reserve.

How to enhance efficiency of China's national commodity reserve system? The emphasis should be: speeding up the establishment of reserve system and establishing national commodities reserve system by the laws; establishing "big reserve management system" and managing all of national commodities reserve coordinately; adjusting structure, scope and scale of the commodity reserve; establishing the scientific operation mechanism for the national reserve enterprises and insuring the increase of state-owned assets.

It is necessary to integrate the management of the national commodities and foreign exchange reserve into the "big reserve system" and establish "national reserve commission" and "national reserve fund". Meanwhile, the "model of two target management of output and price" should be applied in the mechanism of purchase and release of the reserved commodities. If the expected output of national reserved commodities lower or higher than the target output, the authority—"national reserve commission" should pay close attention to the prices on the futures market and cash market, if the prices of reserved commodities lower or higher than the target prices. "national reserve commission" should authorize the reserve enterprises to buying or selling reserved commodities and adjust the market supply and demand.

Power Sector Reforms in India

Prof. R.K. Mishra, Director, IPE

Power sector poses a serious challenge to infrastructure development in India. A recent forecast made by the Planning Commission indicates that India requires an investment of US$ 300 billion for the development of power sector. In terms of per capita power consumption, India is well below China, the US, Russia, France, Germany, Japan and several other countries of the world. The inadequate generation of power and its supply has crippled industry, agriculture, trade, commercial, and domestic sector consumers. The exorbitantly high Transmission and Distribution (T&D) losses have made power an expensive input and constrained India's global competitiveness. Globalization, macro and micro economic reforms and outmoded framework governing functioning of power sector in India ushered in its privatization. The vertically integrated power industry in public sector has been disintegrated into generation, transmission, distribution and regulatory sectors. The power sector has been opened up to the foreign players. The Electricity Act, 1910 was first replaced be Electricity (Supply) Act in 1948 and amended several times till 1998 in which year Electricity Act, 1998 was promulgated to permit the presence of foreign direct investment in power sector. Earlier, during 1986-1990, the Electricity Supply Act, 1948 was amended to permit the entry of domestic private producers in power sector and ensure for them a rate of return of 16 per cent on capital employed at 68 per cent of the use of installed capacity with one per cent additional rate of return per two points of enhancement in capacity utilization resulting in a 32 per cent rate of return at 100 per cent capacity utilization. The 2003 Electricity Act represents a paradigm change allowing the presence of multiple buyers and suppliers. The trading of power has been facilitated by setting up appropriate institutions and steps are under way to promote power markets in India. However, the privatization of power has not been a smooth exercise. The issues concerning the linkage of fuel, debt-equity mix, land acquisition, pricing, law and order, access to capital markets in India and abroad, allocation of risks, labour market and fiscal incentives have obstructed privatization of power. The regulation has been posing serious challenges due to capture of regulator and suboptimal internal functioning of regulatory institutions in the absence of qualified staff and training. The subsidization has emerged as a major impediment resulting in unreasonable tariffs for the industrial, commercial and domestic consumers. The price of power generated per unit during the post reform and privatization era has not been consumer friendly. The terms and conditions acceded to domestic and foreign players for their participation have created a lack of level playing field between the public and private sectors. The failure of some success stories has taken a great toll on reforms and privatization of power sector. It is necessary to search answers for some questions: Have power sector reforms and privatization improved customer satisfaction? Have power sector reforms and privatization improved profitability and productivity of power utilities in India? Have they enhanced competition? Whether power sector reforms and privatization led to increased quantum of investments and technology up-gradation, and brought about changes in internal dynamics of organization?

This paper will provide an assessment of efficacy of power sector reforms and privatization in India through quantitative and qualitative analysis and case studies of Andhra Pradesh, Orissa and some other States.

Financial Sector Reforms

Prof R.K. Mishra, Director, IPE & Ms Lakshmi Kumari, Assistant Professor, IPE

In the Indian financial system, the banking system occupies a predominant position and it has come a long way to grow into a mature and stable banking system at present. The nationalization and subsequent massive expansion of bank branches provided the much needed fillip to banking habits of the population; extension of bank credit formed an important element of the massive programme of poverty eradication. The Government used bank resources for funding its large public expenditure. The large pre-emption of bank resources which at one point exceeded 63%, led to automatic monetization of fiscal deficit. Total regulation of interest rates which were more often pegged at artificially low levels, prescription of credit ceilings and directed credit programmes led to "financial repression" and distortions in allocation of resources.

As a result, banks came to work under a protective environment. In the absence of transparency in their operations, banks booked incomes which were not realized; profitability was relegated to the background and banks were saddled with assets of poor quality. Eventually, as the costs became unsustainable, some of the banks started incurring losses and accumulated them even to the extent, of wiping away their entire net worth. In 1990-91, the Indian economy faced unprecedented external crisis arising out of macro-economic imbalances. The resolution of the imbalances was attempted through the twin process of stabilization in the short-term and structural reform over the medium and long-term. Although attempts were made earlier to bring about changes in the financial sector a, cohesive strategy for reforms came about with the report of the Narasimham Committee (1991). The broad aim of the reform process was clear. With the gradual opening of the economy, financial sector cannot be kept in isolation. Accordingly, a movement from financial repression to liberalisation had to be achieved through a shift from an inventionist approach to market-based mechanisms. This was to lead to improvement in operational efficiency, i.e. reduction in costs of financial intermediation and allocational efficiency, i.e. allocation of resources to the best possible uses.

This paper proposes to look into the banking sector reforms concerning prudential norms, asset liability match, bank supervision, technologisation, productivity of the banking system, competition, and internationalization, regulation and portfolio transformation during the period of economic reforms.

The Impact of Sub Prime Mortgage Crisis on Chinese Economy

Dr. Ma Xiaofang, Associate Professor, Department of Economics, CNSA

Sub prime Mortgage Crisis in USA started in late 2006, which upgraded into a global financial storm in August, 2007. Quite a number of financial institutions such as property and hedge funds went bankruptcy and stopped redemption. Investment and commercial banks gave warning signals of profit loss and the global stock markets slumped. The governments of developed countries put more than 500 billion dollars to the markets within two weeks. Many economists think if the crisis continues, it will have great impact on global financial markets, and the US economy and the world economy will fall into recession. In order to review this crisis deeply, analysis should be done to find out reasons behind it. Three risk links can be found in this financial accident: the prosperity of property market enhances the standard release of the mortgage loan and innovation in the products of mortgage loan; securitization leads to credit risk transfer from property financial institutions to capital markets; the increase of benchmark interest rate and the weakness of property market become the main fuse. In order to reveal the trend of crisis and inspire the Chinese economy, this essay, first of all, tries to explain why sub-prime loan crisis took place and what are the risks in asset securitization; secondly, it shows the effect of sub-prime loan crisis on Chinese financial market and Chinese economy; last but not least, some suggestions and measures are offered on how to avoid such crisis.

Changes of Monetary Policy in China

Dr. Xu Jie, Associate Professor, Department of Economics, CNSA

The past decade has seen significant improvement in China's monetary policy (MP, for simplicity). China's central bank (People's Bank of China, PBC) plays more and more important role in macroeconomic regulation, and policy effectiveness increases steadily. Some new features in MP operation emerge in the past few years, which can be found in more flexible exchange rate regime, deliberate employment of policy instruments, more transparent operations of policy, market agents more sensitive to monetary policy change, and market-oriented reform enhancing effectiveness of MP.

Capital Market Reforms

Prof. R.K. Mishra, Director, IPE

The importance of capital market in any economy can not be over emphasized. The development of capital market is vital for the growth of real economy. A significant feature of developed capital market is the degree of its integration and interaction with major sectors of the Economy. A stronger capital market promotes sound and sustainable financial system. The growth and development of Indian Capital Market, in particular during the last decade has been *spectacular.* The impact of international trends of the developed and emerging capital markets was evident in India also. The turnover in developed markets has grown more sharply than that in emerging markets. This is a fact that financial Stock markets worldwide have grown in size as well as depth during the last 10 years. The aggregate turnover of all markets has grown nearly 9 times from US $ 5.5 Trillion in 1990 to US $ 47.9 Trillion in 2000. U.S. Securities Market *doubled* its share in total turnover between 1990 and 2000.

India accounted for 1.1 % total turnover during the year 2000, in spite of the fact that it has the largest number of listed companies in the world. The market capitalisation of all listed companies taken together on all markets of the world increased by 245% from US $ .4 Trillion at the end of 1990 to US $ 32.3 Trillion at the end of 2000. The share of U.S. in worldwide market capitalisation increased from 38.5% as at the end of 1995 to 46.8% as at the end of 2000. The share of India Listed Companies accounted for 0.5% of total market capitalisation. The market capitalisation as per out of COP in India stood at 41.3% at the end of the year 1999. The Table 1 shows the position of Indian Capital Market in terms of *International* comparison.

The Deregulation, Liberalisation and Globalisaltion of the *Indian* Economy has provided much needed impetus to the Capital Market for its growth and development. The earlier reforms facilitated faster growth and the latest one focused on strengthening the functioning of the Capital Markets in *India* by adoption and implementation of best international practices, systems and products. This trend will definitely increase the efficiency and effectiveness of Indian Stock Market.

This paper makes an attempt to critically examine the capital markets reforms in India since the onset of economic reforms in July 1991 and points out the directions of its future growth and development. It lists the important initiatives undertaken as reform measure, discusses the impact of such measures on the content and working of capital markets, looks at the changes in the global perspective and sump up the key features of the changes in the direction of the capital markets.

Monetary Reforms in India

Prof. R.K. Mishra, Director, IPE & Dr. J. Kiranmai, Assistant Professor, IPE

The economic reforms programme commenced in 1991 with two components: stabilization and structural adjustment. The role of monitory policy was considered a very important component as the money supply affects prices, on the one hand, and influences liquidity, on the other. The term money supply for the purpose of this paper will include both the monetization and credit and would therefore examine the impact of credit control measures initiated by the central banking authority from time to time ranging from direct to indirect measures.

Building Up a Universal Social Service System, Promoting Comprehensive Modernization of Economic Society

Prof. Xu Zhengzhong, Department of Economics, CNSA

From the perspective of human society development, the world has experienced two modernization phases which includes two leaps of social economy precede formation that includes from agriculture-based to industry-based society, and then pass to knowledge-based society. Facing the new situation which builds up cores in term of globalization, being knowledgeable and informatization, the governments all over the world now are taking the challenge from converting of culture and economic formation of society. Considering from the angle of Human-Society development, Germany is the first country which creates Social Security System, its social productivity has exceed the productivity summation of UK and France, which makes the Germany become economic power worldwide. Face to Japan's huge competitive pressure, the American has caught the chances which come from Information revolution and Knowledge revolution, and taken the lead in applying new strategy, adjusting the national economic, social, and cultural framework to lead human society stepping into new civilization of knowledge society. At present times, all nations around world commonly face the new pattern whose key technology filtered among Nami technology, information technology, biology technology and cognize technology, and all these urge and form new technology culture, new commercial module, social function system. Nowadays, the countries all over the world have set up the core of Nanotechnology, the complementary of information technology, biological technology and Cognitive Science to create new business model and Social Operative Mechanism based on new technology and cultures. At present, all nations commonly Through the thirty-year innovation, Chinese economy and social development have greatly succeeded, under the new historical situation, how to take the challenge of new generated culture, to be a power in world wide" and achieve double leaps in terms of being from agriculture-based to industry-based society and then to knowledge-based society, how to hold the responsibility of moving world economy plate to orient" the reverting of technology and culture, innovation of Social Operative Mechanism, to set up the Universal social Service System is the key.

Social Sector Reforms

Dr. Seeta Mishra, Assistant Professor, Post Graduate A.V. College & Dr. Lalitha Shanth Kumar, Senior Administrative Officer (Research), IPE

Economic reforms should be accompanied with human face and also social restructuring through educational, health and employment sector reforms. Economic reforms sans social sector reforms result in social inequity and unrest. In a democratic society, the populace expresses its disenchantment by a popular vote against such policy. This paper presents the poverty estimates in India, critically looks at the debate going on about the methods of measurement of poverty, analyses the programmes initiated to combat poverty and exclusion, and suggests finally, a broader framework for the elimination of the twin problems from the Indian society. Some broad features of poverty and exclusion in India such as rural and urban poverty, agricultural poverty, gender and poverty, and economic reforms and poverty have also been discussed in this paper. The paper begins by providing the backdrop of poverty and development policy in India. The concluding section of the paper sums up the major issues relating to poverty and exclusion in India.

Fiscal Competition and Fiscal Accountability: Evidence from Unitary and Federal Countries

Prof. Shi Hongxiu, Department of Economics, CNSA

This paper aims at discussing how the fiscal competition among governments influences fiscal accountability. Between subordinate and higher level governments, despite their high integration, central or federal government would possibly yield to local governments due to information asymmetry. Although macroeconomic stability is one of central government's primary responsibilities, to many local governments it has externality, local governments would prefer fiscal expansion. If independent interest boundary exists between governments, fiscal competition as well as bad effects it brings could not be avoided, even the vertical integration has been improved. In this issue, political ideology always submits to economic logic.

Taking the Equalization as the Aim: Proposals of improving the Financial Transfer Payments System. Chinese governments will improve the public finance system as they work to ensure equal access to basic public services and establish development priority zones. The dialectical relationship between promoting the equalization of basic public services and establishing the priority zones should be considered roundly. To promote the public finance system especially to promote the system of transfer payments, these two different political aims should be balanced. The design of the system of transfer payments of China has some serious substantial and procedural defects. The paper provides some proposals for promoting the system of transfer payments, including to conforming the different kinds of transfer payments, to conforming the fiscal resources, to advancing the system of supervision and the system of performance assessment of transfer payments, and to making a law to restrict the behaviors of transfer payments etc.

Introduction: the status quo of the basic public services and the issues of the financial transfer payments system

1.1 The status quo of the basic public services

    1.1.1 There are large gaps of finance among the different areas in China.

    1.1.2 There are large gaps of public services among the different areas in China.

1.2 The main issues of the financial transfer payments system

      1.2.1 The design of the transfer payments system has some serious substantial defects.

      1.2.2 The design of the transfer payments system has some serious procedural defects.

The dialectical relationship between promoting the equalization of basic public services and establishing the priority zones

2.1 The dialectical relationship between promoting the equalization of basic public services and establishing the priority zones

      2.1.1 The former is a goal in certain phase of history; and the latter is along-term goal.

      2.1.2 The former is a synthesis goal; and the latter is a single function goal.

      2.1.3 Over a long period of time, the former is the means to realize the policy target; and the latter is the genuine policy end-result and target.

2.2 Some regions will pay high prices to build the priority zones, and more financial supports should be provided to these regions.

2.3 Different transfer payments targets should be realized by different transfer payments means.

2.4 Pay attention to the core word: BASIC

Some proposals of improving the financial transfer payments system

3.1 To accelerate the establishment of a unified, standardized and transparent system for transfer payments;

3.2 To enlarge the size and proportion of general transfer payments;

3.3 To abolish the revenue return gradually;

3.4 To conform the diverse transfer payments to two kinds forms: general transfer payments and special transfer payments;

3.5 To conform the fiscal functions and to integrate the financial resources;

3.6 To advance the system of supervision and the system of performance assessment of transfer payments;

3.7 To make a law to restrict the behaviors of transfer payments.

Asymmetrical Power-Division and its Rectification among Chinese Governments—The Necessity to Improve the Public Service Capability

Dr. Fan Jida, Department of *Economics, CNSA*

After the reform of "revenue-sharing-scheme" financial management system in 1994, the Chinese government's public finance relation presents as the characteristic of asymmetrical power-division. The large difference between town and country, the high speed of economy growth and imbalance among different regions are related to asymmetrical power-division. The way to rectify asymmetrical power-division is not simply to realize symmetrical power-division among governments. In order to realize the aim of equalization of public service, we should take measures such as re-dividing administrative power between different governments, adjusting tax power reasonable and further consummating transfer payment system.

Economic Reforms in China With Reference to Privatization of Public Enterprises

Prof. R.K. Mishra, Director, IPE

Chinese Economy is being intensively studied by several scholars and institutions. Chinese economic reforms and privatization of its public enterprises are of great significance to India, which launched its economic reforms program in 1992. The sequencing, putting in place appropriate institutional structure, and an optimal trade off between the equity and growth and the pace of privatization have surfaced as major issues confronting policy makers in India engaged in formulating and implementing the economic reforms program which have entered a crucial stage wherein they are required to traverse from the center to the states.

Stages of Economic Reforms in China

Chinese reforms commencing in 1979 have passed through three stages. In the first stage, extending from 1979 to 1984, Chinese Government liberalized agriculture, withdrew controls, modernized industry and its fundamental structure in the national economy. In the second stage, beginning from 1984 and stretching up to 1991, the leadership reforms occupied the center stage. The leadership reforms concerned themselves with the emergence and continuation of leadership committed to the development of Chinese society with a specific perspective of achieving the rate of growth 10% per annum for the next 20 years. During this stage, Chinese economic reforms also transformed the political structure. During this stage Chinese overhauled their agricultural, industrial, fiscal, financial infrastructure and trade policies. The current stage of reforms began in 1991, and continues to hold its way in the present decade of 21st century. It deals with marketising the political structure and the economy. This is the most crucial stage of reform which has helped Chinese in preserving their socio-political and economic systems, on the one hand, and superimposing on this tripod on the element of market economy, on the other. During this stage of reforms, Chinese have mounted an ambitious program of privatizing public enterprises. The privatization drive, which has taken off during this stage, has led to privatization of 1,00,000 public enterprises out of a total of 2,66,000 public enterprises in China. The enterprise reforms have transformed public enterprises into self-reliant entities.

The economic reforms have transcended the expected benefits. The allocations to the central government of the total resources have increased from 40%-50%. The preponderance of government agencies is being questioned. The roles and responsibilities of the remaining government organs have been classified. The strong hold of the bureaucracy has been substantially weakened. The number of departments of Chinese government has been reduced form 40 to 28. The over-sized Chinese bureaucracy has been trimmed from a massive number of 30,000 to 10,000. The number of bureaucrats belonging to the provincial governments has declined from 55,000 to 28,000. A new system of evaluation of civil servants has been introduced which favors action and discourages bias in favour of accumulating files. The bureaucracy at the level of local administration is also getting leaner and meaner.

Focus of the Paper

The present paper looks at public enterprise reforms in China within the broad ambit of economic reforms therein. An attempt has been made to study privatization and non-privatization reforms, techniques and modalities of privatization, marketisation process of public enterprise in respect of mobilization of funds, operational and commercial autonomy and the post-privatization efficiency. The issue of equity and growth in relation to privatization and the labour related issues pertaining to privatization have also been studied besides discussing the comparative aspects of public enterprise reforms in India and China.

Industrial Sector Reforms in India

Prof. R.K. Mishra, Director, IPE

Industrialization has been long recognized as a strategy of economic development. Industry occupies an important place in the developmental of India. The contribution of industrial sector has registered a decline in the gross domestic product. However there has been a renewed emphasis on industrial development in the XI Plan of the country. The industrial sector comprises small, medium and heavy industries. These were shackled by letter of intents, industrial licenses, permits, quotas, and various regulations. After the on set of economic liberalization the policy of broad banding, automatic approvals, FOIs, competition and elimination of monopoly, productivity, access to capital markets, cheaper industrial finances, joint ventures, etc, made their foray in the industrial sector. This paper makes an attempt to bring out the industrial sector reforms measures, the impact thereof on industrial development and the status of industrial sector in the pre and post industrial reforms period. The paper benchmarks the industrial sector reforms and their efficacy with the counter parts of India in the various regions.

Visits to Different Places

Visit to Government of Shijingshan District (Training Base)

This is a new economic area developed as a recreation center. A detailed presentation about the district and its development was made by Dr Ms Hang Wang, Vice Governor, Senior Economist. The district comprising of many industrial units which are eco friendly and a theme park has been developed.

Dotman is the Beijing's Cyber Recreation District located in the Shijingshan District. The team interacted with Mr Jason Hoa, MBA Executive President, Dotman, on the working projects in the center. The center developed software relating to animation and online children games. The center is proposing to have some tie-ups with Indian IT firms for further development. The team was accompanied by Mr Cui Juhang, Deputy Director General, International Division, CNSA, Ms Connie Zhang, CNSA and other official from Shijingshan District Office.

Tianjin Institute of Public Administration and
Tianjin Economic Technological Development Area

Prof Li Yadong, Director, Tianjin Institute of Public Administration received the team and Prof Zang Xueying, Department of International Strategic Development, Tianjin Institute of Public Administration made a presentation on the Tianjin becoming the new economic zone in the costal area. The district of Tianjin is under the direct control of the Central Government. Tianjin is an ancient city and has an history from 1885. The city has lot of cultural heritage and is 120 km away from Beijing. 50 Km away from Tianjin city districts is the newly developed Tianjin Economic Technological Development Area (TEDA) where the foreign investment ventures get the highest returns in China. To meet the development requirements, three sub zones have been established outside TEDA viz. Micro Electronic Industrial Park, Yat-son Scientific and Industrial Park and Chemical Industrial park. To date, there have been 15,000 plus foreign investment enterprises settling down in Tianjin for manufacture and trading business including more than 200 world famous multinations.The per capita GDP of the district in US $ is 6022 during 2007 compared to the GDP of US $ 3126 in 2001. The fiscal revenue of TEDA increased to 1204 Yuans during 2007 compared to 451 Yuans during 2003. The area provided good capital incentives, tax free holidays, low paid electricity, English medium schools and colleges for foreign investors. By the end of 2007, TEDA has accumulatively approved 4485 foreign, Hong Kong, Macao and Taiwan funded enterprises from 74 countries and regions.

FRIDAY 6 JUNE 2008

Shanghai Institute of Public Administration

The team visited the Shanghai Institute of Public Administration. A detailed presentation was made by Dr Wang Zhiping, Director and Professor, Department of Economics and Management at the Shanghai Institute of Public Administration on the Economic Development in Shanghai. He elaborated the three 'Cs' of Shanghai ie Important Economic 'Center'; Dynamic high-tech 'Cluster' and Expected World Class 'City'. The city has emerged as a main business center with information technology, finance, automobile, fine chemicals, metallurgy and biological industries. The world's only commercial magnetic levitation (no wheels) line was in operation. The city has the largest port handling a cargo of 560 million tones during 2007. The city has two international airports ie Hongquiao Airport and Pudong Airport. The new industrial area has been developed on the bank of the river Poo and named the area as Pudong New Area. The main aim of the city is to transform Shanghai into an International Metropolitan Center and also one of the worlds finest economic, finance, transport and trade Centers.

Seminar Schedule

PROGRAMME

Sunday 1 June 2008	:	Registration
Monday 2 June 2008	:	

0900-1015

Opening Ceremony
Convenor: Prof. Zhou Shaopeng,
Department of Economics, CNSA

Welcoming Address
Prof. Han Kang, Vice President, CNSA

Keynote Speech 1 : *Prof. Han Kang, Vice President, CNSA*

Keynote Speech 2 : **An Overview of 30 Years' Economic Reform and Opening Up in China**
Prof. Wang Jian, Director-General,
Department of Economics, CNSA

Keynote Speech 3 : **An Overview of Economic Reforms in India**
Prof. R.K. Mishra, Director,
Institute of Public Enterprise (IPE)

1015-1025 **Group Picture**

1025-1040 **Tea Break**

1040-1230 1st Plenary Session: Economic Reforms
Convenor: Prof. Li Xuefeng,
Department of Economics, CNSA

Speech 1 : **Prospect of the Economic Development between 2008 and 2020**
Prof. Wang Haibo,
Chinese Academy of Social Sciences

Speech 2 : **Economic Reforms in Agriculture Sector in India**
Prof. Naresh Sharma, Department of Economics,
University of Hyderabad

Speech 3 : **Economic Reforms in China**
Prof. Huang Hengxue, School of Government Management, Peking University

Speech 4	:	**Second Generation Reforms in India (State Level Reforms)**
		Dr R.K. Mishra, Director,
		Institute of Public Enterprise (IPE
		Dr. Seeta Mishra, Assistant Professor,
		Post Graduate AV College Secundrabad
Speech 5	:	**Development Approach Similarity between China and India and Their Strategic Choices**
		Prof. Zhang Zhanbin,
		Department of Economics, CNSA
1230		**Lunch**
1330-1510		**2nd Plenary Session: Public Enterprise Reforms Convenor: Prof. R. K. Mishra, Director, IPE**
Speech 1	:	**Performance of Public Enterprises in the Era of Economic Liberalization**
		Prof. R.K. Mishra, Director, IPE
		Dr. Janaswamy Kiranmai, Research Associate, IPE
Speech 2	:	**SoEs Reform and Development of the Nonpublic Sector of the Economy in China**
		Prof. Zhou Shaopeng,
		Department of Economics, CNSA
Speech 3	:	**Political Economy of State Level Pubic Enterprises Reforms in India**
		Dr Venkateswara Rao, IAS, Principal Secretary,
		Government of Karnataka, Bangalore
		Dr. Janaswamy Kiranmai, Research Associate, IPE
Speech 4	:	**An Analysis on Mainland China's Economic Growth and Policy between 1992 and 2006**
		Prof. Li Xuefeng, Department of Economics, CNSA
Speech 5	:	**Policy Restructuring for Industrial Cluster Upgrade in China**
		Dr. Li Jiangtao, Associate Professor,
		Department of Economics, CNSA
Speech 6	:	**Economic Reforms in China with Reference to Privatization of Public Enterprises**
		Dr R.K. Mishra, Director, IPE

1510-1530		**Tea Break**

1530-1720   **3rd Plenary Session: Prospects and Challenges**
Convenor: Dr. Hui Shuangmin,
Department of Economics, CNSA

Speech 1   :   **Industrialization Dilemma and Civilization Model Innovation under Resource and Environment Restrictions in Large Countries**
Prof. Zhang Xiaode,
Department of Economics, CNSA

Speech 2   :   **China and India: Economy Prospects vs. Challenges**
Prof. Dong Xiaojun,
Department of Economics, CNSA

Speech 3   :   **Technology Reforms: A Case Study of E-Governance in India**
Dr. Suri Subrahmanyam Suribohtla,
Associate Professor, IPE
Dr. Lalitha Shanth Kumar,
Senior Administrative Officer (Research), IPE

Speech 4   :   **Consummating National Commodity Reserve System and Enhancing Stabilization of Macro Economy**
Prof. Zhang Qing, Department of Economics, CNSA

Speech 5   :   **Power Sector Reforms in India**
Prof. R.K. Mishra, Director, IPE

1720-1830   **4th Plenary Session: Capital market and Monetary policy**
Convenor: Prof. Naresh Sharma,
Department of Economics,
University of Hyderabad

Speech 1   :   **Financial Sector Reforms**
Prof. R.K. Mishra, Director, IPE
Dr. Janaswamy Kiranmai, Research Associate, IPE

Speech 2   :   **Capital Market in China**
Dr. Ma Xiaofang, Associate Professor,
Department of Economics, CNSA

Speech 3	:	**Changes of Monetary Policy in China** *Dr. Xu Jie, Associate Professor,* *Department of Economics, CNSA*
Speech 4	:	**Fiscal Policy Reforms in India** *Prof. R.K. Mishra, Director, IPE* *Dr. Janaswamy Kiranmai, Research Associate, IPE*
1900		**Welcoming Dinner**

Tuesday 3 June 2008

0900-1030		**5th Plenary Session: Social Sector Reforms** *Convenor: Prof. Zhang Qing,* *Department of Economics, CNSA*
Speech 1	:	**Building Up a Universal social Service System, Promoting Comprehensive Modernization of Economic Society** *Prof. Xu Zhengzhong,* *Department of Economics, CNSA*
Speech 2	:	**Social Sector Reforms** *Dr Lakshmi Kumari Ch, Assistant Professor, IPE* *Dr. Lalitha Shanth Kumar,* *Senior Administrative Officer (Research), IPE*
Speech 3	:	**Fiscal Competition and Fiscal Accountability: Evidence from Unitary and Federal Countries** *Prof. Shi Hongxiu, Department of Economics, CNSA*
Speech 4	:	**Taking the Equalization as the Aim : Proposals of improving the Financial Transfer Payments System** *Dr. Cai Chunhong, Associate Professor,* *Department of Economics, CNSA*
Speech 5	:	**Asymmetrical Power-division and Its Rectification among Chinese Governments—The Necessity to Improve the Public Service Capability** *Dr. Fan Jida, Department of Economics, CNSA*
1030-1050		**Tea Break**

1050-1120		**Closing Ceremony**
1120		**Lunch**
Afternoon		**City Tour in Beijing**
Evening		**Cultural Show**

Wednesday 4 June 2008

0900-1200	:	Visit to Government of Shijingshan District (Training Base)
1400	:	Departure for Tianjin
1630	:	Arrival at Tianjin Institute of Public Administration

Thursday 5 June 2008

Morning	:	Visit to Tianjin Binhai New Area
Afternoon	:	Presentation on Economic Development in Tianjin
1905	:	Departure for Shanghai by Flight MU 5148
2050	:	Arrival at Shanghai

Friday 6 June 2008

Morning	:	Presentation on the Economic Development in Shanghai by Shanghai Institute of Public Administration
Afternoon	:	Visit to Pudong New Area
Evening	:	Departure for New Delhi

Future Collaboration

Co-operation between Dragon and Elephant should be continued in future. CNSA and IPE have agreed to cooperate for 3 years initially in future to provide valuable proposals to both the governments in the following areas by way of visits to study the development of special economic zones, exchange of information, dialogues, seminars etc on economic development reforms in both the countries. This may also result in some collaborative publications.

INFRASTRUCTURE

Study the broad base growth areas in infrastructure development, financing and all the connecting facilities.

DEVELOPMENT OF SEZ

The process of converting wastelands into SEZs is noteworthy. Research can be done in this area in order to give suggestions to the Indian government in setting up SEZs in India.

POLLUTION CONTROL

The environmental issues of both the countries will be studied in order to suggest necessary pollution control measures like, waste management techniques, and to protect the environment from global warming. Research will be carried out on various social problems concerning poverty, unemployment in both the countries for bringing changes in the government policies towards the eradication of these problems.

Incentives offered by the Government for up-liftment of the industries either in SEZ or in rural areas will be studied in depth for development of first generation entrepreneurs to provide employment opportunities.

The basic needs of the rural areas will be studied in detail and the steps to be taken for adopting in our country to improve the standard of living will be taken up on priority basis.

Visits to the rural areas and actual industries. The authorities who are providing procedural steps as documentation have to be obtained and studied. The government scheme for providing employment in rural areas for about 100 days announced by Government of Andhra Pradesh will be studied in detail for further development and the procedures to be adopted for implementation. Similar model or the other being followed as a Chinese model will also be studied in collaboration and the effective methods to be taken up and to be followed as a cohesive model will be worked out.

The IT scenario in both the countries will be taken up for study and further development to be made individually and also to make it effective will be studied for further implementation.

Preparations for the Next Seminar—
Exhaustive Blue Print

The Chinese team comprising academicians and policy makers would be visiting India during January 2009 to participate in the return seminar; the tentative programme for the return seminar would be as follows:

Day 1   :   Arrival at the Indira Gandhi International Airport Delhi Stay at Hotel

Day 2 & 3 :   IPE-CNSA seminar on Public Enterprise Reforms in India at SCOPE Conference Hall

Day 4   :   Arrive in Hyderabad Visit to Hi-tech city, ICICI Biotechnology Park, local Sight seeing

Day 5 & 6 :   IPE-CNSA seminar on Economic Reforms

Day 7   :   IPE-CNSA—Govt of Karnataka (DPE) one-day seminar on public enterprise reforms

Day 8   :   Visits

Day 9   :   Departure to Bangkok, Beijing.